Praise for *What every teacher needs to know about psychology*

"This is a must-read book for every beginning teacher. And even the most experienced teachers [will find much of interest] here. I certainly did."
   Dylan Wiliam, Emeritu[s ...]

"In an era when policy mak[ers ...] qualified, this book explore[s ...] that underpin all teaching a[nd learning.]"
   Alex Quigley, Director of Teaching and Learning at Huntington School and author of *The Confident Teacher*

"A book of rapacious research, relentless drive and keen intellect. It works as an entry point into the history of cognitive psychology, presenting findings from an array of inter-related areas with such clarity that the previously forbidding is easily understandable to even the most distracted of ingénues. The key thing with this work though is that the evidence is not just presented and left to grow cold, but is sifted and judged so that easily implemented recommendations are made as to how a teacher might use such research."
   Phil Beadle, author, *Rules for Mavericks*

"This book fills this yawning gap in our collective understanding of the way our students think and behave. Didau and Rose enable teachers to beat a path between the intellectual rigours of their subject and the patchy prior knowledge of their students. I look forward to seeing a copy of this book in every staff room I visit."
   Stephen Adcock, Deputy Director Academies, United Learning and co-author of *Headstrong: 11 Lessons of School Leadership*

"Every teacher, at any stage of their career, should read this book. It makes you think and challenges some of the assumptions, so that we approach the latest fad with a healthy scepticism and a determination to self-evaluate our own impact."

Jackie Beere, author, trainer and school improvement consultant

"In these days of such monstrosities as 'brain based learning' and the pursuit of 'the answer' when it comes to 'how to teach', this book offers salvation. What Every Teacher Needs To Know About Psychology should be the first stop and, more importantly, the last stop on every teacher's itinerary into this field. Disarmingly well written, and accessible even when it deals with some difficult concepts this book can serve as the teacher textbook for this area."

Martin Robinson, teacher, consultant and author of *Trivium 21st Century*

"...manages to strike the importance balance between the world of cognitive psychology and practical application in the classroom. If you are interested in how students think and learn and want to use that knowledge at the chalk face, this is the book for you."

Liam Collins, Headteacher of Uplands Community College and vice-chair of the Headteachers' Roundtable

"I predict that a great many students will benefit from their teachers having read this terrific book. A very helpful and accessible guide to understanding the complexities of learning."

Phil Stock, Assistant Head, Greenshaw High School

"The perfect blend of research and thought-provoking questions for schools to grapple with. The beauty of the approach is that it opens up a range of issues and presents the research and then lets schools debate and move forwards."

Oliver Knight, Headteacher at Greenwich Free School and author of *Creating Outstanding Classrooms*

WHAT EVERY TEACHER NEEDS TO KNOW ABOUT...
PSYCHOLOGY

DAVID DIDAU **NICK ROSE**

A John Catt Publication

First Published 2016

by John Catt Educational Ltd,
12 Deben Mill Business Centre, Old Maltings Approach,
Melton, Woodbridge IP12 1BL

Tel: +44 (0) 1394 389850 Fax: +44 (0) 1394 386893
Email: enquiries@johncatt.com
Website: www.johncatt.com

© 2016 David Didau and Nick Rose

All rights reserved.

No part of this publication may be reproduced, stored in a retrieval system, transmitted in any form or by any means, electronic, mechanical, photocopying, recording, or otherwise, without the prior permission of the publishers.

Opinions expressed in this publication are those of the contributors and are not necessarily those of the publishers or the editors. We cannot accept responsibility for any errors or omissions.

ISBN: 978 1 909717 85 5

Set and designed by John Catt Educational Limited

Contents

Thanks and acknowledgements	7
Foreword by Professor Robert Coe	8
Introduction – What every teacher needs to know about psychology	10
Part 1 – Learning and thinking	**14**
How students learn and think	
1. Evolutionary psychology	17
2. Prior learning and misconceptions	26
3. Working memory	34
4. Cognitive load	43
5. Long-term memory and forgetting	51
6. Context and transfer	62
7. Practice and expertise	70
8. Feedback	82
9. Assessment	89
10. Effective instruction	109
Part 2 – Motivation and behaviour	**120**
What motivates students to learn?	
11. Beliefs	124
12. Expectations	134

13. Goal setting	140
14. Mastery	146
15. Rewards and sanctions	151
16. Intrinsic and extrinsic motivation	164
17. Self-regulation	171
18. Restorative practice	181
19. Social norms	190
20. In-group and out-group	199
Part 3 – Controversies	**208**
Professional scepticism	
21. Cognitive development	219
22. Attachment	228
23. Stress and resilience	237
24. Neuroscience	247
25. Individual differences	254
26. Creativity	265
Conclusions and further reading	272
Index	276

Thanks and acknowledgements

Writing a book is a collaborative process and, as always, too many people have contributed in so many small ways that it would be impossible to thank each of them directly. Two people we need to single out for special thanks are Dylan Wiliam whose questions, comments and suggestions have greatly enhanced the book and Rob Coe for writing the foreword and for taking the time to point out where our understanding of assessment was unclear.

Particular thanks should also go to Martin Robinson, who gave permission for extracts from Nick's chapter in *Trivium into Practice* to be reproduced in Chapter 1: Evolutionary psychology. Others who have taken time to read the time to read early drafts and make helpful suggestions are Pedro de Bruyckere, John Tomlinson, Yana Weinstein, Cindy Wooldridge, Cristina Milos, Oli Knight and Greg Ashman.

We also need to thank Jonathan Barnes and Alex Sharratt at John Catt for putting up with our chaotic working practices and slipshod approach to the whole thing. Well done on making us look so good.

Finally, thanks to everyone who has read and commented on our blogs over the years – your contributions have certainly helped to shape our understanding of what every teacher needs to know about psychology.

David & Nick, June 2016

Foreword

When I was teaching in schools, some twenty years ago, my sense was that you would be hard pushed to find advocates for a list of 'what every teacher needs to know about psychology' that went beyond a few snippets of Piaget and Vygotsky. Many teachers would recall dry 'theory' sessions on Piagetian Stages or the Zone of Proximal Development in their pre-service training that were widely seen as irrelevant once they actually got into schools. As a trainee teacher, I recall a group of real teachers, hardened by time at the chalk-face and made cynical by repeated experience of having to dodge barmy initiatives promoted by experts and bosses, giving the following advice:

"Lecturers in the university have to justify their existence with all that pointless theory – they'd be worried Education is not a proper subject without it. And they need something to cover for the fact that they couldn't hack it in the classroom. But once you start working in a school you'll soon forget all that stuff, and you'll never miss it."

Perhaps things have moved on, but writing a substantial book full of psychological theory for teachers does not seem like an obvious proposition for a best-seller. Do all teachers really need to know this?

Actually, I think they do. All too often, attempts to promote educational evidence, research and theory have seemed unconvincing to teachers, but this book does three things really well. First, it is appropriately selective in the evidence it presents: to meet the standard for 'what every teacher needs to know' the psychological research must be both rigorous and relevant. Second, it challenges a lot of traditional practice and ideas about teaching. The case for a scientific approach is at the heart of the thinking behind the book. Intuition, common practice and folk-wisdom can all be wrong, and often are, so we need something more trustworthy. Of course, this kind of challenge may not be welcome to every teacher, but Didau and Rose take no prisoners here. Third, and crucially, it connects the research to its implications for practice in classrooms. Every chapter contains a list of direct implications of the evidence discussed for teaching.

Interestingly, Piaget does get most of a chapter devoted to his work, though you have to wait until Chapter 21, and the discussion is mostly quite critical. Vygotsky gets a couple of passing mentions. The work of plenty of other psychologists gets a good airing on a very wide range of topics and it will be a rare teacher who can claim they knew all this already. Indeed, the scale and range of content covered is enormous and is likely to overwhelm anyone who tries to read it start to finish. To engage with the ideas deeply and avoid overloading working memory – about which plenty more follows – most people should probably take it in small doses.

In the last few years there seems to have been a significant growth of interest from teachers and policy makers in research evidence and a scientific approach to understanding and improving education. In the space of a decade in England, randomised controlled trials in education have gone from being almost unheard of to being commonplace. A number of robust and accessible summaries of relevant research have become widely known by teachers. Social media, led by teacher bloggers and tweeters, has helped create communities of teachers who want to engage with research and discuss the ideas and their implications. There is an appetite for research evidence and an increasingly critical and sophisticated research stance. In that context it would be nice to think that maybe a book like this could be a best-seller.

What we still lack is the translation of all this theory into scalable models for practice. Even if teachers know about, for example, Bjork's idea of 'desirable difficulties', they still have to work quite hard to plan their own teaching to incorporate spacing, interleaving and retrieval practice into the learner's experience. They must work from first principles, building the tools they need to use. The landscape is still one where a few pioneers forge a route through a challenging environment, working hard to gain every step of the journey. We don't yet have the infrastructure of roads, railways and settlements that would allow mass travel, but slowly and inevitably it will come. This book helps to bring that closer.

Robert Coe,
Professor in the School of Education and Director of the Centre for Evaluation and Monitoring (CEM), Durham University,
July 2016

What every teacher needs to know about psychology

When we began this project, many of the teachers we spoke to about it responded enthusiastically, saying things like, "Great! It's about time someone wrote about how we can use all that therapy stuff with our students." Others groaned and admitted to hating "all that touchy-feely crap". This is *not* that kind of book. One of the many motivations for undertaking this venture was to challenge the notion that psychology is synonymous with therapy. Clinical psychology – that branch of the subject concerned with the assessment and treatment of mental illness and behavioural problems – is enormously worthwhile but not, in our opinion, what teachers really need to know about. This book considers the broader science of the study of the mind and human behaviour. We have chosen to focus on those aspects of psychology which consider how children learn and what teachers can do to better help them learn.

Much of what we do in classrooms is intuitive, steered by what 'feels right', but all too often what feels right proves a poor, sometimes treacherous guide. Although what we know about the workings of the human brain is still pitifully small, the science of psychology can and has revealed certain surprising findings that teachers would do well to heed.

But the relationship between psychology and teaching is an uneasy one. Research often falls into one of two camps – the blindingly obvious and the obviously wrong. Some findings are dismissed because everyone already knows them and others because they run counter to what everybody knows. But both categories of research can be made to bear fruit, the first because quantifying and qualifying what 'everybody knows' gives it power and importance, the second because the human mind is lamentably prone to prejudice and bias.

Over the past few decades, psychological research has made real strides into understanding how we learn, but it's only in the last few years that education has become aware of these insights. Part of the problem is a tendency amongst teachers to resist being told 'what works' if it conflicts with intuition. Dylan Wiliam says:

> *To build a bridge, you need to know about the behaviour of steel and stone when compressed and when stretched, but knowing all this will never tell you what the bridge should look like. In the same way, psychology will never tell teachers how to teach, but there are now clear principles emerging about how we learn best; principles that teachers can use to make teaching more effective, such as the fact that spaced practice is better than massed practice and the benefits of frequent classroom testing for long-term retention.*[*]

One of the criticisms of psychology is that it's not 'hard science'. Although the social sciences cannot claim the same credibility as the natural sciences, they can still be held up to the rigours of the scientific method. Nobel prize winning physicist Carl Weiman argues that rigorous education research is not so very different from 'hard' science as some might want to suggest. Good science has the power to make useful predictions; if research can be used to inform our actions then it is useful. It's unnecessary to accurately control and predict how every student in every context will behave or learn, just as a physicist has no need to control or predict how every single atom will behave in a physics experiment. All that's necessary is that we can predict an outcome that is both meaningful and measurable.

This tells us that the insights of psychology, gleaned over many years and predicated on well-designed, repeatable tests that build on prior research and which produce broadly consensual meaningful and measurable outcomes, should not be dismissed as unlikely to work in the classroom. If the scientists are right, we could make a profound difference to how well our students learn. If all our empirical evidence turns out to be wrong, no one's died. It may not be worth betting your life on, but it outweighs the risk of going with a hunch.

Whilst we cannot and should not relinquish our professional judgement in the

---

[*] Wiliam, D. in Didau, D. *What If Everything You Knew About Education Was Wrong?* (205: ix)

face of outlandish claims, we should at least be aware of what scientists have discovered about learning, thinking, motivation, behaviour and assessment over the past few decades.

This though is far easier said than done. Every year thousands of research papers are published, some of which contradict each other. How can busy teachers know which research is worth investing time in reading and understanding? This book is an attempt to lay out the evidence and theoretical perspectives on what we believe are the most important and useful psychological principles of which teachers ought to be aware. That is not to say this book contains everything you might ever need to know – there is no way it could – it is merely a primer. We hope that you are inspired to read and explore some of the sources for yourself and see what other principles can stand the scrutiny of investigation and find a home in your classroom.

We're not claiming that psychology provides quick and easy answers to the difficult problems of teaching and learning, but that it can help us ask better questions about our classroom practice. Some of what we present may be surprising, some dubious, but some in danger of being dismissed as 'blindingly obvious"*. Before embracing or dismissing any of these principles we urge you to interrogate the evidence and think carefully about the advice we offer. While nothing works everywhere and everything might work somewhere, this is a guide to what we consider the best bets from the realm of psychology.

How to read this book

Obviously enough, this is your book and you can choose to read (or not read) it in any way you want. That said, it might help to know that we haven't written a book which we're expecting readers to simply devour from cover to cover.

We've organised the areas of psychology we've chosen to discuss under three broad headings: learning and thinking, behaviour and motivation, and controversies. Within each of themes, we've given some thought to the most logical way to sequence the material but it's important to note that the chapters are not intended to read in any kind of strict order. Each individual chapter is meant to stand alone so that busy teachers can dip into and read about the aspect they feel most currently pressing. We've taken some care to point out where ideas in one chapter connect with concepts explored in another chapter but these are merely suggestions rather than directions. As a consequence, we've

---

*   Before you give in to this temptation, we recommend reading Gregory Yates' monograph, "How Obvious": *Personal reflections on the database of educational psychology and effective teaching research*. It can be found here: http://www.unisanet.unisa.edu.au/edpsych/research/HowObvious.pdf

deliberately repeated or revisited material in different sections of the book as an acknowledgement that readers may not yet have encountered explanations or ideas that are important or useful in the understanding of other ideas.

While this is by no means an encyclopaedia of psychology, we've imagined that teachers might use it as a handy reference work to support their practice and professional development. In our most excited moments we've hoped that the material we've written could prove useful as a course of professional study or as professional reading designed to complement training or investigation into various aspects of teaching. But, of course, we'd be more than pleased if you simply read it.

References

Weiman, C. (2014) 'The Similarities Between Research in Education and Research in the Hard Sciences', *Educational Researcher*, 43(1), 12-14.

Wiliam, D. (2015) Foreword to Didau, D. *What If Everything You Knew About Education Was Wrong?* Carmarthen, UK: Crown House Publishing Ltd.

Part 1
Learning and thinking

How students learn and think

Learning and thinking are terms used carelessly in education. If we are to discuss the psychology of learning then it makes sense to begin with precise definitions.

Learning

Let's first consider learning. The definition we will use in this book is *the retention and transfer of knowledge and skills*. Another helpful definition is to see learning as a change in the way we see and understand the world. Learning then has three related aspects: retention, transfer and change. This is not to say that something that has been forgotten was never learned – forgetting is an important part of learning, as we'll see in Chapter 5 – but it does suggest that if you can't remember something or are unable to apply it then it would be hard to argue you had really learned it.

If we accept that in order for learning to meet this definition it must be durable (it should last) and flexible (it should be applicable in different contexts) then we should also accept that it cannot be observed in the here and now. The only way to see if something has been retained over time and transferred to a new context is to look at what students can do later and elsewhere.

One of the most useful and important concepts for teachers to understand is the distinction between learning and performance. Performance is what students can do. It is all that we can ever observe. Learning takes place inside a student's mind and as such cannot be observed directly.

We can make inferences about learning based on the performances we see, but performances at the point of instruction are a very poor predictor of learning. What students can do in a lesson – or in response to feedback – tells us very little about what they might be able to do elsewhere and later. Teachers provide cues and prompts to increase students' performance in lessons and students are skilled at mimicking what they think teachers want to see and hear. This mimicry might result in learning but often doesn't.

Most counter-intuitively, psychologists have found that reducing current performance can actually increase future learning. In certain circumstances it seems that if students struggle to perform well during instruction their memory of what was learned is more flexible and durable.

Each item in memory has a storage strength and a retrieval strength. Storage indicates how well an item is embedded in long-term memory and retrieval indicates how easily an item can be brought to mind when needed.[*] Attempts to increase retrieval strength improve performance in the short term but very quickly fade. It appears that trying to retrieve something from memory too quickly can interfere with our ability to store it more strongly. That said, if we wait until we've started to forget something, retrieval practice increases our ability to recall it in the long term. The best way to increase storage strength is to allow memories to fade before trying to retrieve them. Surprisingly, forgetting improves long-term memory.[†] (See Chapter 5 for a more detailed explanation.)

Robert Bjork and colleagues have suggested that the best way to make items in memory more flexible and durable is to introduce 'desirable difficulties' at the point of instruction.[‡] Bjork defines a difficulty as desirable if it makes retrieval practice harder in the short term but acts to increase retention and transfer. The desirable difficulties which have the best evidence base are spacing, interleaving, variation, testing and reducing feedback.

Thinking

There are two common usages of the term 'thinking'. One holds that thinking is everything that the conscious mind does. This would include perception, mental arithmetic, remembering a phone number, or conjuring up an image of an elephant-headed zebra. We might also include the many varieties of unconscious thought but whilst unconscious cognitive processes may well be tremendously important in shaping the way we make sense of the world, we

---

[*]   Bjork, R. & Bjork, E. (1992)
[†]   Storm, B. et al (2008)
[‡]   Bjork, R. (1994b)

are using 'thinking' in its conscious sense. Simply equating thinking with any and all conscious cognitive processes is too broad to be useful. Thinking is an essentially active process and therefore distinct from the more passive 'thought'. Thought is the result of thinking and thinking is the struggle to get from A to B.

So, thinking is conscious and it is active. It is the kind of deliberative cognitive process that allows us to make new connections and create meaning. It is dialogic: it has the quality of an internal conversation between different perspectives, although this is not always immediately obvious. And it is linguistic: verbal for those of us who use spoken language, visual for those of us who use sign language to communicate with others and with ourselves.

This is not to say that language is essential for thinking[*] but it is certainly connected. We can think things we cannot say but we cannot say anything we cannot think. Although we can catch glimpses of thought untethered to language, we can only really become conscious of what we can put into words. Thought then, for our purposes, is the inner dialogue we have with ourselves.[†]

In this section of the book we will look at what psychology has to tell us about how students learn and think and what we as teachers can do to harness this knowledge.

References

Bjork, R. A. (1994b) 'Institutional impediments to effective training', in Druckman, D. & Bjork, R.A. (eds.) *Learning, remembering, believing: Enhancing human performance*, Washington, DC: National Academies Press.

Bjork, R. A. & Bjork, E. L. (1992) 'A new theory of disuse and an old theory of stimulus fluctuation', in Healy, S. Kosslyn & Shiffrin, R. (eds.) *From Learning Processes to Cognitive Processes: Essays in Honor of William K. Estes* (Vol. 2), Hillsdale, NJ: Erlbaum, pp. 35-67.

Pinker, S. (2015) *The Language Instinct: How the Mind Creates Language*, London: Penguin.

Reiber. R.W. & Carton, S.C. (1998) *The Collected Works of L. S. Vygotsky: Problems of General Psychology*, Volume 2, New York: Springer.

Storm, B. C., Bjork, E. L. & Bjork, R. A. (2008) 'Accelerated relearning after retrieval-induced forgetting: The benefit of being forgotten', *Journal of Experimental Psychology: Learning, Memory, and Cognition*, 34(1), 230-236.

---

[*] That is the Sapir-Whorf hypothesis: the idea that certain thoughts an individual thinks in one language cannot be understood by those who think in another language. Most psycholinguists have roundly dismissed this notion.

[†] This is by no means uncontroversial and it should be understood that condensed internal dialogue is quite different and distinct from expanded external dialogue. It is perhaps instructive to read Lev Vygotsky's essay 'Thinking and Speech' as well as Stephen Pinker's *The Language Instinct*.

Chapter 1
Evolutionary psychology*

Most social animals, even invertebrates, are attracted to the presence and behaviour of members of the same species. This requires very little flexibility in intelligence or capacity to socially learn, but still allows these animals to exploit food resources or discover good nesting sites. However, many non-human animals also appear genuinely capable of social learning. Difficult cognitive tricks like imitation – for example, birds imitating a local 'dialect' of song – and emulation – for example, tool use in chimpanzees – lie at the heart of this ability. These can form 'traditions', observed in primates and some other species of mammals, birds and even fish. In this sense, a 'tradition' is a durable characteristic of a group of individual animals which is created and sustained through repeated social learning.

Beyond passing on and sustaining a clever trick or two, to what extent do other animals possess culture? Some anthropologists, like Miriam Haidle, suggest that a basic cultural capacity might be recognized where there exists a diversity of traditions within a social group. The great apes appear to exhibit this diversity of tradition – to a lesser degree, perhaps so too do some other primates and cetaceans. However, even the most advanced forms of non-human animal culture lack a key feature of human culture: a 'cumulative culture', where more complex cultural forms are built upon existing ones.

The philosopher Daniel Dennett suggests that Darwinian evolution depends upon a high fidelity of transmission. If information suffers too many copying

---

* Extracts from this chapter first appeared in Martin Robinson's *Trivium in Practice* (2016), published by Crown House and are used here with their kind permission.

errors, good tricks can be lost from the population as quickly as they might appear. At some point the accuracy with which cultural information was able to be passed on seems to have crossed some sort of threshold, allowing cultural evolution to take off. Chimpanzees might discover a good foraging trick and (if by fortune it is directly observed and imitated), it might be passed on to their troop, but it appears they lack the cognitive architecture required for cumulative culture. Early hominids may have been able to accumulate culture, but without the technology to represent and store these ideas, they could swiftly become lost through accident or poor communication.

This ability to code and decode notional culture allows us to become time travellers within the realm of ideas. Writing allows us to reach across the sands of time to the occasional diamonds that emerged from the dust. According to psychologist Susan Blackmore, it allowed some "good, useful, true, or beautiful" ideas to travel across this brief period of written history and survive to this day (Blackmore, 2007: 4). Indeed, in the information age, our ability to store and communicate notional culture appears almost unlimited. I say almost unlimited, for there is perhaps one pretty fundamental limitation: our brains are basically the same as those of Upper Palaeolithic humans.

In *Educating the Evolved Mind*, David Geary argues for a distinction between two types of knowledge and ability: those that are biologically primary and emerge instinctively by virtue of our evolved cognitive structures, and those that are biologically secondary and exclusively cultural, acquired through formal or informal instruction or training. Evolution through natural selection has built brains that eagerly and rapidly learn the sorts of things which benefited our capability to survive and reproduce. These primary forms of knowledge and ability are not inflexible, but they readily process quite restricted classes of information. Geary divides these biologically primary domains into folk psychology (interest in people), folk biology (interest in living things), and folk physics (interest in inanimate objects). He suggests that we have a motivational bias towards learning such things as peer interaction, play hunting of other species, and exploration of the physical environment within these primary domains. So adaptive were these kinds of knowledge that over time we evolved the ability to create symbolic representations of experiences and techniques like storytelling to communicate these experiences.

Geary also points out that children's inherent motivational bias to adapt folk knowledge to the local social environment will often conflict with the need to engage in activities that will result in secondary learning – interacting with your friendship group will always feel more important and fun than doing homework. Another reason why children may struggle with motivation in school is that the cognitive resources we use to learn are well adapted for biologically primary knowledge, but have been co-opted for the purposes of learning secondary knowledge. Learning to read or learning mathematics are not 'natural' human activities – in the sense that these technologies have been around for such a short time that evolution through natural selection hasn't had much of a chance to shape our brains to learn them as easily as we learn 'folk knowledge'. As a result, such activities are typically much more difficult and take more effort.

The problem for teachers is that working memory (see Chapter 3) is well adapted to processing the sorts of information and solving the sorts of problem related to biologically primary knowledge. Humans appear to have exapted this cognitive resource to deal with biologically secondary knowledge acquisition – and, as a result, we find such learning difficult.

Psychologists often use the term 'schema' (*pl.* schemas or schemata) when talking about the encoding and retrieval of information from our long-term memory. First introduced by psychologists such as Piaget and Bartlett, a schema can be thought of as an organized framework representing some aspect of the world and a system of organizing that information. The classic example used frequently in psychology is going to a restaurant (we've no idea why; perhaps psychologists can't cook). The schema for getting a table, ordering food and drink, and paying for the meal, makes visiting a new restaurant for the first time, even in another country, a pretty straightforward process, as we deal with new situations by linking them to things we've encountered in the past. Most of the time we can rely on pre-existing schemata as a heuristic, or rule of thumb: it requires little thought and acts like a cognitive 'shortcut' when dealing with new information.

Schemata provide a quick and painless way to deal with new information and allow us to cope with complex changes in the environment or social situation by quickly drawing on our prior experiences. They can also get in the way when learning. Schemata readily form around biologically primary knowledge and act as rough-and-ready rules, intuitive but also often stereotyped or based on misconceptions. When drawing upon schemata we make minimal use of working memory – it simply doesn't need very much conscious reasoning. Daniel Kahneman, in *Thinking, Fast and Slow*, describes this as 'system 1 thinking': fast, effortless, based on emotions and stereotypes, and usually subconscious. As a result, it leaves decision making open to a wide variety of cognitive biases. These biases represent essential ways in which humans are irrational in their thinking and decision making, but probably emerged because they were in some way adaptive in our evolutionary past (e.g. Geary (2007) suggests such cognitive biases form the basis of primary 'folk knowledge'). Many examples of these biases and the ways in which these may influence the decisions made in schools are discussed in David's book, *What if Everything You Knew about Education was Wrong?*

Kahneman contrasts this fast 'schematic' processing with system 2 thinking, which is slow, effortful, logical and conscious. We can relate this to what's happening when working memory becomes heavily involved in the processing of new information. It's hard and we don't especially enjoy it. The brain has evolved to make efficient use of schemata (which form most readily around the 'folk knowledge' needed to survive and reproduce) and when a schema doesn't fit we possess only limited mental resources for conscious problem solving (see Chapters 3 and 4). To quote psychologist Daniel Willingham, "Your brain serves many purposes, and thinking is not the one it serves best."[*]

Humans have only very recently, in evolutionary terms, started to significantly accumulate biologically secondary knowledge (science, mathematics, art, literature, engineering, computing etc.). Geary suggests that these cultural advances have resulted in an ever-growing gap between folk knowledge (easy and intuitive) and this growing cultural knowledge base (more difficult to learn) needed for living in society, and that schools emerged in societies to close the gap between the two. Education, in its broadest sense, is what makes *homo sapiens* such a unique kind of animal.

Into the classroom

Evolution through natural selection has shaped our minds to rapidly learn the sorts of behaviours which helped survival and reproduction over the course of our evolutionary past. Things like first spoken language acquisition, developing a basic sense of number, basic motor skills, spatial awareness and social skills arise universally and are easily 'discovered' without the need for explicit teaching of any kind (indeed it would be a waste of time and possibly counterproductive). We're highly motivated to learn this kind of material and it comes to us with minimal effort.

However, the majority of the learning children do in school involves cultural-specific knowledge which has often taken decades (in many cases centuries or perhaps millennia) to be discovered by humans. For example, whilst spoken language has emerged spontaneously all over the world, written language is a very recent cultural trick. We may rapidly develop a simple sense of small numbers, but there's an enormous amount of culturally specific learning

---

[*] Willingham, D. (2009: 4)

required to become functionally numerate (let alone a decent mathematician). This kind of learning is effortful and difficult – because evolution through natural selection has not had time to shape our minds to rapidly learn this way.

As a consequence, we're forced to use our limited working memory resources to learn this material. It requires considerable motivation as it takes considerable conscious effort to do this, though (as we'll see) the material we already know actively helps this become easier over time.

Theory of Mind and the ability to teach

To what extent does effective teaching involve a biologically secondary set of knowledge and skills and to what extent is it a biologically primary ability? Effective teachers appear to anticipate how students think about their subject and to use this insight to ask effective questions. The ability to infer how other people think and feel is referred to by psychologists as 'Theory of Mind' (ToM). ToM enables a person to explain and predict the behaviour of other people by inferring the mental states which cause that behaviour. The philosopher Daniel Dennett calls this the 'Intentional Stance"* – understanding that other people's actions are goal-directed and arise from their beliefs or desires.

Strauss, Ziv and Stein (2002) proposed that ToM is an important prerequisite for teaching. A few other animals, for example chimpanzees, appear to teach conspecifics in a limited way, but only humans appear to teach using the ability to anticipate the mental states of the individual being taught. They point to the fact that the ability to teach arises spontaneously at an early age without any apparent instruction and that it is common to all human cultures as evidence that it is an innate ability. Essentially, they suggest that despite its complexity, teaching is a natural cognition that evolved alongside our ability to learn.

Strauss, Ziv and Stein taught pre-school children how to play a board game, and then observed that child's behaviour when teaching another child. The study identified a range of teaching strategies:

- Demonstration – teacher actively shows learner what to do, e.g. moves the train on the track and stops at a station.
- Specific directive – teacher tells the learner what to do right now, e.g. "Take this".
- Verbal explanation – teacher explains to the learner a rule or what he/she should be doing, e.g. "You got green. You can take the cube".
- Demonstration accompanied by a verbal explanation.

---

* Dennett, D. C. (1989)

- Questions aimed at checking the learner's understanding – "Do you understand"? "Remember"?
- Teacher talk about own teaching – teacher shares with the learner his/her teaching strategies, e.g. "I will now explain to you how to play".
- Responsiveness – teacher responds to utterances or actions of the learner, e.g. answers questions when a learner errs and demonstrates or verbally repeats a rule.

They found that five-year-olds appeared to have a more advanced understanding of teaching compared to three-year-olds: relying more on verbal explanations, more responsive to the learner's difficulties, along with asking questions aimed at checking the learner's understanding.

From his studies of imitation in infants, the psychologist Andrew Meltzoff suggests ToM is an innate understanding that others are "like me" – allowing us to recognise the differences in the physical and mental states apparent in others by relating them to our own actions, thoughts and feelings'. In essence, ToM is a bit like the ability to use your own mind to simulate and predict the states of others. Baron Cohen has suggested that a functioning ToM involves both affective and cognitive components – the ability to emotionally respond to another's mental states and the ability to understand another's mental state. People likely vary on a spectrum across both of these components. He has suggested that psychopaths, for example, probably have a very high functioning cognitive ToM (required to be able to deceive and manipulate people) but 'zero negative' empathy for others.

It seems likely that great teachers need both: the ability to model other people's thought processes (e.g. how students think about a subject), balanced by an empathetic concern for others. However, if teaching is essentially a natural ability, then potentially a great deal of professional development may involve trying to teach the sorts of biologically primary abilities we can discover easily for ourselves. So, an important question might be: exactly what is the biologically secondary, 'technical' or 'professional' body of knowledge or set of skills required of an effective teacher, which can actually be taught?

One possible part of the answer to this question is 'pedagogic content knowledge'. In the Sutton Trust report 'What makes great teaching?' the idea of what knowledge makes a great teacher was defined as this:

---

* Baron Cohen argues that individuals on the autistic spectrum lack ToM, and struggle with the idea that other people can have different mental states to their own – often assuming that other people will share what they think and know.

(Pedagogical) content knowledge (Strong evidence of impact on student outcomes)

The most effective teachers have deep knowledge of the subjects they teach, and when teachers' knowledge falls below a certain level it is a significant impediment to students' learning. As well as a strong understanding of the material being taught, teachers must also understand the ways students think about the content, be able to evaluate the thinking behind students' own methods, and identify students' common misconceptions. (2014: 2)

Whilst a great deal of what we do in the classroom is always going to be instinctual, there's a lot to learn about the way children think about the subjects and topics we teach, and how we can help them learn. The next chapters will take a look at how psychological research into memory and learning might provide a promising basis for the parts of teaching which require conscious effort like planning a lesson or designing the sequence of a curriculum.

What every teacher needs to know about evolutionary psychology

- Understanding the evolution of how we learn asks some difficult questions about the curriculum we put in front of children. Whilst they will be highly motivated and engaged when they have opportunities to socially interact and develop other biologically primary abilities, these are things they would probably learn independently without giving up curriculum time.

- We shouldn't be surprised that students often seem less motivated by school as they get older. Biologically secondary learning is effortful and difficult and we're adapted to prefer the sorts of primary learning because it was adaptive in our evolutionary past.

- A key idea in the psychology of learning is the 'schema'. Learning new information requires secure foundations (schemas) of prior knowledge. There are likely to be some concepts, facts or ideas that are more 'foundational' than others.

- How do students 'select' which schema to use when tackling questions or problems in lessons? Perhaps, as Geary implies, the more our subject relies upon biologically secondary knowledge, the more readily a student will rely upon a misconception based on their prior 'folk knowledge'.

- A final possible implication is the use of storytelling or narrative structure in teaching; Willingham makes the point that stories have a privileged place in memory. Our brains have adapted to readily recall stories, and he suggests we might use the abstract structure of stories (he suggests causality, conflict, complications and character) within a sequence of learning. How might we exploit this adaptation of memory to help students build firmer foundations of knowledge?

- Teaching involves the 'impossible task' of mind reading – not only identifying gaps in a student's knowledge, beliefs or skills but also whether they hold incomplete or distorted ideas. In addition, great teachers make countless, unconscious inferences about students' emotional and motivational states (are they attentive, tired, bored or confused?) and react intuitively to these states. Teaching is such a complex task it is probably impossible to 'do it consciously'.

- However, there is potentially a body of knowledge which might help to guide conscious tasks like planning and curriculum design. To do this well appears to require in-depth knowledge of a subject area, but also a firm understanding of how children think and learn.

References

Baron-Cohen, S. (2001) 'Theory of mind and autism: A review', *International review of research in mental retardation: Autism*, 23, 169-184.

Blackmore, S. (1999) *The Meme Machine*, Oxford: Oxford University Press.

Blackmore, S. (2007) 'Imitation Makes Us Human', in Pasternak, C. (ed.), *What Makes Us Human?* Oxford: Oneworld Publications, pp. 1–16.

Coe, R., Aloisi, C., Higgins, S. & Major, L. E. (2014) *What makes great teaching? Review of the underpinning research*, London: Sutton Trust.

Dennett, D. C. (1995) *Darwin's Dangerous Idea*, London: Penguin.

Dennett, D. C. (1989) *The intentional stance*, Cambridge, MA: MIT press.

Didau, D. (2015) *What If Everything You Knew About Education Was Wrong?* Carmarthen, UK: Crown House Publishing Ltd.

Geary, D. C. (2007) 'Educating the Evolved Mind: Conceptual Foundations for an Evolutionary Educational Psychology', in Carlson, J. S. & Levin, J. R. (eds.), *Educating the Evolved Mind*, Greenwich, CT: Information Age, pp. 1–99.

Haidle, M. N., Bolus, M., Collard, M., Conard, N., Garafoli, D., Lombard, M. ... & Whiten, A. (2015) 'The nature of culture: an eight-grade model for the evolution and expansion of cultural capacities in hominins and other animals', *Journal of Anthropological Sciences*, 93, pp. 43-70.

Kahneman, D. (2011) *Thinking, Fast and Slow*, New York: Farrar, Straus and Giroux.

Meltzoff, A. N. (1999) 'Born to learn: What infants learn from watching us', in Fox N. & Worhol J. G. (eds) *The role of early experience in infant development*, Pediatric Institute Publications, Skillman, pp. 145–164.

Piaget, J. (1961) 'The Genetic Approach to the Psychology of Thought', *Journal of Educational Psychology*, 52: 275–281.

Strauss, S., Ziv, M. & Stein, A. (2002) 'Teaching as a natural cognition and its relations to preschoolers' developing theory of mind', *Cognitive Development*, 17(3), 1473-1487.

Willingham, D. (2009) *Why Don't Students Like School? A Cognitive Scientist Answers Questions about How the Mind Works and What it Means for the Classroom*, San Francisco, CA: Jossey-Bass.

Chapter 2
Prior learning and misconceptions

Prior knowledge is the most important difference between students, certainly far more important and useful for teachers to be aware of than any of the concepts discussed in Chapter 25 on individual differences. Students' minds are not a blank slate; when children arrive at school they already know lots of stuff. Even though students in the same lesson might all go through essentially the same learning process, their background knowledge, experiences, interests and motivations can be wildly different. According to Graham Nuthall, whenever teachers begin a new topic, on average students already know about half of what they're told – it's just that they each know a different half.[*] Obviously enough, this prior knowledge affects how students acquire new knowledge and skills; what is already known interacts with the material being learned. In Chapters 3-5 we will discuss how memories are formed and schemas of learning established. Then in Chapter 7 we will explore the differences between novice and expert learners.

As discussed in the previous chapter, when we learn new ideas and pieces of information our minds organise it all into *schemas*. A schema is a web of interrelated information that allows us to keep track of everything we've learned. Say you learn about the Roman practice of *decimation* – the method Roman generals used to punish cowardly or disobedient legionaries by forcing them to kill one in ten of their comrades – then this information may be

---
[*] Nuthall, G. (2007: 35)

categorised as 'Roman', 'history', 'school stuff', 'stuff about killing', 'disgusting stuff' and a whole range of other potential categories. This item of information is interesting because it links to so many different schema and so is relatively easy to recall. But if you learn how to do long division, then this might only be stored in the 'maths' schema and therefore be tricky to retrieve when you might need the information elsewhere.

Nuthall says that, "learning does not come directly from classroom activities; learning comes from the way students experience those activities."[*] When students are given new information, they hold it in working memory as they connect it to other new information and experiences and evaluate it against known concepts. If the new information is sufficiently integrated then it will be 'learnt': that is, retained in long-term memory.

Since what you learn depends on what you know, knowing what students know and can do when they come into the classroom, or before they begin a new topic of study, will help us design lessons that build on student strengths and acknowledge and address their weaknesses. Daniel Willingham says, "students come to understand new ideas by relating them to old ideas. If their knowledge is shallow, the process stops there."[†]

There are two related processes at work here:

Conceptual *growth* – learning more about what is already known.

Conceptual *competition* – misconceptions continue to influence our thinking even after new understandings are learned.

Conceptual growth is relatively straightforward, conceptual competition is not. The psychologist Robert Siegler has suggested that the way we learn is like waves overlapping as the tide comes in; although the movement up the beach is inexorable, it is hesitant and sometimes results in false starts. At any given time, children think in a variety of ways and their understanding ebbs and flows as new understandings overlap with existing understandings. The frequency of these ways of thinking shift gradually and more advanced ways of thinking are constantly being introduced.

Many misconceptions are widely held, predictable and therefore easily anticipated by a teacher with sound pedagogical content knowledge, but they are probably impossible to completely dislodge for several reasons. Most obviously, students are generally unaware that the knowledge they possess is erroneous. Why else would they believe it? Some misconceptions can become

---

[*]   Nuthall, G. (2007: 103)
[†]   Willingham, D. (2010: 72)

deeply entrenched in students' thinking and as new information is embedded into their faulty schemas the belief in bad ideas is further entrenched. Some misconceptions are based on folk knowledge, as discussed in Chapter 1 – things that just seem intuitively correct.

Geary identifies at least three distinctive forms of folk knowledge which lead to children making these kinds of misconceptions: folk psychology, folk biology and folk physics. All three branches of folk knowledge appear to have evolved to help us survive and thrive; folk psychology describes our intuitive fascination with other people and ourselves, whereas folk biology and physics help us to make sense of the world around us. Often though, these intuitive folk understandings are at odds with scientific explanations of how the world actually works. None of this makes much difference to our survival from an evolutionary perspective, but can be pretty annoying from the perspective of education.

There's an obvious link between folk biology and physics and their associated academic disciplines and Geary has suggested that the schemas associated with folk psychology are important in learning to read and write. He speculates that, "the invention of written symbols emerged from the motivational disposition to communicate with and influence the behaviour of other people (e.g. morals in the Bible); thus, writing-reading is predicted to be dependent on folk psychological communication systems. More precisely, learning to read and write involves co-opting primary folk psychological systems."[*]

Problematically, misconceptions tend to be resistant to instruction[†], as whole rafts of students' prior knowledge will compete with the new schemas being taught. Geary points out that, "Not only is the gap between folk biology and the knowledge base of the biological sciences widening at a rapid pace but also the inferential biases of this folk system may sometimes interfere with the comprehension of scientific models of biological phenomena." There are similar problems with folk understandings of physics: the knowledge base of the physical sciences is exponentially larger than the knowledge base of folk physics, and in some cases (e.g. quantum mechanics) the accompanying conceptual models bear little resemblance to the naïve concepts of folk physics.

One argument is that we can induce cognitive change through conceptual conflict. Because students rely on pre-existing notions to understand and

---

*   Geary, D. (2005: 504)

†   It is important to note that the term instruction is used here to mean more than 'telling' – we use it to mean both the process of teaching and the role of the teacher to help students learn. See Chapter 10 for a breakdown of what we mean by effective instruction.

function in the world, they may not easily discard their ideas and adopt a new way of thinking. Simply presenting a new concept or telling students that their views are inaccurate is unlikely to result in conceptual change. Students need to take an active role in reorganising what they know. Cognitive conflict strategies can be effective tools in teaching for conceptual change. The trick is to create situations where students' existing conceptions about particular phenomena or topics are made explicit and then directly challenged in order to create a state of cognitive conflict or disequilibrium. Cognitive conflict strategies are aligned with Posner et al's theory of conceptual change in that their common goal is to create the four conditions necessary for conceptual change: students must become dissatisfied with their current conceptions and accept an alternative notion as intelligible, plausible, and fruitful.

This leads to a discussion of threshold concepts. These are the conceptual areas where students routinely get stuck but upon which further understanding depends. Meyer and Land suggest a threshold concept will most likely possess certain important qualities. Some of the adjectives we could apply to these concepts are:

- **Integrative:** Once learned, they are likely to bring together different parts of the subject which you hadn't previously seen as connected.
- **Transformative:** Once understood, they change the way you see the subject and yourself.
- **Irreversible:** They are difficult to unlearn – once you've passed through it's difficult to see how it was possible not to have understood before.
- **Reconstitutive:** They may shift your sense of self over time. This is initially more likely to be noticed by others, usually teachers.
- **Troublesome:** They are likely to present you with a degree of difficulty and may sometimes seem incoherent or counter-intuitive.
- **Discursive:** The student's ability to use the language associated with that subject changes as they change. It's the change from using scientific keywords in everyday language to being able to fluently communicate in the academic language of science.

Until a student has passed through a particular threshold, they will be in a state of liminality (a state of ambiguity or uncertainty). Moving from knowing to not knowing is a lot less straightforward than we think. Often, when it appears that someone has made rapid progress they are merely mimicking what they think we want them to do. We can memorise things in isolation, but as teachers we would argue that this is a necessary but not sufficient component of learning. Students may begin by 'mere mimicry' but knowing requires that they integrate new information into their schema of prior knowledge*. It is this process of integration that leads to long-term retention and the ability to transfer – at least to a degree – between contexts.

Into the classroom

If we want students to truly understand anything more than the superficialities of our teaching then we need to stop trying to rush them through liminal space. The false certainty of easy answers – successful in-lesson performance – might actively be retarding learning. But we have a problem: we're genetically predisposed to avoid uncertainty. To survive the various threats they faced, our ancestors evolved to make rapid assessments rather than ruminate. If it looks like a duck or, more to the point, if it looks like a snake, we're better off assuming it's a snake rather than having an ontological debate. It's easy to see how a preference for dithering might quickly have been selected out of the gene pool. We are naturally risk averse and are much more sensitive to threats than we are to opportunities for growth and enhancement.

This really is a challenge. Rushing to certainty is the problem but we hate the cognitive conflict caused by uncertainty. The reason it's so problematic is that the rush to certainty leads to maximising short-term performance, which leads to mimicry, but acts to reduce learning in the longer term.

It's possible to see glimpses of students' current understanding of a specific subject area by conducting a diagnostic assessment prior to instruction on a topic, though in practice these often reveal relatively little. Unless such assessments are very well designed, students tend only to recall what is foremost in their minds; just asking students to record what they know will not be enough. Even if we carefully craft the kind of questions that can reveal faulty thinking, we will only ever have a very rough guide as to what students actually think. That said, we would at least be able to see if major, more obvious misconceptions are being used and address them accordingly.

One possibility is a model-based reasoning approach, which asks students to generate, test and revise a model of their understanding of a topic. Students begin by using their knowledge of the topic to make a prediction about the

---

* We could teach you to say the word 'ysgol' in the absence of any context and you could, with some practice reliably repeat the word back to us. There's been a change in long-term memory – a psychologist might say you've learnt it – and technically you have. However, this is an incomplete notion of 'knowing' something – some element of 'parroting back' is often necessary, but not sufficient for our role as teachers. As well as remembering it, we'd want you to know the meaning of the word and when you might use it. (In case you didn't know, ysgol is the Welsh word for school.)

outcomes of an experiment or the likely developments of a text and explain their reasoning. This mental model can then be tested – either by reading on, conducting an experiment or observing a phenomenon – to see whether they are correct. Any deviation between what was predicted and what occurred should then be discussed, questioned and used to refine the model: what might be a better way of thinking about the topic?

As we've already said, diagnostic assessment doesn't have to just be a test. Direct measures like tests, concept maps, interviews etc. may all be useful but so, sometimes, are more indirect methods like student self-assessment, reports and inventories of topics that have already been studied. However we go about assessing what students know, some sort of benchmark allows us to have a rough idea of how much they've learned at the end of a teaching sequence.

> **What every teacher needs to know about prior learning**
>
> Teachers need to bring about significant conceptual change. Some strategies that have might be effective include:
>
> - Ask students to write down their pre-existing conceptions of the material being covered. This allows you to explicitly assess their preconceptions and provides them with an opportunity to see how far their understanding has come after learning the new concepts.
> - Find conceptions which are correct and build bridging analogies to the new concept or theory to be learned.
> - New concepts or theories should be presented in such a way that students see them as plausible, high quality, intelligible and generative.
> - Use model-based reasoning, which helps students construct new representations that vary from their intuitive theories.
> - Use diverse instruction, wherein you present a few examples that challenge multiple assumptions, rather than a larger number of examples that challenge just one assumption.
> - Help students become aware of their misconceptions and present them with examples which contradict their understanding.
> - There may be value in presenting students with experiences that cause cognitive conflict. Experiences that can cause cognitive conflict are ones that get students to compare misconceptions alongside, or at the same time as, correct concepts. However, be

aware that students need a degree of background knowledge to 'wrestle' effectively with the conflict otherwise they may ignore the conceptual differences you are trying to illustrate, or even become more convinced of the misconception (called the 'backfire effect' in psychology).

- Use case studies – concrete, real world scenarios with accompanying references – as teaching tools to deepen understanding of new material and reduce misconceptions.
- Help students self-repair their misconceptions. If students engage in a process of 'self-explanation' then recalling correct concepts is more likely. Self-explanation entails prompting students to explain text aloud as they read.
- Once students have overcome their misconceptions, engage them in debate to strengthen their newly acquired understanding.

We should certainly try to find out what students know before we start teaching, and since this is an impossible job, we ought to focus on exposing the misconceptions predicted by folk understandings of academic subjects.

References

Blunt, J. R. & Karpicke, J. D. (2014) 'Learning with retrieval-based concept mapping', *Journal of Educational Psychology*, 106(3), 849.

Clement (1993) 'Using Bridging Analogies and Anchoring Intuitions to Deal with Students' Preconceptions in Physics', *Journal of Research in Science Teaching*, 30(10), 1241-1257.

deLeeuw, N. & Chi, M. T. H. (2003) 'Self-explanation: Enriching a situation model or repairing a domain model?', in Sinatra, G. M. & Pintrich, P. R. (eds.) *Intentional conceptual change*, Mahwah, NJ: Lawrence Erlbaum Associates, Inc, pp. 55-78.

Duit, R. (1999) 'Conceptual change approaches in science education', in W. Schnotz, S. Vosniadou, & Carretero, M. (eds.), *New Perspectives on Conceptual Change*, Oxford: Pergamon, pp. 263-282.

Eryilmaz, A. (2002) 'Effects of conceptual assignments and conceptual change discussions on students' misconceptions and achievement regarding force and motion', *Journal of Research in Science Teaching*, 39(10), 1001–1015. doi.org/10.1002/tea.10054

Geary, D. C. (2005) 'Folk knowledge and academic learning', in Ellis, B. J. & Bjorklund, D. F. (eds.) *Origins of the social mind*, New York: Guilford Publications, pp. 493–519.

Holding, M., Denton, R., Kulesza, A. & Ridgway, J. (2014) 'Confronting scientific misconceptions by fostering a classroom of scientists in the introductory biology lab', *American Biology Teacher*, 76(8), 518–523.

Johnson, M. & Sinatra, G. (2014) 'The influence of approach and avoidance goals on conceptual change', *Journal of Educational Research*, 107(4), 312–325. doi:10.1080/002 20671.2013.807492

Karpicke, J. D. & Blunt, J. R. (2011) 'Retrieval Practice Produces More Learning than Elaborative Studying with Concept Mapping', *Science*, 331, 772. http://memory.psych.purdue.edu/downloads/2011_Karpicke_Blunt_Science.pdf

M. Teresa Lechuga, Juana M. Ortega-Tudela, Carlos J. Gómez-Ariza (2015) 'Further evidence that concept mapping is not better than repeated retrieval as a tool for learning from texts', *Learning and Instruction*, 40, 61-68.

Mayer, R. E. (2011). *Applying the science of learning*, Boston, MA: Pearson.

Meyer, J. H. F. & Land. R. (eds.) (2006) *Overcoming Barriers to Student Understanding: Threshold concepts and troublesome knowledge*, London: Routledge.

Meyer, J. H. F., Land. R. & Bailie. C. (eds.) (2010) *Threshold Concepts and Transformational Learning*, Rotterdam: Sense Publishers.

Nersessian, N (1999) 'Model Based Reasoning in Conceptual Change', in Magnani. L., Nersessian, N.J. & Thagard, P (eds.) *Model Based Reasoning in Scientific Discovery*, Dordrecht, Netherlands: Kluwer/Plenum, pp. 5-22.

Novak & Cañas (2008) *The Theory Underlying Concept Maps and How to Construct and Use Them*, Institute for Human and Machine Cognition, Technical Report IHMC CmapTools 2006-01 Rev 2008-01 http://cmap.ihmc.us/docs/theory-of-concept-maps

Nuthall, G. (2007) *The Hidden Lives of Learners*, Wellington, NZ: NZCER Press.

Pashler, H., Bain, P. M., Bottge, B. A., Graesser, A., Koedinger, K. R., McDaniel, M. & Metcalfe, J. (2007). *Organizing instruction and study to improve student learning* (NCER 2007-2004), Washington, DC: U.S. Department of Education, Institute of Education Sciences, National Center for Education Research. Retrieved from http://ies.ed.gov/ncee/wwc/practiceguide.aspx?sid=1

Posner, G. J., Strike, K. A., Hewson, P. W. & Gertzog, W. A. (1982). 'Accommodation of a scientific conception: Toward a theory of conceptual change', *Science Education*, 66, 211-227.

Raghavan, K. & Glaser, R. (1994) 'Studying and Teaching Model-based Reasoning in Science, Technology-Based Learning Environments', NATO ASI Series, 137, pp 104-111.

Savinainen, A. & Scott, P. (2002). The Force Concept Inventory: A tool for monitoring student learning, *Physics Education*, 37(1), 45–52.

Siegler, R. (1998) *Emerging Minds: The Process of Change in Children's Thinking*, Oxford: Oxford University Press.

Willingham, D. (2010) *Why Don't Children Like School?* San Francisco, CA: Jossey-Bass.

Chapter 3
Working memory

Everyone has taught lessons where students leave your classroom confident they've understood a tricky concept only for them to have forgotten it by the next time you see them. Essentially, the problem of helping students develop knowledge and understanding involves two aspects of memory: working and long-term memory. Obviously, we want children to have long-term memory of the stuff we've been teaching, but one of the obstacles to this is limitation of our working memory.

Our capacity for long-term memory appears huge.* However, our brains have not evolved to be some enormous data storage device; they have evolved to be 'just good enough' to help us survive and reproduce. Our memories are reconstructive rather than recordings, associative rather than predictable, cue dependent rather than reliable. Our ability to remember has adapted to help us learn important survival information and function in our social environment, and is not well adapted for learning about science, mathematics, literature,

---

* No one really knows the upper limit of long-term memory capacity. Clues exist – for example cases of hyperthymesia (Marilu Henner who played Elaine in the long-running US sitcom *Taxi* is a famous example). Hyperthymesia is a condition where an individual possesses extraordinarily detailed autobiographical memory – being able to recall precise details of everyday life events since childhood. A recent study (Bartol et al, 2015) attempted to estimate this capacity by looking at how much information might be stored at each synapse (the tiny gaps between neurons which control the flow of information in the brain). Scaling up from their sample, they judged that the total memory capacity of the brain was in the region of a petabyte (a million gigabytes) which – to give you some sense of scale – is roughly the total contents of the World Wide Web. The estimate of human long-term memory capacity has increased over the years.

art history and so on. The science-fiction trope of being able to plug in and download information as and when we need it is a fantasy. Although human beings may have an enormous capacity to store information long-term, we need to learn it first – and that requires new information to squeeze through the 'bottleneck' of working memory.

The Working Memory Model (WMM), developed in 1970s by Alan Baddeley and Graham Hitch, is one of the most robust theories within cognitive science. As you'd expect for a scientific theory, it has been refined a number of times since the original model, but the basic elements of the model have survived the process of empirical testing very well.

Before Baddeley and Hitch proposed working memory, Atkinson and Shriffin's Multi-Store Model (MSM) had been the dominant theory. The MSM presented memory processes as a fairly linear progression from a sensory store (which momentarily holds perceptual information – quickly lost unless attended to), to a short-term memory (STM) store (which held information through rehearsal – e.g. silently repeating it to yourself) to a long-term memory (LTM) store (information held indefinitely after sufficient rehearsal).

Baddeley and Hitch reviewed a large number of brain injury cases and identified a number of findings that simply couldn't be explained by the MSM. For example, the case of KF, who was able to process and recall visual information but was unable to retain some types of verbally presented information. From these various case studies, Baddeley and Hitch saw that STM was not a single store, but a more complex multi-component process.

Overall, the WMM proposes that what was called STM is actually the active part of LTM – the two are not separate stores. There are four main components to the WMM, which coordinate together when we try to process new information. It's often described as the part of memory that is engaged when trying to calculate mental arithmetic or reading a sentence. If you feel like you're doing conscious, effortful thinking, then your working memory is active (though some psychologists have questioned the reverse – whether working memory always requires conscious awareness*).

---

* For example: Soto, D., Mäntylä, T. & Silvanto, J. (2011) 'Working memory without consciousness', *Current Biology*, 21(22), 912–913

The components of working memory

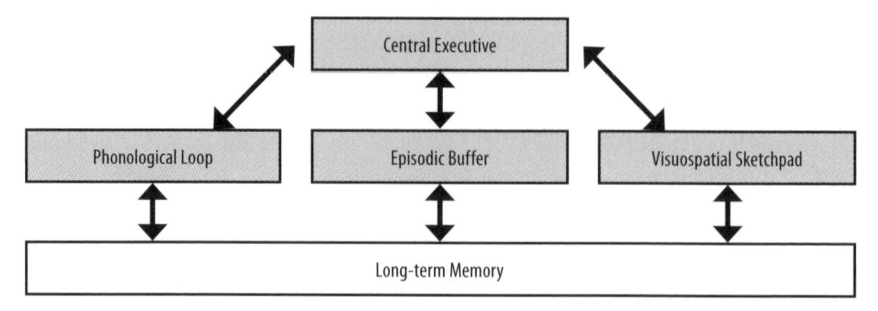

Figure 1: A model of Working Memory

The Central Executive (CE) acts a bit like a supervisor. As information comes into WM, the CE focuses attention to the information – selectively attending to one stimulus over another where there are competing stimuli (e.g. listening to the teacher's voice rather than watching the people playing football outside the window). It's not entirely under conscious control; even when we are highly motivated to focus attention on something, an unexpected stimulus (especially one which might represent a threat) can quickly tear our attention away. As any teacher will know, even your best class will stop listening to you the moment a bee flies in through a window.

The CE is related to the concept of 'executive functioning' which, along with managing attention, helps us do things like problem solving, reasoning and planning, but also allows us to inhibit action or speech within appropriate norms. These functions develop rapidly in early childhood, then slowly throughout adolescence and early adulthood – reaching a peak in our mid-twenties before gradually beginning to decline.

The CE can call upon three 'fluid' or 'dynamic' sub-components to help process new information:

The Phonological Loop (PL) deals with speech and sometimes other kinds of auditory information. This store is itself divided into sub-components, the phonological store (sometimes called the 'inner ear') and the articulatory process (often referred to as the 'inner voice'). Together they act sort of like an echo and temporarily store about two seconds' worth of verbal information before it decays or is overwritten.

This is the part of memory we use to consciously rehearse verbal information to hold it in memory, for example trying to remember a phone number while we search for a pen. The PL (specifically the articulatory mechanism) also converts some visually presented material into an auditory form (e.g. converting graphemes to phonemes when presented with an unfamiliar word) and this is helpful as typically visual materials are more difficult to retain through rehearsal.

The Visuo-Spatial Sketchpad (VSS) briefly holds visual information and the spatial relationships between objects. It may also hold onto some kinaesthetic information (relating to the movement and positions of your body). Again, this is simply a temporary store and the information quickly decays unless it is rehearsed.

An example I use when teaching is this: When I was a kid, my light switch was on the other side of the room from the bed. My room wasn't exceptionally tidy, so it was a nightly challenge to navigate back across the room without stepping on something or stubbing a toe. The VSS deals with this kind of problem, holding a brief impression of where things were around me when the light went out.

The Episodic Buffer (EB) was added to the model by Baddeley in 2000 after evidence suggested that there was a need for an additional component to combine the information from the different stores with what we already know. Its principal job is to integrate new information with information already stored in LTM. Cognitive science is still learning more and developing ideas about how this component works in WM.

The EB is one of the reasons why cognitive scientists point to the importance of prior knowledge when it comes to learning new material. By activating the relevant information in LTM, new material can be encoded in a meaningful way and successfully stored. The role of LTM in helping working memory is well established and very easy to demonstrate (e.g. compare the retention of a random sequence of letters – DPL OAM IGGB – to a sequence containing meaningful 'chunks': DOG PIG LAMB).

Implications of working memory

One of the key things to know about working memory is how limited it really is! Being distracted whilst trying to process something frequently means we immediately lose the contents of working memory. We also can't deal with much information at once. Famously, in the 1950s George Miller suggested the capacity of our short-term memory was 7±2 'chunks', but more recent research by Cowan (2001) appears to suggest this was a flattering estimate! Even when working memory capacity is at its highest during early adulthood, we may be limited to handling an average of only about four 'chunks' of information at any one time.

On the other hand, we appear to be able to simultaneously process verbal and visual information without problems. This may help explain how popular systems of mnemonics work (e.g. the ancient loci system where items you want to remember are placed in your 'mind's eye' within a familiar location). 'Dual Coding Theory' suggests that attempting to process the same information both visually and verbally has an additive effect and therefore increases the chance of retrieving the memory in future.

Perhaps unsurprisingly, there's some evidence to suggest that variations in working memory function, particularly the CE, may have a strong influence on student attainment (e.g. Gathercole and Pickering, 2000). There's also evidence to suggest that deficits in working memory underlie some of the specific difficulties children face in school. For example, Gathercole and Alloway suggest that as many as 70% of children with learning difficulties relating to reading score very low on tests of working memory. Differences in working memory may also underlie a number of special educational needs, for example ADHD (attention deficit hyperactivity disorder).

This large variation in children's working memory presents a particular challenge for teachers. Gathercole and Alloway estimate, for example, that in a typical Year 3 class of 30 students they would expect to find three children with the working memory capacity of an average four-year-old, but also three children with the working memory equivalent to an 11-year-old.

It also seems that the causes of poor working memory are more likely to be related to genetic factors than environmental ones. This may explain the fairly disappointing results from intervention programmes intended to improve working memory (for example adaptive training tasks which involve memory exercises which become more challenging if the trainee performs well).

Despite some fairly confident reports claiming that working memory training packages – such as brain training – could help children with ADHD, dyspraxia, ASD, boost IQ and improve school grades, the results are thin. Studies have shown short-term improvements on both verbal and non-verbal working memory tasks, however these did not last long, nor generalise to things like the ability to do arithmetic or decode words. For attentional control, the effects were small to moderate immediately after training, but reduced to nothing in the follow-up. One of the problems with many of these programmes is that they seem to be based on a fairly naïve 'physical–energetic' model: the simple but incorrect idea that repeatedly 'exercising' working memory will lead to it increasing in capacity, perhaps somewhat analogously to strengthening a muscle by repeated use. Despite the popular idea associated with 'growth mindset' (see Chapter 11), in very many ways the brain really isn't like a muscle.

Into the classroom

Working memory as a bottleneck

There is no practical limit to how much we can learn; the complaint that learning new knowledge pushes out old knowledge isn't true. However, our capacity to 'juggle' much new information at once is very limited. When teaching new material, it's worth bearing in mind this limitation – especially as the working memory capacity of children in your class may be quite varied.

Failures in working memory may show themselves as incomplete recall of instructions, missing out or repeating parts of a task, or the child simply giving up as the task seems overwhelmingly complex. Where teachers observe this, it may be worth evaluating the demands being made on working memory. Things to try might include reducing the number of steps in a sequence of instructions, breaking up the new material you introduce and explicitly linking new information to familiar examples. We'll explore more ideas in the next chapter looking at cognitive load.

Performing two tasks which require the same component of working memory can quickly overload our capacity. For example, if you use slides in your lesson which contain a lot of text and then talk over them, your students are forced to process both using the phonological loop. The words on the board are converted into phonemes as the student reads them occupying the phonological loop, but at the same time your words are also being processed by the same component. Inevitably, students either stop reading what's on the board, stop listening to you – or just stop paying attention altogether!

Using separate components simultaneously

On the other hand, we can use different components at the same time without difficulty. Teachers can exploit the fact that the phonological loop and the visuo-spatial sketchpad can be utilised at the same time by providing 'anchor images' to support a complex verbal explanation. For example, in a science lesson, having an image showing the key stages of a complex process (e.g. a simple animation or series of images showing how enzymes work or the difference between longitudinal and transverse waves) as you explain what's happening can help students remember the explanation better.

Many popular systems of mnemonics exploit this capability by encouraging visual and verbal processing of the same information. The loci method (the basis of Sherlock Holmes' mind palace) is one example, but another common one is the keyword method. The keyword method involves linking words together by incorporating them in a mental image together. For example, the French for umbrella is *parapluie* – which sounds a bit like parachute – so a student might memorise this by imagining someone jumping off a roof using their umbrella as a parachute. Whilst mnemonics are only useful for learning fairly limited types of material, like foreign language vocabulary, obscure science terms or people's names and accomplishments, when used appropriately they can be effective.[*]

The importance of prior knowledge

As discussed in the previous chapter, perhaps the single most important implication arising from working memory research is the importance of prior knowledge when learning new material. Whilst attempts to expand the capacity of working memory directly through training programmes have proved disappointing, one surefire way we can build up the complexity of material children can hold in mind is by ensuring they have the background knowledge to help them process the new material we want them to learn.

Knowledge doesn't just sit in long-term memory waiting to be called upon – it appears to actively help to increase working memory capacity within a domain or type of activity. This is a marvellously positive message for educators. Whilst we may be able to do very little to directly improve working memory in a generic way, we can help children to reason in complex and creative ways when they possess lots of background knowledge. The more you know, the more complex and interesting the connection you can make. By ensuring children have a confident grasp of the inflexible knowledge which forms the foundations of new learning, we provide them with a greater 'mental workspace' which they can use for more complex analytical and evaluative tasks.[†]

---

[*] For a much more detailed review of the effectiveness of mnemonics see: Dunlosky, J., Rawson, K. A., Marsh, E. J., Nathan, M. J. & Willingham, D. (2013) 'Improving Students' Learning With Effective Learning Techniques: Promising Directions From Cognitive and Educational Psychology', *Psychological Science in the Public Interest*, 14(1): 4.

[†] A great article explaining more can be found here: Willingham, D. (2006) 'How Knowledge Helps: It Speeds and Strengthens Reading Comprehension, Learning – and Thinking'. http://www.aft.org/periodical/american-educator/spring-2006/how-knowledge-helps

> ## What every teacher needs to know about working memory
>
> - Whilst the human capacity for long-term memory is vast, learning is constrained by the limitations of working memory.
> - We can help students by being broadly aware of their working memory capacity and structuring instructions and tasks so we don't overload them.
> - We should try to teach in a way which avoids multiple demands on the same component of working memory. However, there's an advantage in exploiting different components when teaching new material.
> - Whilst working memory capacity cannot currently be expanded generally, we can readily expand its capacity within particular domains of knowledge. By ensuring children build a firm foundation of background knowledge, we can help them reason and problem-solve in creative and critical ways.
>
> We want our students to reason critically, to be able to apply and evaluate arguments and to be creative in their thinking. Perhaps because teachers tend to be experts in the subject areas they teach, we sometimes lose sight of the fact that novices learn differently to the way we do. In our haste to promote the kinds of skills we want children to possess, do we sometimes underestimate the extensive knowledge we possess which allows us to successfully use those skills?

References

Atkinson, R. C. & Shiffrin, R. M. (1968) 'Human memory: A proposed system and its control processes', in Spence, K. W. & Spence, J. T. (eds.) *The psychology of learning and motivation*. 2, New York: Academic Press, pp. 89–195.

Baddeley, A. D. & Hitch, G. (1974) 'Working memory', in Bower, G.H. (ed.) *The psychology of learning and motivation: Advances in research and theory*, 8, 47–89, New York: Academic Press.

Baddeley, A. D. (2000) 'The episodic buffer: a new component of working memory?' *Trends in Cognitive Science*, 4, 417–423.

Bartol, T. M., Bromer, C., Kinney, J., Chirillo, M. A, Bourne, J. N., Harris, K. M. & Sejnowski, T. J. (2015) Nanoconnectomic upper bound on the variability of synaptic plasticity. *eLife* 4:e10778 http://elifesciences.org/content/4/e10778

Cowan, N. (2001) 'The magical number 4 in short-term memory: a reconsideration of mental storage capacity', *Behaviour and Brain Sciences*, 24(1), 87-114.

Dunlosky, J., Rawson, K. A., Marsh, E. J., Nathan, M. J. & Willingham, D. (2013) 'Improving Students' Learning With Effective Learning Techniques: Promising Directions From Cognitive and Educational Psychology', *Psychological Science in the Public Interest*, 2013; 14(1): 4.

Ericsson, K. A. & Kintsch, W. (1995) 'Long-term working memory', *Psychological review*, 102(2), 211.

Gathercole, S. E. & Alloway, T. P. (2007) *Understanding Working Memory: A Classroom Guide*, London: Harcourt Assessment.

Gathercole, S. E. & Pickering, S. J. (2000) 'Working memory deficits in children with low achievements in the national curriculum at 7 years of age', *British Journal of Educational Psychology* 70, 177-194.

Melby-Lervåg, M. & Hulme, C. (2013) 'Is Working Memory Training Effective? A Meta-Analytic Review', *Developmental Psychology.* 49(2), 270–291.

Miller, G. (1956) 'The magical number seven, plus or minus two: Some limits on our capacity for processing information', *The psychological review,* 63, 81-97.

Otgaar, H. & Howe, M. L. (2014) 'What kind of memory has evolution wrought?' Introductory Article for the Special Issue of Memory: Adaptive memory: The emergence and nature of proximate mechanisms, *Memory*, 22(1), 1-8.

Paivio, A. (1986) *Mental representations: a dual coding approach*, Oxford: Oxford University Press.

Shipstead, Z., Redick, T. S. & Engle, R. W. (2012) 'Is Working Memory Training Effective?', *Psychological Bulletin* 138(4), 628–654.

Willingham, D. (2006) 'How Knowledge Helps: It Speeds and Strengthens Reading Comprehension, Learning and Thinking' http://www.aft.org/periodical/american-educator/spring-2006/how-knowledge-helps

Chapter 4
Cognitive load

In Chapter 2 we gave a brief overview of working memory. There we discussed that, despite our vast capacity to hold information in long-term memory, our working memory is extremely limited (between 3-5 chunks) and becomes overloaded very easily. Greater insight into these problems and some practical ideas about what to do about them comes from the research of John Sweller. Sweller was interested in how teachers could structure their lessons in order to avoid this problem of overload. From the results of numerous experiments, he developed Cognitive Load Theory (CLT) which explains how teachers might optimise the 'load' they place on working memory and help students learn more readily. Essentially, CLT proposes that we want students to think hard about the material we're teaching them without overloading their working memory capacity.

One source of potential overload is the intrinsic difficulty of the material. One obvious source of this difficulty is the number of new elements the student has to juggle in mind at the same time. There's not always much we can do about this as teachers (multiplying 5x8 will always be easier than 5x8x3). However, looking for ways to break up complex material up into simpler sub-components may help. We can focus students on tackling each sub-component separately at first and recombine them later.

Not everything we ask students to do with their working memory is likely to help with the material we want them to learn. A simple example of this is attention switching. For example, having text labels alongside a diagram requires the student to constantly switch attention between the text and the visual image. We can easily reduce this sort of cognitive load by placing the labels at appropriate locations on the diagram.

Problem solving with minimal guidance is also intrinsically difficult, which can be a good thing as it forces children to think hard about the material we want them to learn. However, presenting new material through minimally guided activities can also quickly overload working memory. One reason is that when faced with a novel problem, students tend to use a 'processing intensive' general strategy called means-end analysis in order to find a solution (a bit like old-fashioned chess computers, which looked at every possible move of every possible piece in order to select the best move). Whilst computers are great at this, it's often unsuccessful for students as human working memory capacity is simply too limited to hold all the numerous possible steps towards a solution in mind at once.

For example, science teachers sometimes use practical activities to teach key concepts, like observing the differences in the behaviour of voltage and current in series and parallel circuits. It's not uncommon to discover that students pick up many misconceptions and have weak understanding when later assessed. CLT would explain this as a problem of students trying to juggle too many things at once in their heads, and dropping most of what the teacher wanted them to learn. The lack of familiarity with the key terms and concepts involved means that the practical approach left their understanding of circuits deeply muddled.

The role of long-term memory

A key implication of Sweller's theory is that the presence of schemas (see page 19) in long-term memory effectively reduces the load on working memory. A 'chunk' is the unit of working memory capacity (you can think of it as a collection of elements having strong associations with one another). Although working memory capacity is very limited, the ability to chunk information together allows us to hold more information in mind at once. Essentially, the schema informs you how elements of new information can be grouped together as a chunk.

For example, compare the difficulty of recalling the following sequences of numbers:

6010 8112 9166

1066 1812 1966

The bottom list of digits will be much easier to recall because your long-term memory allows you to group them together as (hopefully meaningful[*]) dates. Therefore, rather than trying to hold 12 items in mind you only have three.

When engaged in a working memory task the presence of schemas essentially reduces the load on working memory. As a consequence, additional capacity is freed for other things educators would like students to be able to do (like reasoning and analysis). Schemas not only form the basis of long-term memory storage but also help overcome working memory limitations.

The loading on working memory is reduced where individuals have a strong background of prior knowledge. Familiar information is said to be organised in our long-term memory as schema, allowing us to work with a larger chunk of new information as if it were one item. So having automatic access to these schemas helps overcome something of the limitations of our working memory. This is why, for instance, many people argue for the memorisation of multiplication tables. For example, if the student doesn't have to mentally calculate 5x8 this will reduce the load on working memory and they will find 5x8x3 easier to 'hold in mind'.

Not all learning is equally hard

Not all material is equally intrinsically difficult. Our brains are adapted to rapidly solve complex problems related to things that might affect our survival and reproduction. David Geary calls this 'biologically primary knowledge' (see Chapter 1) and it seems that the load on working memory appears to be greatly reduced where this sort of knowledge is involved. For example, syllogistic reasoning is notoriously difficult, but we can solve the same problems readily when put into the context of something we've evolved to do, like spotting if someone is breaking a social rule.

A classic illustration of this is the Wason selection task[†]. The abstract version of this task goes a bit like this: Imagine you have four cards on a table in front of you. On each card there is a letter on one side and, if you flip it over, a number on the back. The cards you can see have the letters 'D', 'F', '3' and '5' on them. Which cards would you need to turn over to test the rule that if there's a 'D' on one side of a card, then the opposite side will have a '3' on it?

Only about 10% of people successfully identified the correct solution in Wason's

---

*   The Battle of Hastings, Tchaikovsky's 1812 Overture and England's only victory in the World Cup!

†   The example which follows is adapted from Cosmides, L. & Tooby, J. (1992). 'Cognitive Adaptions for Social Exchange', in Barkow, J., Cosmides, L. & Tooby, J. (eds.) *The adapted mind: Evolutionary psychology and the generation of culture*, New York: Oxford University Press. pp. 163–228.

original study.* One explanation for this difficulty is that we have evolved the capability to rapidly solve complex social problems – but struggle with abstract logical ones because we haven't evolved similar 'mental modules' to deal with these. The ease with which many people solve a social contextualized version of the task (see below) appears to illustrate this. In schools we want students to be able to use abstract mathematical ideas, so we must not be surprised that they find it effortful and difficult.

Evolutionary psychologists Cosmides and Tooby altered the context of this task to one where the participant had to spot social cheating. The social cheating version of this task was like this: Imagine you have four cards on a table in front of you. On each card there is a drink on one side and, if you flip it over, the age of the drinker on the back. The cards you can see have the letters 'Beer', 'Soda', '21' and '17' on them. Which cards would you need to turn over to test the rule that if someone is drinking beer, then they are over 18 years old?

Most people solve this version of the problem without much difficulty.†

Deep versus shallow processing

CLT suggests that we want students to think hard about the material we want them to learn, but is it merely the quantity of that mental effort which leads to learning, or something about the quality of it?

A useful concept here might be the idea of 'levels of processing' – the idea that mental effort might comprise of more shallow or deeper processing. This experimental observation showed that successful encoding in long-term memory depends on the depth to which new information is analysed.

A simple way to illustrate this is consider the difference between a word search and a crossword, which we've often seen used when familiarising students with new terminology. Word search puzzles are a great example of 'shallow processing'; they can be completed with no understanding of the key words but simply pattern matching the first few letters. Such an activity might require mental effort to complete, but it's unlikely to help very much in learning the

---

*　The correct answer is 'D' – in order to check whether there is a '3' on the back – and '5' to check that there isn't a 'D' on the back (as this would break the rule). Many people pick the card showing a '3' but this isn't relevant to the task. The rule is that where there is a 'D' there must be a '3' on the other side – not the reverse. The '3' card could have any letter on the back without breaking the rule.

†　This problem follows exactly the same structure as the original but most people solve it fairly easily: You check 'Beer' to ensure the person is over 18 and you check '17' to make sure they aren't drinking beer. You don't care what the 21-year-old is drinking – it's not like over 18s *have* to drink beer after all.

new terms. On the other hand, a crossword using the definitions of words as the clues is more likely to encourage deeper, semantic processing of the material.

It seems likely that students stop processing information once the analysis relevant to the task has been carried out. So, if a task merely requires shallow processing of the material then deeper processing will not occur and this won't help them form good long-term memory for the material. This may help explain the idea of 'desirable difficulties' leading to more transferable long-term memory. For example, the 'testing effect' (see Chapter 10) appears to stop working once the recall of material becomes fairly automatic. This implies that it's important to allow a certain amount of forgetting to occur before testing recall, otherwise there's very little mental effort involved and the benefits are lost.

An example of this problem is related to photosynthesis. It's not too difficult to get students to recall the idea that carbon dioxide is absorbed from the air to make glucose, but they won't necessarily transfer that understanding if you ask the question in a different way. Quite famously, when you ask students 'where does the mass of a tree come from?' many answer 'from the soil'.

So, it seems probable that predictable rote practice of recall will likely lose any benefit quite quickly as the responses become fairly automated and require little mental effort. Instead, as soon as basic recall starts to become reliable, we should begin to vary the conditions of practice.

Into the classroom

When planning a sequence of learning, it's worth holding in mind some of these limitations and some of the strategies which can help overcome them. The key is to balance the cognitive load so students are 'thinking hard' about the material we want them to learn without overloading working memory.

It's worth looking at the materials we use when teaching. We've seen already in Chapter 3 that we can 'cheat' working memory limitations is by exploiting the fact that visual and auditory information can be processed simultaneously without creating additional load. For example, using visual/audio presentations (which use visual and verbal processing separately) will be much easier to process than where text and explanation (which both require verbal processing) is used. We also need to be aware that attention is a limited resource. Materials which require students to often switch attention from one part of a page to another will reduce the cognitive resources available for processing that information.

It's also worth bearing in mind that when tackling an unfamiliar topic for the first time, tasks which involve students discovering ideas for themselves or goal-directed problem-solving tasks will likely risk overloading working memory and reduce the amount that students learn. As teachers, we're on safer ground teaching the key terms and concepts fairly explicitly, so they can apply these schemas when tackling tasks which require more complex thinking later on. Other strategies include using 'goal-free' problems (e.g. 'find all the angles in this diagram', rather than 'find x') which may encourage the student to avoid the generic, load-intensive means-end approach.[*] A further strategy is to use a series of worked examples rather than problem-solving exercises early in a sequence of learning (discussed further in Chapter 10).[†]

Of course, these strategies presume that students have little prior knowledge of the topic you are teaching. Where students possess lots of background knowledge, these schemas actively help them 'chunk' information in working memory. This reduces the loading on working memory significantly and allows students to use that extra capacity to tackle more complex processes we want them to be able to do – like critical analysis, evaluation and seeing connections between apparently disparate topics. We can also exploit this by anchoring new, abstract ideas to these concrete and familiar ideas students already possess (e.g. through the use of analogy).

Furthermore, these strategies presume that we're teaching quite abstract 'secondary biological knowledge'. Humans have evolved to solve quite complex problems related to survival and reproduction, so where material is related to 'primary biological knowledge' there's likely to be no benefit in explicitly trying to teach them about it.

Lastly, it may be that it's not simply the quantity of mental effort that facilitates learning but also the quality. To develop long-term memory requires retrieval practice, but that practice needs to relate to the semantic properties of the material (what it means). In order to get the most out of the testing effect, we need to space that practice so recall involves more effort and vary the conditions of practice so recall doesn't become too automatic.

---

[*] For example, Paas and Van Merrienboer (1994) argue that giving novices problems that require them to achieve specific goals can lead to students using a processing intensive method of 'means-end' analysis to achieve it. Means-end analysis, in essence, means the student tries to juggle all the possible sub-steps that minimise the difference between the current state (the problem) and the end state (the goal) in mind – which quickly overloads working memory. A 'goal-free' process encourages students away from this strategy, and focuses attention upon working forward from the information present – one step at a time, rather than trying to hold multiple possible steps in mind at once.

[†] Teachers should be aware of the 'reversal effect' which suggests that as students become more knowledgeable they need less guidance and structure. See Chapter 7 for more detail.

What every teacher needs to know about cognitive load

- We want students to think hard about the material we're teaching them without overloading their working memory capacity.
- Where students are tackling new, fairly abstract ideas, we're probably better off explicitly teaching these ideas rather than introducing them through minimally guided approaches like problem solving or discovery learning.
- Prior knowledge appears to actively help working memory by informing us how to chunk information. Therefore, it helps to reduce the load on memory and make more available for complex tasks like analysis or evaluation.
- We've evolved to solve certain kinds of complex problems very readily. If material is related to the sorts of things we needed for survival and reproduction, they tend to take up little working memory capacity and not benefit from explicit instruction.
- We want to maximize the amount of mental effort related to 'deeper' processing of material. Even reliable strategies like the retrieval practice will lose their benefit if they become too automatic. We can rectify this by starting to vary the conditions of practice.

References

Anderson, M. C., Bjork, R. A. & Bjork, E. L. (1994) 'Remembering can cause forgetting: retrieval dynamics in long-term memory', *Journal of Experimental Psychology: Learning, Memory, and Cognition*, 20(5), 1063.

Chandler, P. & Sweller, J. (1991) 'Cognitive Load Theory and the Format of Instruction', *Cognition and Instruction*, 8(4), 293-332.

Cosmides, L. & Tooby, J. (1992) 'Cognitive Adaptions for Social Exchange', in Barkow, J., Cosmides, L. & Tooby, J. (eds.) *The adapted mind: Evolutionary psychology and the generation of culture*, New York: Oxford University Press, pp. 163–228.

Craik, F. I. M. & Lockhart, R. S. (1972) 'Levels of Processing: A Framework for Memory Research', *Journal Of Verbal Learning And Verbal Behavior*, 11, 671-684.

Endres, T. & Renkl, A. (2015) 'Mechanisms behind the testing effect: an empirical investigation of retrieval practice in meaningful learning', *Frontiers in Psychology*, 6.

Geary, David C. (2007) 'Educating the Evolved Mind: Conceptual Foundations for an Evolutionary Educational Psychology', in Carlson, J. S. & Levin, J. R. (eds.), *Educating the Evolved Mind*, Greenwich, CT: Information Age, pp. 1–99.

Kirschner, P. A., Sweller, J. & Clark, R. E. (2006) 'Why Minimal Guidance During Instruction Does Not Work: An Analysis of the Failure of Constructivist, Discovery, Problem-Based, Experiential, and Inquiry-Based Teaching', *Educational Psychologist*, 41(2), 75–86.

Mousavi, S. Y., Low, R. & Sweller, J. (1995) 'Reducing Cognitive Load by Mixing Auditory and Visual Presentation Modes', *Journal of Educational Psychology*, 87(2), 319-334.

Paas, F., Renkl, A. & Sweller, J. (2003) 'Cognitive Load Theory and Instructional Design: Recent Developments', *Educational Psychologist*, 38(1), 1–4.

Paas, F. G. & Van Merriënboer, J. J. (1994) 'Instructional control of cognitive load in the training of complex cognitive tasks', *Educational psychology review*, 6(4), 351-371.

Sweller, J. (1994) 'Cognitive load theory, learning difficulty, and instructional design', *Learning and Instruction*, 4(4), 295–312.

Sweller, J., Van Merrienboer, J. J., G. & Paas, F. (1998) 'Cognitive Architecture and Instructional Design', *Educational Psychology Review*, 10(3), 251-296.

Van Merrienboer, J. J. G, Kester, L. & Paas, F. (2006) 'Teaching complex rather than simple tasks: Balancing intrinsic and germane load to enhance transfer of learning', *Applied Cognitive Psychology*, 20(3), 343-352.

Chapter 5
Long-term memory and forgetting

Teachers use a variety of techniques to check 'progress' within and between lessons. Typically these include some sort of review or a quiz, or 'exit tickets' where students summarise what they have learnt or answer a question. It would be tempting to believe that successfully answering these questions indicates that the key points of the lesson have been learnt – that they are safely in long-term memory – but as often as not, by the time students attend the next lesson they will have forgotten a lot of it. To understand why this happens, even if you designed the 'perfect' lesson, requires a bit of knowledge about long-term memory and some of the reasons why we forget.

Long-term memory (LTM) isn't a single storage unit but encompasses a number of diverse functions involving different regions of the brain. Psychologists tend to divide LTM into declarative (explicit recall and recognition where memory is consciously available*) and non-declarative memory (implicit memories which can be retrieved without awareness).

Non-declarative memory

Perhaps the most important form of implicit memory for educators is procedural skills – our knowledge of how to do things like tying your shoelaces,

---

* Though whether conscious access is the defining characteristic of these types of memory is debatable – see Henke, K. (2010) 'A model for memory systems based on processing modes rather than consciousness', *Nature Reviews Neuroscience*, 11(7), 523-532.

walking or swimming. In education, important procedural skills include things like decoding phonemes in reading, simple mathematical operations (e.g. times tables) or learning to play a musical instrument. At first, we likely need the task broken down into procedural steps. Each time we repeat an activity we strengthen the neural connections involved. Skills can become automated to the degree that we are no longer able to articulate how we do them. They require minimal conscious effort and are valuable to future learning because we can draw upon them without a significant load on working memory (see Chapter 3).

Associative memory (e.g. priming and simple classical conditioning) is another form of implicit memory. Priming involves unconscious associations between visual stimuli, words or concepts. For example, if I say the word 'BREAD' there's a greater chance you might respond with 'BUTTER' than 'ASTRONAUT'. This kind of memory sometimes hampers our efforts as teachers. For example, in science lessons a question like, 'What type of gas was produced in this chemical reaction?' often elicits the automatic response 'carbon dioxide' because of its common association with the question regardless of the fact that students have been testing for hydrogen! Classical conditioning also involves an unconscious association between a stimulus and a subsequent response. The famous experiments of Ivan Pavlov, where he trained dogs to salivate at the sound of a bell, are likely well known to many readers. By ringing a bell shortly before the presentation of food, the dogs learnt an association between the two and began exhibiting the reflex behaviour normally provoked by food at the sound of the bell alone.

Lastly, there are things like habituation, where you unconsciously learn to ignore a constant stimulus (like tuning out the hum of your computer or the whine of your tinnitus) and sensitivity, where exposure to a stimulus makes you more likely to respond strongly to it for some time afterwards (e.g. having been frightened by a wasp you seem temporarily hyper-alert to the buzzing sounds from flies).

Declarative memory

Declarative memory – made up of semantic and episodic memory – is probably the area of long-term memory which causes teachers most anxiety. Semantic memory is the ability to recall facts, meaning and concepts independent of the situation or event where we learnt them, whereas episodic memory is the ability to reconstruct the events of our lives with reference to the time, place and emotional context of these events.

Some of the earliest experiments into semantic memory were carried out by Hermann Ebbinghaus in the 1880s (successfully replicated in a recent study by Murre and Dros). This research sought to find the relationship between the amount of information retained in memory and the duration of time since the material was learnt. It's worth noting that he conducted these experiments with himself as the subject based on an intense schedule often up to three sessions per day over seven months. He studied lists of nonsense syllables practised until he could perfectly recall them twice in a row and then examined his performance over repeated sessions.

These experiments formed the basis of the well-known 'forgetting curve': the negatively exponential curve indicating the decay of information that occurs in the first minutes and hours after learning. Likewise, the 'learning curve' (how fast new information is learnt) is also exponential, with the quickest gains on the first try and increasingly smaller gains on subsequent attempts. He also calculated the 'savings' (i.e. the amount of time saved on the second learning trial as a result of having had the first) and discovered that each learning attempt tended to be quicker than the last. The presence of these savings demonstrate that *even when we believe we have completely forgotten previous learnt material we can relearn it faster.* Even when we are unable retrieve it, much information is still stored in long-term memory.

These two systems of declarative memory are linked together in several ways. For example, semantic memories may eventually become 'stand alone' from the context in which we learnt them, but they are probably initially derived from our episodic memory. Episodic memory (e.g. of a particular lesson) underpins semantic memory (e.g. the key terms and concepts of the lesson) at first, only becoming more generalised and independent of the event gradually over time. Often students can remember episodic details of lessons without being able to recall any semantic information.

This link between episodic and semantic memory is one reason why exploiting a narrative structure can be a powerful way to help children learn facts and concepts. Daniel Willingham argues that stories occupy a privileged position in memory, perhaps because they tap into the episodic processes which underpin the beginnings of semantic memory. He suggests that structuring a lesson in a way which captures some of the key elements of stories, such as conflict between characters or obstacles which must be overcome to achieve a goal, make the semantic elements of the lesson easier to comprehend and recall.

Another example of this link is the influence of context on recall. A study by Godden and Baddeley asked divers to memorise lists of words, some on land and some underwater, then asked them to recall the words when either the context was the same (e.g. learning and recalling underwater) or different (e.g. learning on land, but recalling underwater). They found that when the context was the same, participants tended to have better recall of the information. However, these context-dependent effects on memory tend to be relatively small compared to other factors. There may be some benefit to students revising under conditions close to the conditions of the exam (e.g. sat at a table in silence), but extension of this principle to situated learning environments is probably misleading (see Chapter 7).

Likewise, semantic memory may sometimes influence episodic memory. For example, research into eye-witness memory has shown that giving witnesses misleading information about an event can alter their recall of that event. A famous study by Elizabeth Loftus and John Palmer showed participants a series of films involving car collisions and found that the estimation of how fast the cars were travelling could be manipulated by changing the verb used in the question. Where participants were asked 'About how fast were the cars going when they hit each other?' they gave lower speed estimates compared to where the word 'hit' was replaced by a more intense verb like 'smashed'. The language used appeared to create a 'fact' about the collision which influenced the participant's memory for the 'event' they had witnessed.

Another example comes from a well-known experiment in which Frederic Bartlett examined the reconstructive character of memory using a culturally unfamiliar folk story called 'The War of the Ghosts'. Participants read the story twice at their own pace and attempted to reproduce the story a number of times. Bartlett found that the stories changed in the retelling: the participants created a new story from fragments and snippets of the original. Participants would omit material they found unfamiliar, irrelevant or unpleasant, but would persistently recall otherwise trivial details of the story. The reproductions tended to dramatise and rationalise the material so it fit the more familiar format of a Western folk story. Overall, the reconstructions were moulded to the framework of prior knowledge – the schema – already possessed by the participants.

We can link these ideas to the problems students face learning new material when they possess misconceptions related to the topic of study. For example, in a science lesson where students are learning about forces, they will possess a great deal of 'folk physics' (see Chapter 1) about the behaviour of objects being pushed or pulled. One natural observation, given things like friction and air resistance, is that objects will naturally slow down of their own accord after being given an initial push. So, students already possess naïve schemas – misconceptions (see Chapter 1) – related to forces (e.g. the idea that you need to constantly apply a force to make an object travel at the same speed) which continue to assert themselves after a lesson where the correct schema has been taught (i.e. that objects will travel at a constant speed until another force affects it). Unless the new schema is used repeatedly, it's likely that 'The War of the Forces' story will revert to the more familiar 'folk physics' conception.

The power of forgetting

Most of us believe that as we learn we build up memories and as we forget these memory stashes decay. This is wrong. Hermann Ebbinghaus noted that when we 'lose' information – such as French vocabulary or the process for working out the circumference of a circle – we can relearn this information much faster than if we had not previously learned it. This would seem to suggest that information isn't really forgotten but lurks somewhere beneath conscious awareness as memory engrams.

The rate at which students forget depends on all sorts of factors including their prior knowledge, motivation to learn, the contextual cues present at the time of instruction, how long information needs to be retained and, most crucially, the type of material we want students to learn. Some things are stickier than others; we're excellent, for instance, at remembering stories.

Ebbinghaus first conducted his experiments into remembering and forgetting in the 1880s. He wanted to test the outer limits of memory and so practised trying to retain lists of nonsense syllables. He found that, on average, we predictably forget about 70% of what we study within a few days. As the graph below shows, the curve of forgetting is initially very steep and then flattens off.*

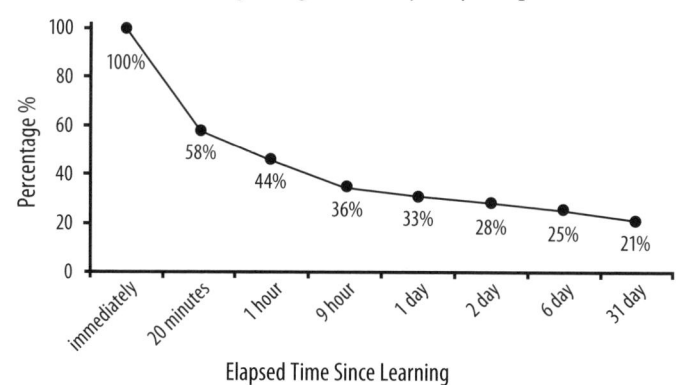

Figure 1: Ebbinghaus' forgetting curve

Although it would be foolish to say exactly how much each individual student will remember and forget, what's useful to know is that forgetting is both endemic and predictable – people forget at broadly similar rates over time.

---
* It's important to remember that the forgetting curve is based on the average score of a group of students (or one student learning and forgetting lots of things). In reality, you might remember each piece of information today and forget it tomorrow. The forgetting curve just shows the average tendency.

Unlike 19th century psychologists, we're probably not interested in remembering nonsense. Most of what we want students to learn is much more memorable, but even so, the likelihood of getting the correct answer in a test decays steeply at first and then levels off.

As discussed in Chapter 3, for all practical purposes our capacity to store new information appears limitless – our brains have sufficient space to comfortably store every experience we're likely to have over our lives. Despite that, sometimes we cannot access or retrieve these memories. In an attempt to explain this, Robert and Elizabeth Bjork came up with the New Theory of Disuse. They explain that everything we've ever encountered has retrieval strength (how easily we can recall that thing right now) and a storage strength (how well we know something; the quantity of schema to which an individual item is linked). Retrieval strength correlates with our ability to recall information when we want it and storage strength is, simply, how deeply embedded individual items are in schemas. Although retrieval strength completely determines our ability to recall memories, it's storage strength that governs how *quickly* we forget and regain information.

Some things – like the formula for finding the circumference of a circle, or the first line of *Pride and Prejudice* – have extremely high storage and retrieval strengths; we can recall these things whenever we need them because we've accessed the memory so many times over such a long period.

Other items are well stored but we're not always able to recall them when needed. What about all the other mathematical formulas and lines of poetry you will have learned? At one time you may have been able to bring them to mind with ease, but now it's a struggle. Sometimes we *know* we know something we can't remember – it's on the tip of our tongue but we can't bring it to mind. We've all suffered from the frustrating phenomenon of knowing we know something but being unable to dredge it up from the murky recesses of our minds. Just because a memory is stored does not mean we will always be able to access it.

Then there are items with poor storage strength but high retrieval strength. These are things we've tried hard to memorise through repetition or by outsourcing our memories to pen and paper or an electronic device*. As teachers, we give students cues and prompts to prevent them forgetting content, but then we're surprised when they've forgotten it next lesson. Sometimes when students are taught new information they write it down. Once it's down on

---

*   A good example of this is when staying in different hotel rooms over a number of successive nights. Your current room number has high retrieval strength, but low storage strength. The next night your new room number will be readily recalled, but the number of a previous night's room is swiftly forgotten.

paper they can relax. It seems that by focusing our attention on something and attempting to increase its retrieval strength, we might prevent it being stored. This is called retrieval-induced forgetting.

Counter-intuitively, if we really wanted to remember new information, the best approach might be to allow ourselves to forget it first. The higher the retrieval strength of an item of memory – that is, how easy it is for us to recall a piece of information *right now* – the smaller the gains in storage strength from additional study of practice. So, if something is highly accessible, virtually no learning can happen. No matter what you do, there will be no additional increases in storage. But, and this is the exciting part – as we forget and retrieval strength dips, when we study or practice there's a noticeably larger increase in storage strength. As Robert Bjork puts it, "Forgetting, rather than undoing learning, creates the opportunity to reach additional levels of learning."* So as time passes and we forget some of what we were able to retrieve, any re-presentations of information will result in a boost to learning in the long term. Contrary to our expectations, harnessing the power of forgetting might be the best way to increase the amount we learn.

Into the classroom

However well planned an individual lesson may be, the likelihood is that the material you wanted students to learn will quickly fade or become distorted in long-term memory. Happily, there are a variety of methods we can use to overcome some of these: the key is to exploit strategies which encourage students to practice the retrieval of information.

Where we want students to learn some sort of procedural skill, breaking the skill down into component features and encouraging students to practise each of these components (before eventually combining them) can lead to that skill becoming automatic in future. This sort of 'rote practice' can be very helpful to future learning. As discussed already in the chapter on cognitive load (see Chapter 4) such automated procedural knowledge can be employed without putting additional load on working memory.

However, strictly rote methods of retrieval practice may work well for word lists and nonsense syllables used in psychology experiments, but be insufficient for the consolidation of semantic memory. Priming effects build up around the characteristic ways that teachers ask questions, leading to a reliance on semantic association rather than conscious processing that links to semantic memory. To

---

* From a Go Cognitive interview with Robert A Bjork on The Theory of Disuse and the role of Forgetting in Human Memory: http://gocognitive.net/interviews/theory-disuse-and-role-forgetting-human-memory

avoid this, it's useful to vary the routes by which semantic memory is accessed – by varying the conditions of practice. This can be done by asking students to retrieve knowledge in slightly unpredictable ways or by creating questions which require the semantic knowledge to be applied rather than only recalled.

When it comes to semantic memory, we saw from the Ebbinghaus studies that we forget abstract information very quickly. However, we can take some comfort from the fact that effort to memorise information that we forget isn't wasted. It seems we relearn previously-learnt-but-apparently-forgotten material more quickly each time and retain it for longer and longer periods. B. F. Skinner's famous quip, "Education is that which remains, if one has forgotten everything he learned in school"[*] may, in part, be true. We may quickly lose conscious access to material we have learnt, but some of it is retained implicitly in memory and greatly enhances our future efforts to learn related material in future.

Our ability to remember facts, meaning and concepts we learn in school likely starts as a form of episodic memory for the context of the occasion where we are exposed to them. Ideally, we want semantic memory to generalise from this specific context – so that it becomes 'stand alone' and independent. However, we can exploit this link between episodic and semantic memory through the use of stories and narrative structures within sequences of learning. It seems likely, given writing is such a recent technology compared to the long history of oral transmission of culture, that our brains may be adapted to readily process and store information presented in story form. We can also make use of other encoding effects by combining visual images with words and by asking students to physically locate these rich sensory memories along mental pathways. This is the basis of the ancient Greek memory technique often called *the method of the loci*.

Context can also sometimes help us retrieve long-term memory: similarities between the conditions of learning and the conditions of recall can act as a retrieval cue. Whilst these effects are quite small, they may be useful in circumstances where it is relatively easy to create context where we will need the information in future. Encouraging students to revise in conditions quite similar to an examination may give them a small edge when trying to retrieve the material they need in the exam itself. However, generally we want students to have semantic memory of the material they learn independent of the context in which they learnt it. Whilst contextual cues may appear to accelerate learning, they may also impede it if the student becomes overly reliant upon

---

[*] The full quote is, "It has often been remarked that an educated man has probably forgotten most of the facts he acquired in school and university. Education is what survives when what has been learned has been forgotten." Skinner (1964: 484).

them. The key is to remove 'scaffolding' after students have experienced successful encoding to prevent them becoming dependent on external support. Scaffolding is explored in greater depth on page 130.

Prior knowledge is probably the most powerful influence on future learning, but it can sometimes be a double-edged blade. Students will have schemas related to many of the topics and concepts we wish them to learn and, where these ideas are inaccurate, the new information may be distorted. It's important that teachers are aware of the typical misconceptions related to a topic of study and plan opportunities to deal with them. Unless the new, correct, schemas are frequently used, students will likely revert to familiar ways of thinking. Merely showing the old ideas to be wrong is insufficient as students may ignore disconfirming evidence or even interpret it as supporting their original beliefs. Rather than rely on ideas about cognitive conflict (see Chapter 21) we may be better off making the access to the new schemas as reliable as possible through spaced, varied, retrieval practice.

What every teacher needs to know about long-term memory

- Procedural memory is potentially very helpful to future learning. Where such procedural skills crop up within a sequence of learning, look to break them up and encourage students to become automatic in using them.

- One of the weaknesses of 'rote' mechanisms of recall is that students remember the way a question is asked and the automatic response. Whilst this can be helpful for procedural memory, it's likely less useful for semantic memory.

- Semantic memory starts from the basis of episodic memory. We can exploit this by using storytelling and narrative structures across a sequence of learning. On the other hand, whilst context effects appear to help memory, we usually want students to recall material independent of the context.

- Students forget most of a lesson within a day, but this doesn't make the learning in that lesson a waste of time. Having forgotten something we have learnt, we relearn it quicker each time it is re-encountered, and retain it for longer and longer periods. This is why a lesson is a poor measure of progress – we need to think about how we consolidate learning across much longer periods of time.

- Whilst prior knowledge provides a huge advantage to future learning, we should be aware of where this involves misconceptions. Memory is readily distorted by the presence of expectations and prior (incorrect) beliefs. We can help overcome this by requiring students to use the new schemas frequently and under a variety of conditions of practice.
- We need to be aware of how information is encoded and held in short-term memory before being stored in long-term memory. If students are expected to pay attention to too much at once they will become overloaded and fail to memorise what they need to learn.
- Learning can be consolidated by being given meaning. Narratives are intrinsically memorable in a way that other means of presenting information are not. We should tell students stories in such a way that they can see links and connections with what they already know so that the information sticks.
- Learning and forgetting occur at about the same rate, and one of the few things we can depend on is that pupils will forget much of what they appear to learn. But whether they seem to know it or not, most of this 'forgotten' knowledge will still be rattling around in there somewhere. And once something has been forgotten it is much easier to relearn.

References

Bartlett, F. C. (1920) 'Experiments on the Reproduction of Folk-Stories', *Folklore*, 31(1), 30-47.

Bartlett, F. C. (1932) *Remembering: A study in experimental and social psychology.* Cambridge, UK: Cambridge University Press.

Bjork. E. & Bjork, R. A. (2003) 'Intentional Forgetting Can Increase, Not Decrease, Residual Influences of To-Be-Forgotten Information', *Journal of Experimental Psychology: Learning, Memory, and Cognition*, 29(4), 524–531.

Cabeza, R. & Moscovitch, M. (2013) 'Memory systems, processing modes, and components functional neuroimaging evidence', *Perspectives on Psychological Science*, 8(1), 49-55.

Dunlosky, J., Rawson, K. A., Marsh, E. J., Nathan, M. J. & Willingham, D. T. (2013) 'Improving students' learning with effective learning techniques promising directions from cognitive and educational psychology', *Psychological Science in the Public Interest*, 14(1), 4-58.

Ebbinghaus, H. (1885) *Memory: A contribution to experimental psychology*, New York: Dover.

Geary, D. (2007) 'Educating the Evolved Mind: Conceptual Foundations for an Evolutionary Educational Psychology', in Carlson, J. S. & Levin, J. R. (eds.) *Educating the evolved mind: Conceptual foundations for an evolutionary educational psychology*, IAP, pp. 1–100.

Godden, D. R. & Baddeley, A. D. (1975) 'Context-dependent memory in two natural environments: On land and underwater', *British Journal of psychology*, 66(3), 325-331.

Henke, K. (2010) 'A model for memory systems based on processing modes rather than consciousness', *Nature Reviews Neuroscience*, 11(7), 523-532.

Loftus, E. F. & Palmer, J. C. (1974) 'Reconstruction of automobile destruction: An example of the interaction between language and memory', *Journal of verbal learning and verbal behavior*, 13(5), 585-589.

Murre, J. M. & Dros, J. (2015) 'Replication and Analysis of Ebbinghaus' Forgetting Curve', *PloS one*, 10(7), e0120644.

Skinner, B. F. (1964) 'New methods and new aims in teaching', *New Scientist*, 122(5), 483-484.

Tulving, E. (1972) *Episodic and semantic memory 1. Organization of Memory*, London: Academic, 381(4).

Willingham, D. (2004) 'Ask the Cognitive Scientist: The Privileged Status of Story', *American Educator*. http://www.aft.org/periodical/american-educator/summer-2004/ask-cognitive-scientist

Chapter 6
Context and transfer

As we've seen, learning has to be retained, but it also needs to be transferable to new contexts. The types of contexts we are concerned with in education include subject domains (e.g. history or mathematics), specific tasks/problems (e.g. a textbook problem to solve), social interactions (e.g. caretaking routines between a parent and child), and situational/physical settings (e.g. home, classrooms, examination halls). Unfortunately, what we learn does not spontaneously or automatically generalise to new contexts and so teachers need to facilitate this process.

Back in 1901, Edward Thorndike developed the Principle of Identical Elements which states that transfer depends on the level of similarity between training and performance environments. We haven't really moved on much since then. In the 1920s, Smith and Guthrie described two unpublished, small-scale experiments that studied environmental context-dependent memory in humans. The first involved learning four sequences of ten nonsense syllables; two lists were learned inside a laboratory, and two were learned out of doors. Recall was tested 72 hours later, half in the laboratory, and half out of doors. Thus, two lists were relearned in the same environmental context in which they had been originally studied, and two were tested in altered environmental contexts. Eight of the ten subjects found relearning improved when in the same surroundings in which the first learning had taken place. In the second experiment learning and recall was tested with and without the odour of peppermint oil. Results again showed context-dependent memory effects in relearning, using a typing task to assess learning and retention. Thus, these two experiments both found that unfamiliar materials were more easily remembered when the contexts in which material was first encountered were reinstated. This has since become known as the context reinstatement effect.

Because transfer is affected by the context of original learning, students can learn in one context, yet fail to transfer to other contexts. One study found that street children could perform complex mathematics when making sales in the street but were unable to answer equivalent problems presented in a school context.[*] In another study, subjects did very well at making supermarket best-buy calculations despite doing poorly on similar paper-and-pencil mathematics problems.[†]

Types of transfer

So-called 'far transfer' between different subject domains – the idea that you could learn the skill of analysis in history and then apply it physics – is much more difficult than is often supposed. Experts (those who know a lot about a particular subject domain) find it far easier to transfer their knowledge to new contexts than novices (those who know little within a subject domain). This is not to claim that an expert physicist is more able than a physics novice to apply what they have learned in physics to history, just that they will find it more straightforward to transfer their knowledge to other areas of physics. As we'll see in the next chapter, expertise is highly specific and experts and novices think in qualitatively different ways.

Susan Barnett and Stephen Ceci's research has laid the building blocks for us to begin to understand the processes involved in transferring material learned from one context to another. In their 'taxonomy for far transfer' they identified several factors that affect transfer.

The first three are concerned with the type of *content* being transferred: whether it is a learned skill, a change in performance or a feat of memory. The other six are connected with the *context* in which the transfer takes place: the knowledge domain (whether learning can be transferred between the domains of, say, history and biology), the physical context (from one place to another), temporal contexts (from one time to another), the functional context (between the academic and non-academic settings) and social contexts (between group situations and individual situations) and the modality (whether material can be transferred between speech and writing). In school, students may be able to transfer what they have learned from a history classroom to the examination

---

[*] Carraher, T. & Carraher, D. (1985)
[†] Lave, J. (1988)

hall but be unable to transfer the skill of analysing historical source material to analysing literary texts.

Barnett and Ceci conclude that instances of far transfer are rare, but under the right conditions can happen, and may even turn out to be predictable. However, it is probably more productive for teachers to consider the possibilities of 'near transfer'. Transfer from one problem to another within a course, from one year in school to another, from the classroom to the examination hall, between school and home, and from school to workplace. Our ability to retrieve information is heavily context dependent – we link what we know to related subject matter, times, places, people and feelings. These contextual links provide cues or prompts which helps us to retrieve what we need when we need it. The trouble is, when we learn a thing in one context we rely on environmental cues in order to recall it, when we change the context the absence of those cues can cause us to be unable to retrieve what may have been secure in another location.

Some kinds of near transfer appear quite straightforward, and when subjects are asked questions which are closely related to material they have previously been exposed to, they are able to transfer what they've learned*, but transfer does not seem to occur when subjects are asked questions on related material taken from the same section of a textbook.† The finding seems to be that students have little difficulty in transferring learning when the exact information on which they are quizzed is used in a new situation, but quizzing on *related* information doesn't help students to transfer information, even between closely related topics. This presents obvious difficulties for teachers.

However, Cindy Wooldridge and colleagues have found that when students were *prompted* that they would need to transfer related information to novel situations they were far more likely to successfully apply what they had learned in a new context. It seems that prompting students may be a necessary condition for transfer to occur.

While teachers cannot, of course, predict every conceivable context in which students will need to apply the knowledge and skills they teach, we can prepare students by explicitly informing them that the material being studied will need to be applied to a new context and then provide practice opportunities where they have to apply prior knowledge to novel situations. With luck, this will help students to recognise situations where they can apply what they know when they come up in the future.

---

*   Butler, A. (2010)
†   Wooldridge, C. et al (2014)

The variation effect

Research into the variation effect tells us that by varying the conditions in which instruction takes place, we can make it easier for students to transfer what they have learned from one context to another.

As Marcel Proust well knew, memory is context dependent. We tie the acquisition of new ideas to prior knowledge in environmental contexts. In *How We Learn*, Benedict Carey talks about how he is only able to solve a mathematical proof using Pythagoras' theorem in a particular context:

> I remember it any time I sit alone in some classroom or conference room under dimmed fluorescent lights, like if I've arrived first for a meeting. Those cues bring back the memory of that night and the proof itself (although it takes some fuzzing to get the triangles in place).[*]

The context in which we first encounter an idea creates retrieval cues. They are the visual and autobiographical memory we hang ideas on to. Psychologists have run experiments that show playing particular genres of music[†] or inducing particular emotional states[‡] and then testing participants in conditions which either share or don't share those conditions demonstrates the power of context cues in increasing retention. This would be great if we could exactly recreate the conditions in which we learned when taking a test. Carey's experience is a good example of a widely shared experience – we struggle to transfer what we know into different contexts where retrieval cues are absent.

But by varying the conditions in which we learn maybe we can break our dependence on context cues. Smith, Bjork and Glendale's research into environmental context and memory was probably the first attempt to explore how this might be done. They gave participants a list of words to learn and had them study either in the same room twice or in two separate rooms (one a cluttered basement, the other a windowed office). Three hours later, the students were bundled into a third 'neutral room' and asked to recall as many of the words as they could. Those who studied in the same room managed an average of 16 out of 40 whereas those who studied in two different rooms recalled 24 words. The experiment showed real improvements in subjects' ability to recall the words when the environmental contexts were varied. This has become known as the 'variation effect' and since then there are been many other studies which have replicated these findings and built on this research.

---

[*] Butler, A. (2010)
[†] Smith, S. (1985)
[‡] Weingartner, H. et al (1977)

We need to be mindful that, according to Barnett and Ceci, the more complex material is, the more difficult it becomes to transfer it between contexts. One thing to avoid is attempting to teach generic problem-solving or critical thinking skills, which 'transfer' through some spooky, osmotic process. Privileging transfer over retention is unlikely to be successful as it's impossible to apply something you can't remember. Both processes are equally important functions of improving storage strength and, as such, both benefit from teaching in ways that focuses on embedding learning in long-term memory (see Chapter 4). Teaching ought to contain elements of explicit instruction (explanations and modelling) as well as opportunities for scaffolded struggle and independent practice. Whilst there's no benefit in introducing struggle at the point of encoding (transmission) there do appear to be compelling reasons to believe that certain 'desirable difficulties'[*] at the point of retrieval help to increase students' ability to both retain *and* transfer the content we wish them to learn.

Into the classroom

For learning to be flexible, teachers need to teach a topic or concept in multiple contexts. Nuthall found that he could predict with over 80% accuracy the likelihood of students retaining information six months after instruction if they had encountered new information in at least three different contexts.[†] We should also consider the context of time – *when* the information is taught. Psychologists have known for well over a century that repeated exposure to information on the cusp of forgetting improves storage strength in memory. This is the spacing effect. It seems probable that varying contexts will only strengthen this effect further. (See Chapter 10 for more detail on using the spacing effect in instruction.)

Whilst it's sensible to suggest that teachers can benefit from knowing what their students know and making connections between this prior knowledge and future learning, we should be cautious about the idea that we can ever reliably know what it is our students know. Nuthall found that in a class of 30 students, most students would already know about half of what they were being taught, but each would know a different half. If we were to assess students' prior knowledge before teaching each new topic, we would be unlikely to find out much to help us in our teaching. We might do better to assume that students' prior knowledge provides useful opportunities and contexts to use and practice this knowledge.

---

[*]   Bjork, R. (1994)
[†]   Nuthall, G. (2007: 80-81)

One thing we must be extremely cautious about is the idea that we can expect students to solve problems in the way experts do in the hope that this will make them more expert. A feature of expert problem solving is to organise facts around general principles, but knowing this is of little help to novices, as they don't know enough to see how new problems relate to these general principles. This is why 'critical thinking' is so hard to teach. Daniel Willingham points out that the reason experts are able to engage in critical thinking so readily is because they have deep domain knowledge and can see beyond the surface structure of a problem, whereas novices tend to possess less background knowledge and thus tend to focus on superficial features of a problem.

Teachers should consider the power of narrative to provide a powerful and enduring context for learning. Stories have a psychologically privileged status because they help us to make causal connections between information and context. It's always useful to construct explanations in terms of their narrative structure with beginnings, middles and ends; cliffhangers, characters and conflict. As Willingham says:

> *Screenwriters use the first 20 minutes – about 20 percent of the running time – to pique the audience's interest in the characters and their situation. Teachers might consider using 10 or 15 minutes of class time to generate interest in a problem (i.e., conflict), the solution of which is the material to be learned.*[*]

Harnessing the variation effect

If we want students to perform at their best in the exam hall, we should vary the rooms in which they are taught. Ideally, every lesson would take place in a new room to prevent memories being tied to specific contexts, but this would be both impractical and annoying. Maybe the best we could do is to timetable each lesson in a given week in a different classroom, but this would be only slightly less problematic.

A workable solution for individual teachers is to vary seating plans as much as possible. Sometimes students can struggle to retrieve information when they move seat during a lesson. Changing the physical and emotional context even to this small degree can disrupt students' ability to recall and transfer. If a student spends a term or a year sitting in the same seat every lesson then they will see the same things every lesson and will have similar interactions with the students sitting next to them. They will become dependent on those strong visual and emotional cues. If learning is tied to these cues, when the ties are severed, the learning seems to unravel.

---

[*] Willingham, D. (2007)

If students are regularly moved they encounter a greater variety of sight lines and thus a greater and more unstable range of visual cues. Their ability to transfer what they learned *within the classroom* improves. It might seem inefficient to have a different plan for each class each lesson, but if you're prepared to put up with some short-term disruption for a long-term gain, the pay-off might be that they learn more.

> **What every teacher needs to know about content and transfer**
>
> What every teacher needs to know is the principle that transfer between contexts needs to be facilitated.
>
> - Transfer is difficult, but can be improved if students are explicitly told that the information they are studying will need to be applied in new and related contexts.
> - Learning is contextual – students will associate subject matter with environmental and emotional cues. Varying seating plans as much as is practical to ensure learning is not tied to fixed environmental cues.
> - Context relates both to subject matter and to environment; we need to consider how students apply skills learned in one part of the curriculum in another part and how they might apply knowledge learned in the classroom in the exam hall.
> - Transferring between contexts is difficult because we rely on these cues when attempting to retrieve information.
> - Experts find transfer easier because they are more likely to understand organising principles and see connections; novices don't know enough to make these connections even if they are taught how experts think and work.
> - Teachers can construct narratives to build more durable and flexible knowledge which is more likely to be transferred between contexts.

References

Barnett, S. M. & Ceci, S. J. (2002) 'When and where do we apply what we learn? A taxonomy for far transfer', *Psychological Bulletin,* 128, 612-637.

Bjork, R. A. (1994) 'Memory and Metamemory consideration in the training of human beings', in Metcalfe, J. & Shimamura, A. (eds.) *Metacognition: Knowing About Knowing,* Cambridge, MA: MIT Press, pp 185-205.

Bransford, J. D., Brown, A. L. & Cocking, R. (eds.) (2000) *How people learn*, Washington, DC: National Academies Press.

Butler, A. (2010) 'Repeated testing produces superior transfer of learning relative to repeated studying', *Journal of Experimental Psychology: Learning, Memory, & Cognition*, 36, 1118-1133.

Carey, B. (2014) *How We Learn*, London: Macmillan.

Carraher, T. N., Carraher, D. W. & Schliemann, A. D. (1985) 'Mathematics in the street and in school', *British Journal of Developmental Psychology*, 3, 21-29.

Lave, J. (1988) *Cognition in Practice: Mind, Mathematics, and Culture in Everyday Life*, Cambridge, MA: Cambridge University Press.

Mayer, R. (2008) *Learning and instruction*, Upper Saddle River, NJ: Pearson.

Nuthall, G. (2007) *The Hidden Lives of Learners*, Wellington, NZ: NZCER Press.

Roediger, H. L. & Karpicke, J. D. (2006) 'The power of testing memory: Basic research and implications for educational practice', *Perspectives on Psychological Science*, 1, 181-210.

Saxe, G. B. (1991) *Culture and cognitive development: Studies in mathematical understanding*, Hillsdale, NJ: Erlbaum.

Smith, S. & Guthrie, E. R. (1921) *General psychology in terms of behavior*, New York: Appleton.

Smith, S. M. (1985) 'Background Music and Context-Dependent Memory', *American Journal of Psychology*, 98(4), 591-603.

Smith, S. M., Glenberg, A. & Bjork, R. A. (1978) 'Environmental context and human memory', *Memory & Cognition*, 6, 342–353.

Sousa, D. A. (2011) *How the brain learns* (4th ed.), Thousand Oaks, CA: Corwin.

Thorndike, E. L. & Woodworth, R. S. (1901) 'The influence of improvement in one mental function upon the efficiency of other functions (II). The estimation of magnitudes', *Psychological Review*, 8(4), 384.

Weingartner, H., Miller, H. & Murphy, D. L. (1977) 'Mood-State-Dependent Retrieval of Verbal Associations', *Journal of Abnormal Psychology*, 86(3), 276-284.

Willingham, D. T. (2007) Critical thinking: Why is it so hard to teach?, *American Educator*, 31(2), 8.

Wooldridge, C., Bugg, J., McDaniel, M. & Liu, Y. (2014) 'The testing effect with authentic educational materials: A cautionary note', *Journal of Applied Research in Memory and Cognition*, 3, 214-221.

Chapter 7
Practice and expertise

Whenever the going gets tough, well meaning mothers remind their children that 'practice makes perfect'. It turns out this is wrong. Practice makes permanent. And the more we practice the less demanding the practice becomes. What we repeatedly do we get good at, and if we practice doing the wrong things, we'll get better at doing things badly. So, while practice is certainly necessary for us to acquire long-term knowledge and skill, as well as unpicking exactly what sort of practice we should be encouraging in our students, we also need to make sure we're not consolidating mistakes and misconceptions.

At any given moment, students experience vast quantities of information during the course of a normal school day, but only a relatively tiny portion of this is processed in working memory (see Chapter 3) and it becomes increasingly harder to retrieve from long-term memory (see Chapter 5).

As we've seen, how well we are able to currently perform does not equate with learning. This is problematic because teachers are only ever able to see students' current performance. Although a test taken in a new context will allow us to make strong inferences about what is likely to have been learned, we can never directly observe how successfully they will be able to perform in the future. A performance can only ever be a proxy for learning.

Of course, practice only takes us so far: intelligence and motivation will also affect how well students are able to perform, but in all domains of learning, we only become expert with major investments of time. The amount of time it takes to learn material is roughly proportional to the amount of material there is to learn: the more there is learn, the more you need to practice.

Not all forms of practice are equal. Rote learning – repeating a task over and over – is often dismissed as a laborious, brute force method of engraving routines in long-term memory but it can certainly be effective, as anyone who has learned multiplication tables by chanting them aloud can testify. But it is perhaps only *purposeful practice*[*] – which involves attention, rehearsal, repetition over time, precise feedback, and getting out of your comfort zone – which enables us to develop expertise. K. Anders Ericsson, a psychologist who has spent his career researching expertise, has investigated dozens of domains and found that whatever the field, experts seem to have various traits in common.

In *Human Performance*, Paul Fitts and Michael Posner identified three distinct phases of practice. When we first begin to practice a new skill we are acutely aware of the process. This is the *cognitive stage*. Think of learning to drive a car: we can feel overwhelmed by having to use three different pedals, the steering wheel, change gear *and* keep an eye on what's going on outside. As we keep practising we move into the *associative stage* where we are less aware of all the different aspects and start to associate them together. We begin to make fewer mistakes and have greater capacity to pay attention to our surroundings. Now changing gear and pressing down the clutch are linked – they occur together without us having to consciously think about it. Further practice takes us to the *autonomous stage*. At this point we can drive a car and have a conversation with a passenger at the same time. Driving can become so automatic that miles can pass by with no conscious awareness of what we're doing. Learning to drive a car can be a useful analogy for learning to teach: at the cognitive stage we struggle to focus on delivering a lesson and on managing students' behaviour; at the associative stage we become more able to consider what students are likely to be learning rather than just what they are doing and at the autonomous stage we can start to treat students as individuals without worrying about whether the lesson will work.

Most people only improve a skill to the point of competency. As performance becomes autonomous we tend to stop improving, as we no longer have to stay conscious of what we're doing. The procedures are stored in long-term memory and our working memory is free to pay attention to new information. This is a good thing – as performing whatever we've practised is now much less demanding – but to improve beyond competency we need to continue paying

---

[*] In the literature on practice, *deliberate practice* has a very precise definition. It is only really possible when studying a body of knowledge for which effective training techniques have been mapped out over time and a practice regimen overseen by an expert coach. It also needs direct completion and objective criteria for mastery. Instead Ericsson suggests we adopt the term *purposeful practice*.

attention and this is what differentiates purposeful practice from just repeating procedures we have already mastered. Thus, it's advisable to consider how we can vary the conditions of practice as students gain mastery so that a degree of effortful thinking is still required and learning continues (see Chapter 10).

Practice is important because it increases the likelihood that learning will be long-term and retrievable; it enhances students' ability to apply elements of knowledge automatically and without reflection; skills that become automatic free up students' cognitive resources for learning more challenging tasks. This is true in childhood and adult years. Practice increases the transfer of practised skills to new and more complex domains and these gains often bring about greater motivation for further learning.

In order to develop real expertise, Anderson has identified three main components of practice: focusing on technique, focusing on specific goals and seeking and receiving feedback on performance. Instead of focusing on what we can do, we should focus on improving what we can't do. We have to consciously challenge ourselves to get better. All this takes effort and most of us decide the effort just isn't worth expending

The difference between novices and experts

We all start life as a novice. As such we think in qualitatively different ways to experts. A novice will know very little about a subject and will have correspondingly little to draw from long-term memory to help them think and make new connections whereas an expert has a rich fund of experiences to draw on. Explicitly teaching students how to become consciously familiar with the methods they use to learn, how and why they work, and when and how to apply them, *could* help them think more like experts but we need to remember that children are *not* experts, and that they only way they're likely to *become* experts is by learning facts about the subjects we teach. Of course what we ultimately want is for students to have a flexible understanding that can be applied to a wide variety of new situations, but this is unlikely to happen by magic. Daniel Willingham explains: "Whenever you see an expert doing something differently from the way a non-expert does it, it may well be that the expert used to do it the way the novice does it, and that doing so was a necessary step on the way to expertise."[*]

The transfer of knowledge or skills to a novel problem requires both knowledge of the problem's context and a deep understanding of the problem's underlying structure. The trouble is, novices and experts think about the topics they are

---

*   Willingham, D. (2010: 110)

studying in very different ways; while it's obvious that they have different amounts of subject knowledge, they also approach problems completely differently. Novices set about solving a particular problem as soon as it's set. This, inevitably, means concentrating on detail and ignoring structure.

In an experiment conducted by Michelene Chi and colleagues, two groups were given a series of physics problems to sort in any way they wished. The first group consisted of relatively novice physics undergraduates. The second group were physics postgraduates. These were the experts. The novices sorted the problems by their surface features – whether they were on inclined places, whether they involved springs, whether they were to do with falling objects etc. The experts categorised the problems by their deep structure: conservation of energy, kinematics, Newton's second law, etc. The finding is that without expertise in a particular subject domain, we find it hard to see the unifying underlying concepts in different examples (see the discussion of the Wason card test on page 45).

As Sweller puts it, "Novices, not possessing appropriate schemas, are not able to recognize and memorize problem configurations and are forced to use general problem-solving strategies such as means-ends analysis when faced with a problem."*

An expert understands the particular problem but also the generalities of this kind of problem. An expert will recognise the probability that a new problem within their field is similar to other problems in important respects. Experts are much more likely to learn something that will be of value for the next time a similar problem is encountered, particularly if any part of it has been challenging.

A major difference, therefore, between the novice and the expert is that the former is more likely to become frustrated, and encounter cognitive overload (see Chapter 3), while the expert will remain interested. Unless highly motivated to succeed, novices need to experience some measure of success or they risk becoming demotivated as they encounter increasing difficulty. Conversely, experts are more likely to become ever more motivated by challenge. This perhaps contradicts some of the popular thinking about the attribution of success we will discuss in Chapter 10.

We need to draw a distinction between rote learning and *inflexible knowledge*. What we ultimately want is for students to have a flexible understanding that can be applied to a wide variety of new situations, but again this is unlikely to happen by magic. Inflexibility is a necessary stepping stone to expertise. Willingham suggests that, "inflexible knowledge is meaningful, but narrow; it's

---

*   Sweller, J. (1988: 259)

narrow in that it is tied to the concept's surface structure, and the deep structure of the concept is not easily accessed. 'Deep structure' refers to a principle that transcends specific examples; 'surface structure' refers to the particulars of an example meant to illustrate deep structure."*

Ideally we would encourage students to think about content in deeper, more abstract terms, so that they are better able to generalise what they learn to new contexts. Regrettably this doesn't work. Because students have yet to pass through the thresholds that lead to expertise, any attempt to shortcut the process is only likely to lead to mimicry and inflexibility. We can't expect them to see deep structure until they've amassed sufficient expertise in the shallows. Before they can generalise to the abstract, students need to learn concrete examples and get used to recognising metaphors and exploring what they mean. We want students to have an understanding of the deep structure of a domain of knowledge, but we have to be patient. We should tell them as much about the surface features of a problem as we can and wait for them to join our dots. As they learn more facts, see more examples and get more practice, they will slowly but surely move towards an expert's understanding of the subject. The more we know on any given subject, the more we'll be able to think about. And the more we're able to think about, the greater our ability to think *with* this new knowledge.

The most important difference between an expert and a novice is that a novice hasn't had time or opportunity to build up the schemas of an expert (see Chapter 4). They haven't yet taken on board the underlying practical – and often tacit – understanding possessed by experts. Learning requires a change in the schematic structures of long-term memory and is demonstrated by progress from clumsy, error prone, slow and difficult performance to smoother, effortless performance. As we become increasingly familiar with the material we're learning, the cognitive characteristics associated with the material are altered so that it can be handled more efficiently by our working memory. In order to be an expert, first we have to be a novice. The problem with many 'independent learning' or discovery approaches is that they attempt to shortcut this process by assuming that if we get novices to work on the kinds of problems experts work on then they will think like experts. Sadly this is not the case. Instead, the strategies we explore in Chapter 10 are the basis for moving students from being novices to the beginnings of expertise.

The reversal effect

The reversal effect refers to finding that as we become more knowledgeable

---
*   Willingham, D. (2002)

within a domain, we need less guidance and structure, so much so that instructional techniques that are most effective for novices in helping to create long-term memory schema become increasingly ineffective as novices become experts. Slava Kalyuga, one of the leading researchers in this area, writes, "instructional guidance, which may be essential for novices, may have negative consequences for more experienced learners."*

As we saw in Chapter 3, when students don't know much about a topic in which they are expected to solve problems they are forced to rely on their fragile working memory, which quickly becomes overloaded. In contrast, experts already possess mental representations, which provide internal guidance. If additional instructional guidance is provided it can result in the processing of redundant information and increased cognitive load as new guidance has to be reconciled with existing internal strategies.

The two main examples of the reversal effect are:

The worked-example effect: Worked examples – a problem statement followed by a step-by-step demonstration of how to solve it – are often contrasted with open-ended problem solving in which the learner is responsible for providing the step-by-step solution. Although novices benefit more from studying structured worked examples than from solving problems on their own, as knowledge increases, open-ended problem solving becomes more effective.

The imagination effect: Imagining a solution can be more effective than being told how to approach a task. When students generate and construct their own mental representations of a task they are likely to better store the information in long-term memory. However for novices structured support is more useful to help alleviate cognitive load.

Into the classroom

As most teachers are only too aware, some students are less than keen to participate in activities that demand intense, focused effort. But beyond 'biologically primary knowledge' (see Chapter 1), effortful thought is a requirement of learning, and without expending that effort students won't see the success it can bring. This leaves us with two considerations:

1. What should effortful practice look like?
2. How can we motivate reluctant students to engage in effortful practice?

In answer to the first of these questions, the trick – in so far as there is one – is to prevent students from cruising along on auto-pilot in the autonomous stage

---

* Kalyuga, S. et al (2003)

and get them to pay the kind of attention required in the conscious stage of skill acquisition. Obviously, poorly designed practice problems may lead to student frustration and less motivation to attempt future practice problems, but what might a well-designed practice problem look like? Crucial here to this last point is an understanding of the testing effect and how low-stakes quizzes can be put together (see Chapter 10).

Can we teach metacognition?

In the 1970s, John Flavell came up with the concept of metamemory and metacognition. Metamemory is the ability to monitor and manage the storage and retrieval of what we've learned and metacognition is the ability to consciously and deliberately regulate and monitor our thoughts. According to John Flavell's original definition of metacognition, we need to be aware we need to be able to think metacognitively. This is intentionality – the notion that metacognition is deliberate and goal directed, involving planning a sequence of actions. This is something teachers need to explain repeatedly. Students need to be told that there are broad principles and general approaches that structure and colour detail, and that they should deliberately seek and consider these before we get bogged down in this detail. But no one spontaneously learns that what isn't learned, isn't learned. Experts not only have extensive specialist knowledge, but can also step back and meta-think rather than plunge straight in. As teachers, we become accomplished at finding the structures of our subjects and isolating the relevant; we learn to tell the difference between general understanding and the deliberate application of general understanding. But we've had to be trained to do this; it is no more 'natural', no more an innate skill for us than it is our students.

Teaching metacognition, or any other meta-skill, demands the deliberate deployment of two venerable and unfashionable teaching methods: scaffolding and modelling. To model critical awareness when reading texts, pupils need to see this way of thinking in action. It must be made obvious that the teacher actually uses such metacognition in real life, that their set of techniques is genuinely useful. When addressing issues or solving problems, teachers must think aloud to show how they use metacognitive techniques. Critical reading presents a perfect opportunity for such modelling. Before and during reading we can actively model the metalinguistic questions and ideas we keep actively running in our minds. We can provide a commentary of our thinking and overtly show how we routinely interrogate texts at the metalinguistic level and are alert to agenda, immediate purpose and wider ambition.

Scaffolding requires that we make explicit, and go on making explicit, the frameworks of metacognition and the deliberate need to build and then invoke them: the need to step backwards; to reach peace of mind; to engender confidence in one's own abilities, experience and common sense and to deploy these; to take a deliberately wide, overall view; to invoke general theory; to consider related issues; to recall similar instances and compare them with present issues; to think generally about situational structure; to critique the present and particular presentation of issues; to consider an author's putative purpose and read in the light of it; and so on. As these are not innate mental habits, and do not transfer well into new situations, the deliberate need to engage in such general, proactive, critical and enquiring thinking about thinking must be made explicit repeatedly. This is explored further on page 130.

Here are some examples of metacognitive techniques we can teach:

- Mnemonics: Teach students to spell difficult words like rhythm (Rhythm Helps Your Two Hips Move).
- Word roots: Demonstrate that finding the meaning of 'revolution' will also shed light on the meaning of 'revolve' and 'revolutionary'.
- Evidence of improvement: Show how an essay becomes more focused and better written as it is redrafted.
- Seeing from another's point of view – subtext: "What we really need to think about is what the author is up to – where are they coming from?"
- Self-reflection: "I approached the task this way because ..."
- Self-monitoring: "Slow down sir! I can't take it all in. Can you tell me bit by bit?"

So, can we teach metacognition? Yes. *But it is not a subject!* Making pupils meta-aware should be part and parcel of the process of teaching the content of the curriculum. We need to find effective ways of scaffolding what we want pupils to learn and modelling the way we want them to apply this learning. If we get this right, we might minimise pupils' inability to transfer knowledge between domains. Arguably, this is what expert teachers do already; we just need to be more explicit about what we're doing and, crucially, why we're doing it.

As for motivation, we can point out every time that practice actually improves their performance. We can also help by designing practice activities that while difficult are possible, and make it clear that we have high expectations that students can improve. The complex interactions of the affective domain will be discussed further in Part 2.

What every teacher needs to know about practice and expertise

If practice makes permanent, teachers need to make sure students are practising the right things in the right ways. The general rule of thumb is that if practice is too easy, students are likely to be in the autonomous stage of skill acquisition and therefore unlikely to improve beyond competency.

But, if practice is too difficult too soon, students' working memory is likely to be overloaded (see Chapter 3), they will get frustrated and will end up encoding failure rather than success.

The most successful practice should follow 'the Goldilocks Principle' and be 'just right': not too hard that students become demotivated and not so easy that they do not improve. In essence, these are the characteristics of the kind of practice students need to engage in if they are to master increasingly complex areas of curriculum content:

- Practice activities and conditions should be varied (see Chapter 10).
- Practice should be distributed (spacing and interleaving – see Chapter 10) over extended periods of time.
- Clear instructions on expectations and criteria should be provided.
- The problem-solving process that students are expected to use must be modelled.
- Complex problems should be broken down into their constituent elements, and students should practice these smaller elements before being asked to solve complex problems independently.
- Students must be provided with worked examples and exemplar answers as well as partially completed sample problems.
- Students must be guided through sample practice problems using metacognitive prompts to help them reflect on how to think while engaged in solving a problem.
- Teachers should wait until students actually need more information to solve a complex problem before giving them more information. This strategy – known as 'just-in-time teaching'[*] – helps keep the amount of information that students must hold in their short-term memories to a manageable level as they practice.

---

[*] See the Just in Time Teaching website for examples: http://jittdl.physics.iupui.edu/jitt/

- Plenty of opportunities for students to practice applying problem-solving skills should be provided before testing them on their ability to use those skills.
- Students will only be able to work independently once they have been taught how to do so. **Here are some important strategies to help make students increasingly independent:**
- Get students to compare problems with different surface structures that share the same underlying structure. By comparing problems, students are more likely to perceive and remember their underlying structure.
- Explicitly model the steps needed to solve a problem and narrate the kind of thinking you, as an expert, would have to go through.
- Deconstruct worked examples, pointing out the connection between surface features and deep structure.
- Encourage students to identify and label the sub-steps required for solving a problem. This makes it easier for students to see the underlying structure of the problem and to apply the procedures they've learned to other problems.
- Alternate concrete examples and abstract representations to help students recognise underlying structures.
- Scaffold the steps required to enable students to produce work beyond their current capabilities – encoding the experience of success and build relevant schematic knowledge in long-term memory.
- As students become increasingly knowledgeable, they need less guidance and structure. Scaffolding should be withdrawn as soon as it is no longer needed.

References

Anderson, J. R. (1996) 'A Simple Theory of Complex Cognition', *American Psychologist*, 51(4), 355-365.

Brame, C. Just-in-Time Teaching (JiTT) https://cft.vanderbilt.edu/guides-sub-pages/just-in-time-teaching-jitt/

Campitelli, G. & Gobet, F. (2011) 'Deliberate practice: Necessary but not sufficient', *Current Directions in Psychological Science,* 20(5), 280–285. doi:10.1177/096372141142922

Catrambone, R. (1998) 'The subgoal learning model: Creating better examples so that students can solve novel problems', *Journal of Experimental Psychology: General*, 127(4), 355-376.

Chi, M. T., Feltovich, P. J. & Glaser, R. (1981) 'Categorization and representation of physics problems by experts and novices', *Cognitive science*, 5(2), 121-152.

Cooper, G., Tindall-Ford, S., Chandler, P. & Sweller, J. (2001) 'Learning by imagining procedures and concepts', *Journal of Experimental Psychology: Applied*, 7, 68-82.

Deans for Impact (2015) *The Science of Learning*, Austin, TX: Deans for Impact. Retrieved from http://deansforimpact.org/pdfs/The_Science_of_Learning.pdf

Dunlosky, J., Rawson, K. A., Marsh, E. J., Nathan, M. J. & Willingham, D. T. (2013) 'Improving students' learning with effective learning techniques: Promising directions from cognitive and educational psychology', *Psychological Science in the Public Interest*, 14, 4-58. doi.10.1177/1529100612453266

Ericsson, K. A., Krampe, R. & Tesch-Romer, C. (1993) 'The Role of Deliberate Practice in the Acquisition of Expert Performance', *Psychological Review*, 100(3), 363-406.

Ericsson, K. A. (2008) 'Deliberate Practice and Acquisition of Expert Performance: A General Overview', *Academic Emergency Medicine*, 15(11), 988-994.

Ericsson, K. A. (2016) *Peak: Secrets from the new Science of Expertise*, London: The Bodley Head.

Flavell, J. H. (1976) 'Metacognitive aspects of problem solving', in Resnick, L.B. (ed.) *The Nature of Intelligence*, Hillsdale, NJ: Erlbaum, pp. 231-236.

Flavell, J. H. (1979) 'Metacognition and cognitive monitoring: A new area of cognitive-developmental inquiry', *American Psychologist*, 34, 906-911.

Glover, J., Ronning, R. & Bruning, R. (1989) *Cognitive Psychology for Teachers*, USA: Macmillan.

Goldstone, R. L. & Son, J. Y. (2005) 'The transfer of scientific principles using concrete and idealized simulations', *The Journal of the Learning Sciences*, 14(1), 69-110.

Kalchman, M., Moss, J. & Case, R. (2001) 'Psychological Models For the Development of a Mathematical Understanding: Rational Numbers and Functions' in Carver, S.M. & Klahr, D. (eds.) *Cognition and Instruction: Twenty-five Years of Progress*, Psychology Press.

Kalyuga, S. (2007) 'Expertise reversal effect and its implications for learner-tailored instruction', *Educational Psychology Review*, 19, 509-539.

Kalyuga, S. (2009) 'Knowledge elaboration: A cognitive load perspective', *Learning and Instruction*, 19, 402-410.

Kalyuga, S., Chandler, P. & Sweller, J. (1998) 'Levels of expertise and instructional design', *Human Factors*, 40, 1-17.

Kalyuga, S., Ayres, P., Chandler, P. & Sweller, J. (2003) 'The expertise reversal effect', *Educational Psychologist*, 38, 23-31.

Kalyuga, S., Rikers, R., Pass, F. (2012) 'Educational implications of expertise reversal effect in learning and performance of complex cognitive and sensorimotor skills', *Educational Psychology Review*, 24, 313-337.

Kerr, H. (n.d.) *The Cognitive Psychology of Literacy Teaching: Reading, Writing, Spelling, Dyslexia (& A Bit Besides).* Available at: http://www.hugokerr.info/book.pdf.

Li, S. et al (2008) 'Working Memory Plasticity in Old Age: Practice Gain, Transfer, and Maintenance', *Psychology and Aging*, 23(4), 731–742.

Moors, A. & De Houwer, J. (2006) 'Automaticity: A Theoretical and Conceptual Analysis', *Psychological Bulletin*, 132(2), 297–326.

Pavlik, P. I. Jr. & Anderson, J. R. (2008) 'Using a Model to Compute the Optimal Schedule of Practice', *Journal of Experimental Psychology: Applied*, 14(2), 101–117.

Pitts, P. & Posner, M. (1967) *Human Performance*, UK: Brooks/Cole Pub. Co.

Renkl, A. & Atkinson, R. K. (2003) 'Structuring the transition from example study to problem solving in cognitive skill acquisition: A cognitive load perspective', *Educational Psychologist*, 38, 15-22.

Richland, L. E., Zur, O. & Holyoak, K. J. (2007) Cognitive Supports for Analogies in the Mathematics Classroom. *Science*, 316(5828), 1128-1129.

Roediger, H. L. (2013) 'Applying cognitive psychology to education: Translational education science', *Psychological Science in the Public Interest*, 14, 1–3. doi.10.1177/1529100612454415

Rosenshine, B. & Meister, C. (1992) 'The use of scaffolds for teaching higher-level cognitive strategies', *Educational Leadership*, 49(7), 26–33.

Simkins, S. P. & Maier, M. H. (2008) *Just-in-time teaching: Across the disciplines, across the academy*, Sterling VA: Stylus.

Singley, K. & J. R. Anderson (1989) *The Transfer of Cognitive Skill*. Cambridge, MA: Harvard University Press.

Spiro, R. J., Feltovich, P. L., Jackson, M. J. & Coulson, R. L. (1991) 'Cognitive flexibility, constructivism and hypertext: Random access instruction for advanced knowledge acquisition in ill-structured domains', *Educational Technology*, 31(5), 24-33.

Sweller, J. (1988) 'Cognitive Load During Problem Solving: Effects on Learning', *Cognitive Science*, 12(2) 257–285, at 259.

Taleb, N. N. (2007) *The Black Swan: The Impact of the Highly Improbable*, London: Penguin.

van Merrienboer, J. J. G., Kirschner, P. A. & Kester, L. (2003) 'Taking the load off a learner's mind: Instructional design for complex learning', *Educational Psychologist*, 38, 5–13. doi:10.1207 /s15326985EP3801_2

Willingham, D. (2002) 'Inflexible Knowledge: The First Step to Expertise', *American Educator* 26(4), 31–33, at 32. Available at: http://www.aft.org/periodical/american-educator/winter-2002/ask-cognitive-scientist.

Chapter 8
Feedback

It goes without saying that we need feedback to help us improve a skill. This has taken on the power of a self-evident truth; there are, however, some intriguing findings from the realm of cognitive psychology that have been widely overlooked in education.

There is no doubt that being given corrective feedback improves our performance in any given area or subject, but, counter-intuitively, a gain in performance may not always result in improved retention or the ability to transfer knowledge or skills between contexts. Sometimes, especially when learning the type of abstract, biologically secondary knowledge (see Chapter 1) taught in schools, evidence from cognitive psychology indicates that giving frequent and immediate feedback simply improves students' performance at the cost of long-term learning[*] and that it might be better to delay and reduce the feedback we give.

A lot of the feedback we get comes through trial and error – when something doesn't work we adjust our technique and try again until we get it right – but we also get lots of feedback from those around us. Of particular importance to teachers is the feedback we give students on their current performance and what they need to do to improve, as well as the feedback we get from them about the effectiveness of our instruction.

Perhaps we've been a little uncritical on just how best we should be thinking about feedback? In the abstract to Hattie and Timperley's seminal paper 'The

---

[*] Schmidt, R. (1991)

Power of Feedback', the authors state that, "Feedback is one of the most powerful influences on learning and achievement, but **this impact can be either positive or negative**."[*] [Emphasis added]

Hattie and Timperley also make clear that, "feedback can only build on something; it is of little use when there is no initial learning or surface information."[†] Sometimes, as the principles of distributed practice (see Chapter 10) make clear, we might be better off repeating instructional sequences.

Attribution theory

Perhaps we need to be less concerned with how we're giving feedback and more mindful about how it is received. Feedback is powerful because it affects what we believe about ourselves and to what we attribute success and failure. In 1958, the Austrian psychologist Fritz Heider first articulated what has become known as attribution theory: how people see the causes of behaviour, and the explanations they make for it.

We can either attribute our behaviour to dispositions (e.g. personality traits, motives, attitudes), or situations (e.g. external pressures, social norms, peer pressure, accidents of the environment, acts of God, random chance, etc.). Heider first observed that we tend to place great weight on internal, dispositional causes rather than on external causes. This is the 'fundamental attribution error'.

Giving feedback can often backfire and have startlingly unintended consequences depending on how students attribute success and failure. When we think about success and failure we find it almost impossible to avoid the fundamental attribution error. The way we perceive success or failure is dependent on three factors:

1. **Personalisation**: the extent to which we believe success is influenced by *internal* or *external* factors. Internal factors are obviously within students' control whereas external factors can be used as excuses on which to blame failure.

2. **Stability**: whether success is perceived to be transient or long-lasting. If success or failure is perceived as *stable* then students may not believe they can improve, whereas if it's *unstable* then they can do something about it.

3. **Specificity**: whether success in one area is interpreted as being likely to lead to success in other areas. Ideally, students should see their success as *specific* rather than *global* so that failure in one area doesn't have to mean failure in other areas.

---

*   Hattie, J. & Timperley, H. (2007: 82)
†   Hattie, J. & Timperley, H. (2007: 104)

In order for feedback to result in improvement, students need to believe that they can do something about their current performance. In other words, students need to receive the message that their success is due to *internal*, *unstable* and *specific* factors.

Response Type	Feedback indicates performance...	
	Exceeds goal	Falls short of goal
Change Behaviour	Exert less effort	Increase effort
Change goal	Increase aspiration	Reduce aspiration
Abandon goal	Decide goal is too easy	Decide goal is too hard
Reject feedback	Feedback is ignored	Feedback is ignored

Table 1: Feedback Effects*

This table illustrates just how easy it is to get feedback wrong. The only desirable outcomes for feedback are that students commit to aiming higher or trying harder. But how often might our feedback result in pupils making less effort, aiming lower and abandoning goals? Sometimes well-intentioned feedback has the effect of making students decide to give up or reduce their aspirations. In some cases, no feedback at all might be preferable. *Just* giving students feedback might be harmful.

Reducing feedback

As well as considering attribution theory, teachers should also be aware of the research conducted on how feedback can be used to increase performance as well as increase learning.

The assumption has been that giving students feedback during instruction will foster durable learning. However, there appears to be some compelling evidence that this might not always be the case. In fact, "delaying, reducing, and summarizing feedback can be better for long-term learning than providing immediate, trial-by-trial feedback... Numerous studies – some of them dating back decades – have shown that frequent and immediate feedback can, contrary to intuition, degrade learning."†

Apparently, "feedback that is given too immediately and too frequently can lead

---

* Dylan Wiliam, Embedded Formative Assessment (2014) based on Kluger and DeNisi's preliminary feedback intervention theory (Kluger, A. N. & DeNisi, A. (1996) 'The effects of feedback interventions on performance: a historical review, a meta-analysis, and a preliminary feedback intervention theory', *Psychological bulletin*, 119(2), 254.)

† Soderstrom, N. & Bjork, R. (2013: 23)

learners to overly depend on it as an aid during practice, a reliance that is no longer afforded during later assessments of long-term learning when feedback is removed."* If our feedback acts as a crutch to prop up performance during the acquisition phase of learning, then we could be unwittingly undermining students' ability to retain and transfer what they're learning.

This does *not* mean that we should avoid giving pupils feedback on how they're doing. But it does suggest that feedback should be scaffolded. Judiciously withholding, delaying and reducing feedback can boost long-term retention and lead to more sustained learning. In a system where external assessment has shifted towards terminal, linear examinations, this may be becoming ever more important.

Into the classroom

If we're concerned with improving learning rather than just boosting current performance, feedback should make students think. Simply giving corrections prevents students from having to think and is an example of Sat Nav feedback: students tend to nod and say, "Yeah, I know," and then carry on as before. There's real benefit from demanding that students struggle to work out what to do for themselves and that feedback should provide hints rather than complete solutions.

As a general principle, it might be desirable to give extensive feedback at the beginning of a course or if teachers have not yet had time to get to know their students, but over time the quantity and frequency of feedback should be reduced to allow students to internalise the procedures for successfully retaining and transferring what they have learned.

Teachers should also be wary of advice that feedback should be given as quickly as possible. There's no doubt that immediate feedback will improve students' performance in the here and now, but delaying feedback and forcing students to remain uncertain for longer can be more effective at increasing retention and transfer. That's not to say there's never a point to providing frequent and immediate feedback – it can be highly motivational to be told you're on the right track and given specific instructions on how to perform that little bit better. As long as it doesn't cause students to misattribute success, praise following small degrees of improvement and encouragement to persist can be helpful. As we saw in Chapter 7, practice makes a great deal of difference and anything that motivates students to practise more is probably worthwhile.

---

*   Soderstrom, N. & Bjork, R. (2013: 23)

The final point to pick over is one of tone. Some reports suggest that students "respond better if feedback minimizes negativity and addresses significant aspects of their work and understanding, in contrast to feedback that is negative in tone and focused excessively on details of student performance that are less relevant to the learning goal."[*] These are emotive terms and probably no teacher would think it desirable to be dismissive or cruel when giving feedback, so to that extent at least, minimising negativity is obviously a good thing. We should be careful though not to confuse this with a prescription to be overly enthusiastic or undeservedly positive. Feedback offered in such a way can backfire and end up convincing students you're either insincere or have very low expectations. The key (if there is one) to all this is the relationship between the donor and the recipient of feedback. If a teacher is respected by their students, there's a good chance feedback will be well received, if the reverse is true, then God help you.

What every teacher needs to know about feedback

- The best advice is that feedback should be:
    - Specific and clear.
    - Focused on the task rather than the student and targeted to increase students' task commitment.
    - Explanatory and focused on improvement, not just verifying performance.
    - Designed to attribute outcomes to internal factors that students can control.
    - Designed to make students consider unstable factors that are dependent on effort.
- It will probably benefit students for teachers to reduce the quantity and frequency of feedback over time to help prevent students becoming overly dependent.
- Much well-intentioned feedback can backfire resulting in students aiming lower or giving up. Feedback is more likely to be effective if it helps students believe that making effort will result in improvement, or that adopting a more challenging goal is worthwhile.
- Ultimately, the way teachers give feedback is irrelevant if it's not received, understood and results in students making progress.

---

*   Top 20 Principles From Psychology For Prek–12 Teaching And Learning. p. 13

> Often, the most important factor in determining the impact of feedback is the relationship the teacher has with the student.
>
> - Feedback and marking are not the same. Despite all the evidence on effective feedback, there is little or no evidence to support most marking practices employed in schools. Feedback and marking are not the same. It is recommended that while there is no best way to mark, marking should be "meaningful, manageable and motivating."*

References

Bjork, R. A. & Bjork, E. L. (1992) 'A new theory of disuse and an old theory of stimulus fluctuation', in Healy, S. Kosslyn & Shiffrin, R. (eds.) *From Learning Processes to Cognitive Processes: Essays in Honor of William K. Estes* (Vol. 2), Hillsdale, NJ: Erlbaum, pp. 35-67.

Brookhart, S. M. (2008) *How to give effective feedback to your students*, Alexandria, VA: Association for Supervision and Curriculum Development.

Butler, A. C., Karpicke, J.D. & Roediger, H.L. (2007) 'The effect of type and timing of feedback on learning from multiple-choice tests', *Journal of Experimental Psychology: Applied*, 13(4), 273-281.

Department for Education (2016) *Eliminating unnecessary workload around marking, Report of the Independent Teacher Workload Review Group*.

Ericsson, A. K., Krampe, R. T. & Tesch-Romer, C. (1993) 'The role of deliberate practice in the acquisition of expert performance', *Psychological Review*, 100, 363–406, doi.10.1037/0033- 295X.100.3.363

Gobet, F. & Campitelli, G. (2007) 'The role of domain specific practice, handedness, and starting age in chess', *Developmental Psychology*, 43, 159–172, doi.org/10.1037/0012-1649.43.1.159

Guzman-Munoz, F. J. & Johnson, A. (2007) 'Error feedback and the acquisition of geographical representations', *Applied Cognitive Psychology*, 22(7), 979-995.

Hattie, J. & Timperley, H. (2007) 'The Power of Feedback', *Review Of Educational Research*. 77(1), 81–112 DOI: 10.3102/003465430298487

Hays, M. J., Kornell, N. & Bjork, R. A. (2010) The costs and benefits of providing feedback during learning, *Psychonomic Bulletin & Review*, 17(6), 797-801.

Kulhavy, R. W. & Anderson, R.C. (1972) 'Delay-retention effect with multiple-choice tests', *Journal of Educational Psychology*, 63(5), 505-512.

---

*   Eliminating unnecessary workload around marking: Report of the Independent Teacher Workload Review Group, p. 5

Leahy, S., Lyon, C., Thompson, M. & Wiliam, D. (2005) 'Classroom assessment, minute by minute, day by day', *Educational Leadership*, 63, 19–24.

Minstrell, J. (2001) 'The role of the teacher in making sense of classroom experiences and effecting better learning' in Carver, S. M. & Klahr, D. (eds.) *Cognition and instruction: Twenty-five years of progress*, Mahwah, NJ: Erlbaum, pp. 121–150.

Metcalfe, J., Kornell, N. & Finn, B. (2009) 'Delayed versus immediate feedback in children's and adults' vocabulary learning', *Memory & Cognition*, 37(8), 1077-1087, doi:10.3758/MC.37.8.1077

Pashler, H., Cepeda, N. J., Wixted, J. T. & Rohrer, D. (2005) 'When Does Feedback Facilitate Learning of Words?', *Journal of Experimental Psychology: Learning, Memory, and Cognition*, 31(1), 3–8

Schmidt, R. A. (1991) 'Frequent augmented feedback can degrade learning: Evidence and interpretations', NATO, ASI series 62, 59-75.

Schmidt, R. A. & Wulf, G. (1997) 'Continuous concurrent feedback degrades skill learning: Implications for training and simulation', *Human Factors*, 39(4), 509-525.

Schmidt, R. A., Young, D. E., Swinnen, S. & Shapiro, D. C. (1989) Summary knowledge of results for skill acquisition: Support for the guidance hypothesis, *Journal of Experimental Psychology: Learning, Memory, and Cognition*, 15(2), 352-359.

Schooler, L. J. & Anderson, J. R. (1990) 'The disruptive potential of immediate feedback', The Proceedings of the Twelfth Annual Conference of the Cognitive Science Society, Cambridge, MA.

Soderstrom, N. & Bjork, R. A. (2013). *Learning Versus Performance*, Oxford Bibliographies Online: Psychology, New York: Oxford University Press.

Vander Linden, D. W., Cauraugh, J. H. & Greene, T. A. (1993) 'The effects of frequency of kinetic feedback on learning an isometric force production task in nondisabled subjects', *Physical Therapy*, 73(2), 79-87.

Weeks, D. L. & Kordus, R. N. (1998) 'Relative frequency of knowledge of performance and motor skill learning', *Research Quarterly for Exercise and Sport*, 69(3), 224-230.

Winstein, C. J. & Schmidt, R. A. (1990) 'Reduced frequency of knowledge of results enhances motor skill learning', *Journal of Experimental Psychology: Learning, Memory, and Cognition*, 16(4), 677-691.

Chapter 9
Assessment

Psychometrics – the study of the measurement and testing of skills, knowledge and education achievement – might seem like a pretty arcane subject in a book about psychology for teachers, but arguably this is one of the least well-understood and most important aspects of education. Dylan Wiliam, in typically bullish form, argues that, "it would be reasonable to say that a teacher without at least some understanding of these issues should not be working in public schools."[*]

There are a number of key concepts every teacher ought to know about assessment:

Validity is commonly defined as the extent to which a measurement corresponds to the real-world thing you're trying to measure. In essence, *are you measuring the things you claim to be measuring?* But, as we discuss below, validity is more usefully applied to the interpretations we make of test scores and the decisions we subsequently make. Some important issues in assessment are 'content validity' and 'predictive validity'. For example, your maths test should have 'content validity' i.e. it covers a representative sample of the maths that you want to assess. It should also have 'predictive validity' i.e. do results on the test predict something about the student's future performance e.g. GCSE result.

Reliability represents the extent to which a measure is consistent. One important issue of reliability is 'inter-rater reliability' – for example, if two English teachers separately marked the same essay, would the marks they give

---

[*] Wiliam, D. (2014: 29)

be in close agreement? If a measurement isn't reliable (e.g. one teacher gives it an A, the other a D) then it is not a valid measurement. Another is 'test-retest' reliability – i.e. if I gave the same test to the same students next week, would they get similar results?

Reliability is a necessary condition for the validity of a measurement. However, a measure can be reliable, but invalid.*

A — Reliable and valid

B — Reliable but not valid

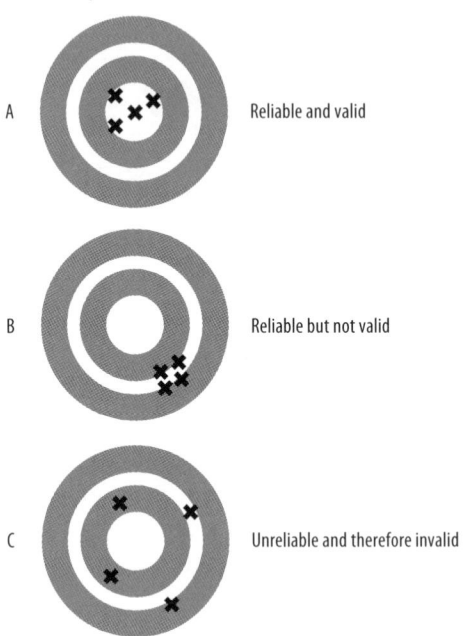

C — Unreliable and therefore invalid

Figure 1: The relationship between validity and reliability.

Shooting at a target: A) is both valid and reliable (the shots are near the centre of the target and close together); B) is reliable, but not valid (the shots are close together, but nowhere near the target); C) is unreliable therefore not valid (the shots are too spaced out).†

---

* The argument that 'a test that is not reliable cannot be valid' is the traditional view. Some scholars argue that an unreliable measure can be valid (reliability is seen as invariance and validity independently seen as unbiasedness). There's a good explanation of various views of reliability here: http://www.creative-wisdom.com/teaching/assessment/reliability.html

† This target metaphor works well in a simple case where the construct has a clear criterion measure against which to compare and validate. In practice, most educational assessments are a bit more complicated than that.

Precision is how 'fine-grain' a measurement is. For example, a weather forecaster could tell you that today will be 'warm' or 'hot' – or tell you it will be 22.5°C or 31.6°C. The latter would be more precise. In assessment, there's a question of how usefully precise the measurement should be. For example, should we tell students that they 'passed' or 'failed' their science test, or that they got an A or a B or a C, or that they got 46.7% correct? The level of precision depends on the random variation we're likely to see. The difference between a student getting 41.1% and 40.9% of a test correct is unlikely to tell us an important or meaningful difference in student ability.

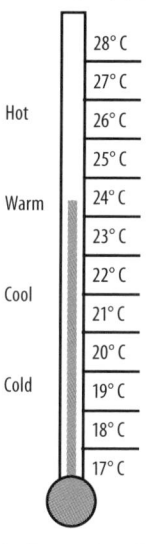

Figure 2: An imprecise thermometer and a more precise one.

Accuracy relates to how 'on target' a measurement is and is closely related to the idea of validity. For example, if my clock is running consistently five minutes slow, then it's not telling the accurate time. In assessment, if I've selected a lot of very easy questions into my history test, then the high marks students receive will not give me an accurate measure of their knowledge of history. Accuracy depends on the extent to which we've introduced a systematic bias in our measurement.

Understanding terms like validity, reliability, precision and accuracy is pretty essential to a full understanding of the uses and limits of testing and assessment.

We should ask ourselves four questions before considering the validity of an assessment:

- How much of what you want to measure is actually being measured?
- How much of what you did not intend to measure is actually being measured?
- What are the intended and unintended consequences of the assessment?
- What evidence do you have to support your answers to the first three questions?

These are important considerations, but here are five further points which all classroom teachers ought to be knowledgeable:

1. Validity is not a property of tests

Dylan Wiliam argues that we need to understand that "validity is best thought of as a property of inferences based on test outcomes rather than as a property of tests."* No test is perfect, after all there's no way an assessment could test *everything* students have been taught, instead it asks a sample of questions from the curriculum (a domain).

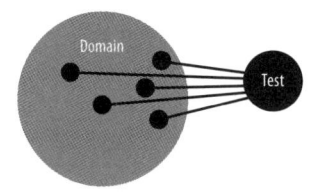

Figure 3: How tests sample from the domain

The difficulty comes in choosing our sample, to best ensure the assessment allows us to draw reasonably valid information about what students have learned. For example, do we create a sample based on what students have learnt today? This week? This term?

There will always be a limit on how much teachers can sample when creating or using assessments for their students. Arguably though, what's more important is the validity of our interpretations of what the assessment outcomes mean. The key question is, to what extent can we infer how much children know about a subject or topic from their performance on the sample of material that we have tested?

2. Validation is the joint responsibility of the test developer and the test user

Validity of an assessment depends both upon the person creating the test and

---

* Wiliam, D. (2014: 29)

the person using the test. With externally assessed exams like GCSEs or A levels, we tend to take it on trust that the sampling of the domain allows us to draw reasonably valid inferences. However, whenever we use a test developed by someone else, we have a responsibility to determine whether the way the developer designed the test actually supports the way we mean to use it. In other words, are we, as teachers, using tests for the purpose for which they were designed? For instance, are we giving the test under similar conditions for which it was designed to be given? If not, then we should be cautious about how we interpret the results. For example, if we give students past examination papers to practice exam technique in class or at home, we will not be able to make particularly valid inferences about how much students have learned or their likely performance in a future exam.

3. The need for reliability increases as the consequences of decisions and interpretations grow in importance

If a student happens to get a low score on a test, to what extent can we infer that it was because they didn't know the material being tested? We need to trust that results of an assessment allow us to make meaningful inferences about students' knowledge, skills, and abilities. The reliability of a test also determines the validity of this inference: unreliable data cannot support high-stakes inferences about student learning. Lots of things can influence the reliability of an assessment. Some of these factors relate to random things affecting the individual students taking the test (e.g. tiredness, health, levels of stress) and some of these relate to the stability of the thing we're trying to measure (i.e. student knowledge and understanding will (hopefully) improve over time).

Perhaps the most important aspect of reliability is whether different markers would give the same piece of work the same grade (inter-rater reliability). It's probably impossible to design an assessment that is totally reliable, but we can increase reliability by narrowing the content or limiting the range of student responses (e.g. use multiple choice rather than short-answer or essays), or by increasing the length of the test. But each of these has trade-off limitations. Narrowing the focus of a test may reduce its content validity, switching to closed answers may limit its predictive validity for exams which involve open or essay-based answers, making longer tests (making longer tests inevitably takes time away from teaching). So, if consequences of decisions are relatively unimportant (e.g. there are no stakes attached to the assessment), we might be better off accepting lower reliability.

We also want to avoid spurious precision. If a student gets 88% on a test we might think they're more able that someone who gets 87%. But this probably isn't true:

these small differences tell us relatively little about a person's ability; rather they tend to represent fairly random variations in individual performance. However, reducing the precision of an assessment doesn't necessarily resolve this problem. We're likely to infer that a student with a B is more able than a student with a C, but this difference in grades might only represent a difference of one mark on the test.

Concerns around reliability and precision become even more problematic when considering progress. If measuring a fixed point is tricky – and it is – then trying to ascertain students' rate of progress between two or more points is devilishly difficult.

Imagine you've given students a test, and provide extra tuition to those who scored below a certain score, then tested them again. If the students have improved it could be they learned more, but might also be because of regression to the mean. Regression to the mean is statistical phenomenon which means that, assuming there's some degree of randomness influencing outcomes, after an extreme result, the next result is likely to be less extreme. So, if the outcome of a test is extreme on its first result, it will tend to be closer to the average on its second – and if it is extreme on its second result, it will tend to have been closer to the average on its first. What this means in practice is that if students do especially well or especially badly, instead of congratulating or remonstrating with ourselves we would do better to remind ourselves of the limitations of assessment and only draw cautious inferences about 'progress'.

All too often, assessments provide data that is both imprecise and inaccurate. Avoiding systematic bias and the need to report 'fine-grain' results increases as the consequences of decisions and interpretations grow in importance. That is to say, the higher the stakes, the more important it is to be sure assessments are both reliable and valid.

4. A test that is fair within the meaning of the standards reflects the same construct(s) for all test takers

To make a valid inference about a student's learning based on an assessment, it should be a fair test. Fairness is an important component of validity, but what does it mean? Should it suggest that all students have an equally good chance of performing well? Well, yes and no. Yes, because it would obviously be unjust to discriminate against certain groups of students, but no because most tests are designed to reveal those differences, not obscure them. This is particularly problematic for students with special educational needs or disabilities. Should physical disabilities prevent students from accessing a test? Of course not. But what about cognitive or emotional issues?

To help us think more clearly about these issues it's useful to distinguish between *adaptations* and *accommodations*. An accommodation is a relatively minor change in the way a test is presented, taken or administered in order to provide fair access but still allow for results comparable to a test that hasn't been accommodated in some way (for example, having a large print version of the test for a student who is partially sighted). An adaptation, on the other hand, is intended to "transform the construct being measured, including the test content and/or testing conditions, to get a reasonable measure of a somewhat different but appropriate construct for designated test takers"* (for example, allowing extra time to complete the test). This is clearly more controversial and opens up discussion about how far a test can be adapted whilst still being fair. "Tests showing real, relevant differences are fair; tests showing differences that are unrelated to the purpose of the test are not."[†]

5. When an individual student's scores from different tests are compared, any educational decision based on the comparison should take into account the extent of overlap between the two constructs and the reliability or standard error of the difference score

If test results are used to monitor or track students, teachers will need to be aware that results might not be as valid as we might hope. When schools report grades or levels to parents throughout the year, what do these grades or levels actually mean? We *think* we know what we're talking about – after all, an A's an A, right? – but very often we're wrong. If the scores we're comparing come from different tests, then we may be comparing apples with pears. We know we're looking at some fruit, but what does this tell us about students' relative achievement? This is even a problem when we try to compare scores from the same test taken at different times.

We also need to be aware that tests measure motivation as well as the skills and knowledge ostensibly being tested. If a test has no meaning for students, they may not be motivated to make much effort. With tests that are low stakes for students but very high stakes for teachers and schools, we need to aware that the inferences we can make may be dubious. Teachers may feel under pressure to narrow the curriculum and only teach the content they decide is most likely to be assessed. Test rubrics can exacerbate this problem by making us aware of 'indicative content'. This content then becomes the extent of the curriculum.

---

*   http://www.apa.org/science/programs/testing/standards.aspx p.59
†   Top 20 Principles From Psychology For Prek–12 Teaching And Learning. p 30.

For instance, if teachers learn that students will be rewarded for using 'fronted adverbials' in their writing they will make sure they teach students to write sentences like, "After a while, we walked back across the field". Fine. But what can happen is that students then conclude that it would be a good idea to write, "Forgettably, he crawled into the shadows." By reducing the curriculum to what's on the mark scheme we have inadvertently ensured that students don't really understand the domain in which they are being assessed.

A test is more likely to allow us to draw valid conclusions on what students have learned when the stakes are moderate for both teachers and students. Very low stakes may mean that the assessment is not treated with any seriousness or preparation, but very high stakes may act to distort teaching and potentially distort outcomes for students (see Chapter 23 on stress and resilience) Furthermore, inferences about teacher effectiveness should only have consequences proportionate to the validity and reliability of that measure – otherwise accountability risks being arbitrary and unprofessional.

Into the classroom

Why interpretation matters

We're awash with data produced by oceans of assessment. As with so much else in life, the having of a thing is not its purpose. Analysing spreadsheets and graphs becomes like gazing, dumbly, into a crystal ball. We need to know how to interpret what these data tell us. And, perhaps more importantly, we need to know what they *can't* tell us. We need to know how to interpret data clearly, appropriately and fairly.

It ought to be obvious that scores from any assessment should generally be used only for the specific purposes for which they were designed. But look at what schools do in practice. What's the purpose of Key Stage 2 tests? Is it to assess the extent to which the Key Stage 2 curriculum has been covered? Is it to infer how much progress students have made across a key stage? Or is it perhaps to see if schools are 'coasting'? How then should we use the data produced? Can we use it to decide how much to pay teachers based on their students' performance? Can we use it to decide how to set students in secondary school? Or maybe we could use it to predict students' GCSE results at the end of Key Stage 4?

Here's a list of a few things assessment data might be expected to do:

- Set or group pupils according to ability
- Diagnose what individual pupils know
- Make promotion or retention decisions

- Share information with parents or government
- Measure the effectiveness of instruction (or learning)

But expecting the same test to produce data that can produce data fit for all these purposes at once is unfair and inappropriate.

The point is, the way we interpret data warps and distorts not only the assessment process, but every other aspect of education it touches. Few tests are bad in and of themselves, it's what's done with the data that determines whether they produce useful data.

Samuel Messick argued that, "Test validation is a process of inquiry into the adequacy and appropriateness of interpretations and actions based on test scores" and designed a framework to help us consider how we ought to inquire into the validity of tests:

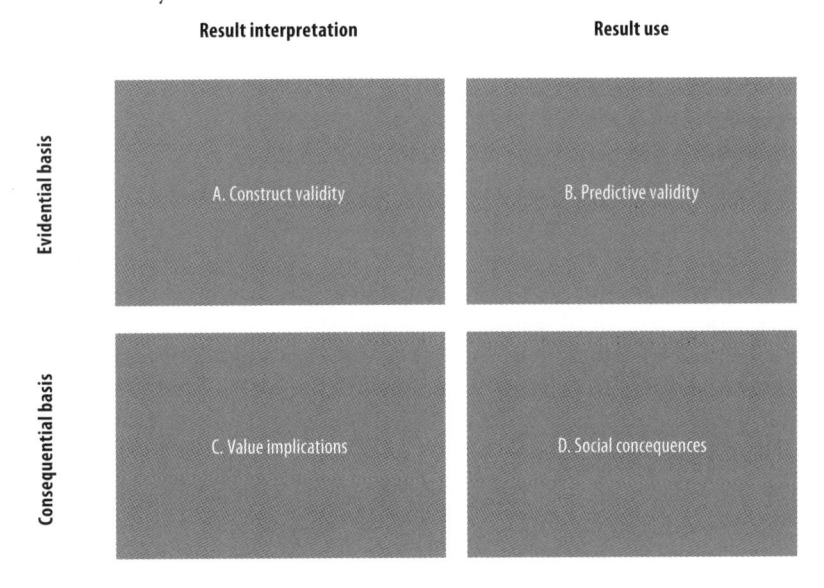

	Result interpretation	Result use
Evidential basis	A. Construct validity	B. Predictive validity
Consequential basis	C. Value implications	D. Social concequences

Figure 4: Messick's framework for the validation of assessments (1989)

Let's look at how it works in practice. Messick suggested that one of the consequences of how tests are interpreted is that those aspects of a domain which are explicitly assessed are judged to be of more value than those which are not assessed. Teachers are busy people. When push comes to shove we only have time to teach what's assessed and so then students may not even be aware that there are aspects of a subject which may in the past have been considered important.

Grammar is an interesting case in point. When I studied English in school, grammar was not assessed and so it wasn't taught. I had no awareness of most of the meta-language used to describe and think about the relationships between words with the results that my understanding of the subject was impoverished. Now, as the pendulum swings, we've decided not to place any value on our assessment of speaking and listening. What will be the consequences?

A. Construct validity – Validity is the extent to which a measurement corresponds the real-world thing you're trying to measure. We can decide that the domain of English can be assessed without a separate assessment of speaking and listening, but do we know what difference this makes to those who rely on test scores to tell them something about an individual? Parents' or employers' interpretation of students' performance in English may assume that the test does, in fact, cover speaking and listening and then students' ability in this area may be judged unfairly. The inferences likely to be drawn by employers about a student with a good grade in English may become less valid as a result. Thus, arguably, if speaking and listening are part of the real-world expectations of someone having a GCSE in English, the exam should include elements that test this in order to have construct validity.

B. Predictive validity – If we omit speaking and listening from GCSE grades, does this reduce the ability of the assessment to predict a student's likely success in further study or future employment? This is the evidential basis of result use: are we using test scores to provide evidence of something which they are not actually measuring? If a student's speaking and listening ability is well correlated with their overall GCSE grade this won't matter, but for those students who perform poorly in writing but well in an oral test then we won't be able to use the results to make useful predications about what the student is capable of.

C. Value implications – The consequential basis of result interpretation is fairly obvious: if we leave out speaking and listening then we send the message that if it's not worth assessing it's not worth studying. Students will be less likely to see the point in activities which involve such skills and, maybe, become less skilled in these areas. Is this what we want?

D. Social consequences – The consequential basis of result use has social implications. I'm of a generation of English teachers who valued speaking and listening because it formed 20% of a student's GCSE grade. We committed curriculum time to teaching and assessing the skills covered by the specification. Some teachers *may* decide that this is so important that they continue to do so despite the changes in assessment, but probably not. And future English teachers will be increasingly unaware that these skills were once valued.

This is all very well, but teachers rarely get a lot of choice about how the data they produce is consumed. Effective teaching no doubt depends on "teachers being informed consumers of educational research, effective interpreters of data for classroom use, and good communicators with students and their families about assessment data and decisions that affect students"* Ideally, teachers would be knowledgeable enough to be able to weigh curriculum and assessment choices to evaluate whether they were fit for purpose. In reality, few teachers have the expertise to be able to do this with confidence. But even if we do conclude that the curricula and assessments we're judged against don't meet the best standards, what should we do?

Whilst it's certainly true that it's important that teachers know how to effectively interpret assessments, it's even more crucial that school leaders are assessment savvy. It's always been the case that the outcome of an inspection is largely dependent on assessment outcomes, but if you know how to interpret data then you can make it sing.

An effective teacher or school leader ought to be able to answer these questions:

1. *What was the assessment intended to measure?* This is harder to answer than you might think. You may have an intuition about what a test is supposed to be assessing but sometimes it's probably helpful to go the horse's mouth and ask.

2. *Do differences in students' performance on the test indicate real and important differences in the achievement that we care about?* It's useful to know how assessments are referenced. Are students being compared to one another (norm, or cohort-referenced)? Or, are students' responses being directly compared to samples of acceptable and unacceptable responses that the teacher or others have provided (criterion-referenced)? This is important because norm-referenced assessments – or more precisely, norm-referenced inferences arising from assessments – disguise the basis on which the assessment is made. Criterion-referenced assessments incentivise teaching to the test in high-stakes settings by specifying the assessment outcomes too precisely.

3. *What are the criteria for cut-points or standards?* How results are reported matters. Raw percentages result in spurious precision while grades or levels result in spurious accuracy. If we don't know about these things, then we will be unable to meaningfully interpret results.

We must also remain mindful of the suitability of assessment data for addressing specific questions about students and their appropriateness for individuals from

---

*   Top 20 Principles From Psychology For Prek–12 Teaching And Learning. p. 31

different backgrounds and circumstances. However we assess students will have both intended and unintended consequences. Whether a test is high or low stakes will fundamentally affect the way students, and teachers, prepare for it and perform. It's important that we keep this in mind when interpreting the data such tests produce. As a general principle, the higher the stakes of the assessment, the less likely it is to produce unpolluted information. Any decision of consequence should be made using as many different sources of information as it's reasonable to collate.

The tension between formative and summative assessment

As readers will be no doubt be aware, summative uses of assessment data are made to establish what students have learned and to provide a quantitative measurement of achievement, whereas formative assessments are intended to establish how students are progressing and provide them with the support needed to arrive at their intended destination. Perhaps a simple heuristic is that summative assessment takes place after instruction while formative assessment is conducted before and during instruction. In order to use assessment data summatively, we must have valid, fair, useful, and reliable sources of information on which to make judgements, but can the same be said for formative uses? The greater part of formative assessment (or Assessment for Learning as it's often dubbed) is made up by teachers on the fly. There are various classroom practices, from the gimmicky (traffic lights, no hands-up questioning, exit passes) to the more conventional (marking books), all designed to allow teachers to judge whether students are on track and to make decisions about future teaching. The problem with all these approaches is that teachers will be making judgements based on current performance, rather than on longer-term outcomes related to learning.

As we discussed in the introduction to Part 1, learning is invisible; we can only ever *infer* learning from performance. We want the skills and knowledge we teach to be both durable and flexible. For learning to be worth the name it has to have resulted in changes to long-term memory so that students will both remember and be able to apply what they've learned in new contexts. Unfortunately we can't see whether students know something later or can do something somewhere else unless we assess them at different times and locations.

As with any abstraction we make up metaphors to help us better imagine what we're discussing. These metaphors are powerful; they can be enormously useful ways of thinking about the world but they can also fatally constrain our thinking. Language is cluttered with dead metaphors – ways of thinking about the world that were once fresh and vital but have, over long use, been trampled into cliché. Most people are unaware that the idea that learning can be seen even is metaphorical; repeated, unexamined usage has tricked us into believing we can *literally* see inside another's head. We cannot.

Why does this matter? There are two reasons. First, if we make judgements on what students appear to have learned within a lesson then we risk mistaking mimicry (see page 15) for learning. This is not to say that immediate demonstrations of learning is never useful, but we need to understand that new and troublesome concepts take time to integrate into patterns of prior knowledge. If we rush students to 'prove' what they have learned they will, often, simply give us the answers they think we want to hear. If they look hesitant or confused we prompt them with eager nods and point to relevant display or previous work in books. All too often they *know* the answer we want them to give with little understanding of what the answer means. But, grateful, we accept these meagre offerings as evidence that learning has taken place. Current performance is often a poor proxy for learning which lead us into making erroneous inferences. It might sound obvious, but if we want students to retain over the long term, we need to assess their long-term retention.

Second, and more importantly, there's a body of evidence that techniques which appear to increase current performance can actually decrease long-term retention and transfer.[*] The better students perform in the here and now, the less likely they are to do well six months later in the exam hall. One possible reason for this is because strong current performance can produce the 'illusion of knowing'. By performing well in the lesson, the student forms an inaccurate judgement of their learning. We remember that we could do something once and fail to notice that the substance of what we think we can do is forgotten. But when students have to struggle and dredge their memories for answers they know that they don't know, there is no comforting sense of familiarity to lull them in a false sense of security. Instead of acting to shore up our ability to retrieve in the short term, making the conditions of recall more difficult (for instance by varying the conditions of practice or interleaving) helps strengthen and embed items in long-term memory. So formative assessments which tell us that students seem to know what we've just taught them tell us little of value. As we saw in Chapter 2, revealing and managing misconceptions is much more useful, but there's even some evidence that getting a wrong answer *now*, helps reduce the likelihood of making the same mistake in the future.[†]

---

[*]   Soderstrom, N. & Bjork, R. (2013)
[†]   See for instance Roediger, H. & Butler, A. (2011)

Summative assessment, on the other hand, is a much more reliable indicator of learning as students' performance is usually judged at a later date and in a different place. We're still only able to see a current snapshot of how they performed on that sample, but that performance will better demonstrate the knowledge and skills have been retained and transferred if there has been a delay between learning and assessment.

Outside of formal exams which have been rigorously constructed and tested, and administered under the strict conditions, the assessments we use in schools are unlikely to have the validity required for us to make robust judgements about student learning. Dylan Wiliam argues that we should think of the validity in terms of the inferences we draw from these assessments rather than a property of our assessments. This makes practical sense – there's little point trying to make every pop quiz or impromptu test a valid psychometric instrument. When we give summative grades based on these kinds of assessments, we risk making an unwarranted inference about the performance of students. On the other hand, there are fewer problems using the evidence gained from these kinds of assessments to draw low-stakes, formative inferences about student learning.

None of this is to argue that formative assessment is useless, just that its goal should be explicitly different to that of summative assessment. Rather than pretending that the assessments typically used by teachers can give us valid, fair, useful, and reliable sources of information which can track student progress in learning, we might be better off seeing their purpose as building students' storage of the knowledge and skills we wish them to remember and apply. Beyond drawing useful formative inferences about student learning from assessment, we can advantage our students by making use of the testing effect.

Testing can (and should) include some of the tricks and techniques we've been misusing and misunderstanding as Assessment for Learning. In fact, it doesn't really matter how we test students as long as our emphasis changes. Testing should not be used primarily to assess the efficacy of your teaching and students' learning; it should be used as a powerful tool in your pedagogical armoury to *help them learn*.

Studying material once and testing three times leads to much better retention than studying three times and testing once.* It doesn't matter whether people are asked to recall individual items or passages of text – testing seems to beat re-studying every time. Now, we all know that cramming for a test works. However, these studies show that testing leads to an increased likelihood that information will

---

*   Psychologists show very consistent replications of the testing effect in laboratories – see for instance, see Karpicke & Roediger (2007) – but these findings have also been observed in the classroom studies undertaken by Nuthall (2007).

be retained over the long term. This implies that if we want our students to learn whatever it is we're trying to teach them then we should test them on it regularly: ideally every lesson. In this way we could help students to become aware of what they actually know as opposed to what they think they know.

A flawed understanding of what formative assessment should actually be for infects much of the advice given to teachers. We've become preoccupied with improving students' current performance in the misguided belief we can reliably collect evidence on students' learning.

Comparative judgement

In his seminal book, *Human Judgement*, Donald Laming explains that human beings are exceptionally poor at judging the quality of a thing on its own. We generally know whether we like something but we struggle to accurately evaluate just how good or bad something is. It's much easier for us to compare two things and weigh up the similarities and differences. This means we are often unaware of what a 'correct' judgement might be and are easily influenced by extraneous suggestions. This is compounded by the fact that we aren't usually even aware we've been influenced.

Some assessments are easy to evaluate; the answer is simply right or wrong. There can be great advantage to designing multiple choice questions (MCQs) which allow us to make good inferences about what students do and do not know, as well as giving us a good idea of their ability to reason and think critically. But, however well designed, MCQs run into a problem with validity in that while they can sample widely from students' domain knowledge, they struggle to sample the ability to synthesise ideas, consider evidence and pursue an analytical line of reasoning at any length. Consequently, many school subjects assess – at least in part – through extended written answers. Evaluating the quality of an essay is a difficult job and so we produce rubrics – mark schemes – in order to indicate how a student might be expected to respond at different mark boundaries. Teachers then read through the essay and attempt, as best they can, to match the content to that indicated in the mark scheme.

The problem is that we are very bad at doing this. As Laming says, "There is no absolute judgement. All judgements are comparisons of one thing with another."[*] He goes on to say that these "comparisons are little better than ordinal"[†]. What this means is that we can reliably put things into a rank order, but that's about it. Mark schemes give the appearance of objectivity but in actual

---

[*]   Laming, D. (2004: 9)
[†]   Laming, D. (2004: 51)

fact when teachers mark a set of essays they often find that half way through they come across an essay that is much better or worse than all the ones they'd marked to that point. This results in going back to change the marks to allow for the new essay to be ranked according to its merits.

Understanding students' performance depends on huge amounts of tacit knowledge. Because it's tacit it's very hard to articulate – even (maybe, especially) for experts. As Michael Polanyi said, "So long as we use a certain language, all questions that we can ask will have to be formulated in it and will thereby confirm the theory of the universe which is implied in the vocabulary and structure of the language."*

In our attempts to break down what experts do we spot superficial features of their performance and make these proxies for quality. For instance, it may well be that a good writer is able to use fronted adverbials and embedded relative clauses, but they would never set out with this as their goal. By looking for these proxies we run the risk of limiting both our own understanding and students' ability.

A solution is to do away with mark schemes and use instead a system of comparative judgement (CJ). Judging is different to marking in that it taps into our fast, intuitive modes of thinking – what Daniel Kahneman has called System 1. Marking, on the other hand, is the slow, analytical thinking characterised by System 2 (see Chapter 1 for more detail).

The idea is that a judge will look at two essays at once and make an intuitive judgement on which is better. For domains where a quick comparison can be made between pieces of work, the number of judgements can be aggregated to form a highly reliable rank order of teacher judgements.† The advantages for teachers are that the process is not only significantly quicker than traditional marking (judgements should be made in about 30 seconds), it's much more reliable and allows for more valid inferences to be drawn.‡

---

* Polanyi, M. (1952) retrieved from https://www.missouriwestern.edu/orgs/polanyi/mp-stability.htm

† The formula Chris Wheadon, founder of No More Marking, recommends is "multiplying the number of scripts you have by 5. So if you have 10 scripts we would advise 50 judgements. Under this model each script is judged 10 times." https://nomoremarking.com/blog/AAGfCvS9xp2aE8Sz

‡ For a detailed description of how to set up a CJ trial in you school, see David's blogs, Proof of Progress Part 1 http://www.learningspy.co.uk/assessment/comparative-judgement-trial-part-1/ and Part 2: http://www.learningspy.co.uk/assessment/proof-progress-part-2/

There are some common misconceptions about comparative judgement: first, there are concerns that it's inaccurate. It's understandable why we might feel sceptical that a fast, intuitive judgement can tell us as much as slow, analytical marking. Surely spending 10 minutes poring over a piece of writing, cross-referencing against a rubric has to be better than making a cursory judgement in a few seconds? On one level this may be true. Reading something in detail will obviously provide a lot more information than skim reading it. There are, however, two points to consider. Firstly, is the extra time spent marking worth the extra information gained? This of course depends. What are you planning to do as a result of reading the work? What else could you do with the time? Second, contrary to our intuitions, the reliability of aggregated judgements is much greater than that achieved by expert markers in national exams. The reliability of GCSE and A level marking for essay-based examinations is between 0.6-0.7. This indicates that there's a 30-40% probability that a different marker would award a different mark. Hence why so many papers have their marks challenged every year. But, if we aggregate a sufficient number of judgements (5 x n) then we can end up with reliability above 0.9. Although any individual judgement may be wildly inaccurate, on average they will produce much more accurate marks than an expert examiner.

For subject areas, where this kind of comparison can be easily made, it puts an end to conversations revolving around sub-levels of progress, or predicted grades, as if they actually meant something concrete. All assessments provide us with a proxy, this point is whether or not it's a good proxy. CJ allows us to make better inferences about learning as an abstract thing because it's so focused on the concrete. The absence of rubrics means we are one step nearer the thing itself. Additionally, not having a rubric also means we are likely to get a more valid sample of students' ability within a domain. Because a rubric depends on attempting to describe indicative content it warps both teaching and assessment; teachers use mark schemes to define the curriculum and examiners search for indicative content and ignore aspects of great work that didn't make it into the rubric.

Another concern is that the presence of a systematic bias might reduce the accuracy of the process (after all a measure can be reliable but still be invalid). However, teacher assessments are more likely to judge the child rather than their work, as investigations into the halo effect have consistently shown (see Chapter 12). We are all inadvertently prone to biases which end up privileging students based on their socio-economic background, race and gender. Whilst concerns that the seemingly irrelevant aspects of students' work – such as the quality of handwriting – affect comparative judgement are fair, theses biases also affect every other form of marking. If anything, comparative judgement is less unfair than marking.

In an ideal world maybe teachers would put the same effort into reading students' work as they put into creating it. Sadly, this thinking has led to the steady rise in teachers' workload and mounting feelings of guilt and anxiety. No teacher, no matter how good they are, will ever be able to sustain this kind of marking for long. But maybe we've been asking the wrong question. Maybe instead we should ask, *if students have put all this effort into their work, is it fair that we assess it unfairly and unreliably?*

It's worth noting that the 30-second intuitive judgement is only desirable during the judging process. When a rank order has been obtained, teachers can use the time to explore much more interesting and personal aspects of the writing, especially where judges make different judgements of the same piece of work.

In essence, comparative judgement is a way of making quick and reliable summative assessments. In order to provide meaningful formative feedback, of course you actually have to spend time reading the work too.

What every teacher needs to know about assessment

- Good sampling involves aligning assessments with what is taught and using a sufficient number of questions overall, and a good variety of questions and types of questions on the same topic.
- Use item analysis to target questions that are too hard or too easy and are not providing sufficient differentiation in knowledge (e.g. 100% of students answered correctly). On the other hand, you may want some items which all students will answer correctly, in order to send a message about the importance of what that item is testing.
- Teachers need to be mindful that inferences based on tests that are valid for one use or setting may not be valid for another.
- High-stakes decisions should be based on multiple measures instead of a single test.
- Outcomes should be monitored to determine whether there are consistent discrepancies across performance or outcomes of students from different cultural groups. For example, are some subgroups of students – for example, students with special educational needs – routinely over-represented at certain grades or levels?

- Teachers should ensure they understand what the concepts of reliability and validity actually mean and how they relate to assessments.
- Assessments can only be used with any reliability when they are used for the purpose for which they were designed. We should avoid drawing conclusions for which there is little reliability or validity.
- We teach what we assess. Teachers need to remember that a mark scheme or rubric only samples from a subject domain and are not the best guide to determining what should be taught.
- Learning and performance are not the same thing. We should avoid drawing conclusions about learning from observing students' immediate performances in lessons.
- Some performances offer more reliable evidence that learning has taken place than others. Ideally teachers should assess what students have learned after a reasonable amount of time has lapsed to be sure students are not just responding to performance cues.
- When making summative assessment judgements, teachers should consider using aggregated, comparative judgements in order to assess students with greater reliability and to make more valid inferences about what students can and cannot do.

References

American Educational Research Association, American Psychological Association, & National Council on Measurement in Education (2014). *Standards for educational and psychological testing*, Washington, DC: American Educational Research Association.

American Psychological Association (n.d.) *Appropriate use of high- stakes testing in our nation's schools.* Retrieved from http:// apa.org/pubs/info/brochures/testing.aspx

Black, P., Harrison, C., Lee, C., Marshall, B. & Wiliam, D. (2003) *Assessment for learning: Putting it into practice*, Buckingham, England: Open University Press.

Brookhart, S. (2011) 'Educational assessment knowledge and skills for teachers', *Educational Measurement: Issues and Practice*, 30(1), 3–12.

Council of Chief State School Officers (CCSSO) (2008) *Formative assessment: Examples of practice*. Retrieved from the CCSSO website: http://ccsso.org/Documents/2008/Formative Assessment_Examples_2008.pdf

Heritage, M. (2007) 'Formative assessment: What do teachers need to know and do?' *Phi Delta Kappan*, 89(2), 140–145.

Karpicke, J. D. & Roediger III, H. L. (2007) 'Repeated retrieval during learning is the key to long-term retention', *Journal of Memory and Language*, 57, 151–162.

Laming, D. (2004) *Human Judgement, The Eye of the Beholder*, Thompson.

Messick, S. (1989) 'Validity', in Linn, R. L. (ed.) *Educational measurement*, Washington, DC: American Council on Education/Macmillan, pp. 13-103

Nuthall, G. (2007) *The Hidden Lives of Learners*, Wellington, NZ: NZCER Press.

Moss, P. A. (2003) 'Reconceptualizing validity for classroom assessment', *Educational Measurement: Issues and Practice*, 22(4), 13–25.

Polanyi, M. (1952) 'The Stability of Beliefs', *British Journal for the Philosophy of Science* 3(11), 217-232.

Roediger, H. L. & Butler, A. C. (2011) 'The critical role of retrieval practice in long-term retention', *Trends in Cognitive Sciences*, 15, 20-27.

Sheppard, L. A. (2006) 'Classroom assessment', in Brennan, R. L. (ed.), *Educational measurement* (4th ed), Westport, CT: American Council on Education/Praeger, pp. 623–646.

Smith, J. K. (2003) 'Reconsidering reliability in classroom assessment and grading', *Educational Measurement: Issues and Practice*, 22(4), 26–33.

Soderstrom, N. & Bjork, R.A. (2013) 'Learning versus Performance', in Dunn, D. S. (ed.), *Oxford Bibliographies Online: Psychology*, New York: Oxford University Press.

Whitehouse, C. & Pollitt, A. (2012) 'Using Adaptive Comparative Judgement to Obtain a Highly Reliable Rank Order in Summative Assessment', AQA.

Wiliam, D. (2014) 'What do teachers need to know about the new Standards for educational and psychological testing?', *Educational Measurement: Issues and Practice*, 33, 20–30. doi:10.1111 /emip.12051

Wiliam, D. (1998) 'The Validity of Teachers' Assessments', Paper presented to Working Group 6 (Research on the Psychology of Mathematics Teacher Development) of the 22nd annual conference of the International Group for the Psychology of Mathematics Education; Stellenbosch, South Africa, July 1998. Available at dylanwiliam.org

Wiliam, D. (2001) 'Reliability, validity, and all that jazz', *Education 3-13*, 29(3), 17-21.

Wylie, C. & Lyon, C. (2012) 'Formative assessment – Supporting students' learning', *R & D Connections* (No. 19). Retrieved from the Educational Testing Service website: http://www.ets.org/Media/Research/pdf/RD_Connections_19.pdf

Chapter 10
Effective instruction

In previous chapters we've explored some of the psychology of how students learn. We've looked at the bottleneck of working memory and the limited capacity of the various components which we use when learning. Overloading this capacity is one reason why students struggle with learning, but we briefly explored some of the research into how we might balance the cognitive load demands we make. We also reviewed some of the research into how long-term memory works and the idea that we primarily store information based on its semantic properties (what it means). However, we readily 'forget' information that we learn unless we make efforts to retrieve it on a regular basis.

Previous chapters also explored some of the ways we might accommodate or exploit these aspects of memory. In this chapter, we want to bring together these various ideas as a summary of how understanding the psychology of learning can be applied to the classroom.

What do students already know?

Psychologists think about long-term memory as organised into schemas, or interconnected webs of concepts, facts, impressions and ideas. When tackling a novel problem, the absence of a relevant schema means we tend to use generic 'processing intensive' strategies. Because we can't 'chunk' the material very effectively, we may quickly overload working memory. The presence of a schema means we can associate items together in larger chunks within working memory. This allows us to hold more information in mind at once, increasing the chance of successfully processing new information, and adding new schemas to long-term memory.

This understanding of the interaction between long-term and working memory has important implications for the way we design a curriculum. Fundamentally, students need a firm foundation in the systems we use to code and decode biologically secondary knowledge (see Chapter 1) such as written grammar and mathematics. Effortless access to times tables, for example, allows students to later tackle more demanding problems (e.g. long division). Having to mentally calculate each component of a maths problem means the cognitive load imposed is much higher. The student quickly loses track of where they are in a procedure or makes simple errors which prevent them from solving the problem. Likewise, effortless grapheme to phoneme conversion allows students to later cope with more complex low-frequency and technical vocabulary. If basic reading is effortful, the process imposes such a large cognitive load that the student is unlikely to pick out relevant information in a maths or science word problem, for example.

Beyond unlocking the secrets of coding and decoding cultural knowledge, we also need to consider the sequence of learning within subjects. Every subject has some basic facts and concepts which are used repeatedly over the course of study and fairly fundamental to understanding that subject. Presenting these basics early in the curriculum and affording students the opportunities to commit these to long-term memory (through the cycle of forgetting and re-learning) will liberate working memory resources later on when we want them to tackle more complex problem solving and application tasks.

Some of what students learn in school is counter-intuitive (i.e. at odds with biologically primary knowledge built up through observation and interaction with the world). Prior knowledge can enhance learning, but where it involves misconceptions it can hamper it. For example, students will have observed that in everyday life a force needs to be applied to make an object move with a constant speed (because they can't see friction and air resistance). When presented with problems involving balanced and imbalanced forces, this 'prior knowledge' leads students to the wrong answers. We've seen that memory tends to 'drift' back towards familiar schema. Thus, it's important to assess these misconceptions and provide carefully paced, explicit explanation which draws attention to the differences between everyday observations or use of key terms and the counter-intuitive reality.

In addition, some of what students learn in school is highly abstract (i.e. quite distant from biologically primary knowledge). Here teachers need to connect the abstract to concrete representations of same concept. One example is using analogies. Good analogies work because they connect a new (abstract) idea onto something students are already familiar with. When using analogies, it's important to explicitly direct student attention to the key similarities between the familiar, concrete model and the unfamiliar, abstract knowledge.

It's also vital that we don't inadvertently introduce misconceptions. For example, in our desire to help students understand the concept of a molecule, it's easy for teachers to drift into unhelpful examples. Developing good explanations and accurate analogies is probably the key area of subject specialist knowledge teachers most need to develop.

How do students best take in new information?

Students learn best when teachers give concrete examples to exemplify abstract concepts and explain how the examples and big ideas connect. Making content explicit through carefully paced explanation, modelling and examples can help prevent students from becoming overloaded. It should be noted that explanation does not mean that the teacher does all the talking while students listen – effective instruction requires interaction, questioning and dialogue.

Additionally, we all receive information through two primary pathways – auditory (for the spoken word) and visual (for the written word and graphic or pictorial representation). It stands to reason that students will find learning easier if teachers use both mechanisms to present new information. Our working memory is made up of several interacting modules, two of which, the phonological loop and the visuo-spatial sketchpad, process information differently (see Chapter 2). Although performing two tasks which require the same component of working memory can quickly overload our capacity, we're able to use different components of working memory at the same time without difficulty. The phonological loop and the visuo-spatial sketchpad can be utilised at the same time by providing anchor images to support a complex verbal explanation. Everybody benefits from experiencing information through more than one modality. Modalities (a feature of materials or presentation) engage students' senses. The more senses engaged, the more likely encoding to long-term memory becomes.

What this means in practice that is speaking at the same time as showing a graphic enhances learning if the two types of information complement one another (e.g. showing an animation while describing it aloud). But if the two sources of information are not complementary students' attention will be divided and their learning impaired.

Richard Mayer (2009) suggests five principles for reducing extraneous cognitive load (see Chapter 4) when designing learning materials: coherence, signalling, redundancy, spatial contiguity and temporal contiguity. Essentially, this means teachers should delete extraneous material, highlight relevant material, avoid unnecessary text, place text near to visuals and make sure spoken words and images correspond. Mayer also found that students learn more from multi-modal instruction (when words and images are presented together) when the words are spoken rather than printed.

Ruth Clark (2015) has investigated the most effective ways to combine words and images and has come up with a number of useful principles to help teachers design better resources and presentations. She suggests that there are four different types of visuals we should be aware of:

- Organisational images – like flow charts, or concept maps – help students to see qualitative relationships in the content they are learning.
- Relational images – pie charts, use of colour to show variation – help to summarise quantitative data.
- Transformational images – animations or overlaying arrows on line drawings to show direction or movement – can help demonstrate changes in time and space.
- Interpretive – some simulations and animations can help students make connections between abstract concepts and concrete examples.

Certain types of visuals are more suitable for specific purposes. Whenever teachers design resources, the type of visual selected should be carefully aligned to the intended purpose.

Whenever we use images or other visuals to present information we should consider the following:

- Combining words and images can help students build coherent mental models of unfamiliar material and concepts.
- A poorly selected visual might actually interfere with learning. Teachers should avoid images which place extraneous demands on students' limited working memory capacity or are distracting because students may focus on unintended or irrelevant features of the image, rather than the parts which relate to our explanation.
- Ideally any text should be incorporated into the image, to minimise the effort of switching attention back and forth and so connections are clear.
- Simple visuals communicate ideas more clearly and concisely. Where possible, use flat two-dimensional images rather than elaborate three-dimensional options.
- When images are self-explanatory it's better to avoid unnecessary words. Conversely, if a diagram is complex, accompanying text may help us process the information.

There's also research to suggest that students can benefit from creating their own visuals. When students are asked to produce drawings whilst reading, they are likely to learn more than they would be writing a summary or other techniques commonly used to help make things stick. We can ease cognitive load by providing partially completed drawings, such as the opening stages of a timeline or some of the connections in a causal relationship diagram. This can be particularly effective when tasks rely on complex problem solving.

What makes explicit instruction effective?

We've seen some simple ideas already. Using stories or a narrative structure within a sequence of learning can help students tap into our evolved propensity for remembering stories. The fact that visual and verbal information can be processed simultaneously without putting additional load on working memory is something teachers should regularly exploit. When explaining new material, it's helpful to find a visual presentation relevant to the learning. Examples include a Venn diagram showing how categories of information can be organised, an animation or representation of a process (e.g. the carbon cycle), a graph showing key information or simply a picture of what you're explaining (e.g. the organelles of a cell).

It's worth being aware that if we try to draw on the same component of working memory more than once, we'll likely overload it. Thus, we should avoid giving a verbal explanation whilst presenting different text on the board. It's also worth considering how we can minimise the amount of attention switching students need to do. Having to shift attention from one part of a page (e.g. a diagram) to another (e.g. some labels) imposes additional load on working memory that probably isn't helpful. Where students need to do this (for example, an exam question using a graph on one page and a description on another to answer a question), try to break the task into component steps and tackle each separately before attempting to combine the components together.

When we use the term 'explicit instruction' we do not mean not simply giving a lecture; whilst 'telling' can successfully get students to process information at a semantic level, most often we need to employ a number of other techniques. As well as providing well-crafted explanations, we want students to think about the meaning of the new material. One way we can do this is to encourage students to pose and answer explanatory questions: the 'how' or 'why' something happened. We can also set tasks which require students to meaningfully organise material (e.g. what are the similarities and differences between two ideas?).

What encourages 'higher order' thinking?

One of the potential problems with teachers pushing for 'higher-order skills' (e.g. as depicted in Bloom's taxonomy) is that it's easy to overlook the importance of that foundation of knowledge which supports everything else. The starting point for the transfer of learning is ensuring students have the background knowledge to understand the context of novel problems. However, in addition, in order to successfully transfer that knowledge to a novel problem, students need to understand the deep underlying structure of the problem.

Where problems involve procedures with lots of steps, there's a risk that working memory will quickly become overloaded. Teachers can use worked examples to reduce the cognitive load involved in learning complex processes and procedures. It may be helpful to start with highly 'scaffolded' examples, for example step-by-step presentations of how to solve a problem. We can help independence by gradually removing this guidance as students tackle more examples so that they are encouraged to tackle more of the steps from memory.

Varying the conditions of practice increases the loading on working memory, but is an important tool for ensuring students are applying mental effort when engaging with material. One way of doing this is to encourage students to compare different types of problems to highlight the same underlying structure. For example, mixing in word problems (which tend to have a fairly concrete basis, e.g. working out the volume of a water tank) along with more abstract problems (e.g. simply applying a mathematical formula) may help students recognise the unifying concepts involved in both.

What facilitates long-term memory for learning?

As noted earlier, the idea that you can judge progress in learning across a lesson is misleading and unhelpful. However well planned a sequence of learning, we have to accommodate the uncomfortable truth that much of what students learn will quickly be forgotten. One of the most robust findings of research into memory is that trying to remember something helps us form long-term memory for that material – what is often called 'the testing effect'. It's important to explain to students that trying to remember something helps memory more than other forms of revision.

Teachers can exploit this aspect of memory in a variety of ways. One technique is to use questions to introduce a new topic. These help 'activate' the schemas relevant to the new learning, re-expose students to ideas they will need in the lesson and also allow the teacher to assess the background knowledge (and any misconceptions) of the students, and hopefully provoke students' curiosity in the process.

Regular low-stakes quizzes and reviews also tap into this testing effect. These can be quick questions on the board at the start of a lesson or multiple-choice quizzes online, or students can use self-tests. The format of the practice of retrieving information probably doesn't matter that much. So, if you've taught students to create mind maps, simply encourage them to practice recreating them from memory. If your students are in the habit of creating flash cards, ensure they are not passively re-reading them, but actively testing memory (e.g. by jotting down what's on the card from memory).

Teachers can also structure sequences of learning so that students gain practice over time. For example, reviewing previously taught content across weeks or months. An easy way to do this is to move from modular to cumulative assessment over the course of the year. Rather than teaching a topic and testing that topic, make sure the test includes other topics covered previously in the year. Cumulative tests ensure that students are exposed to key content on a regular basis and encourages that repeated practice at recalling that knowledge is spaced over time.

As well as distributing practice over time, there may be some benefit to mixing up the types of practice. One strategy (especially in mathematics) is interleaving, where you mix up practice of different types of content when setting problem tasks in lessons. For example, if students are adding, subtracting, multiplying and dividing fractions, typically it's more effective to mix up, or interleave the practice of different problem types, rather than practice just one type of problem then move on to the next.

We generally want students to think deeply about the meaning of material, but there are occasionally rather arbitrary things we might want children to learn (e.g. the order of colours in the visible portion of the electromagnetic spectrum). In these instances, in addition to retrieval practice, techniques like mnemonics (e.g. the acrostic 'Richard Of York Gave Battle In Vain) may be effective. Most of these techniques, like the Loci method and Keyword method (discussed in Chapter 4), utilise the fact we can process visual and verbal material at the same time – and this simultaneous processing may lead to dual coding of the information in long-term memory.

What improves student judgements of learning?

Metacognition – or thinking about thinking – can be a useful process to help students make better progress. One example of where metacognition can play an important role is the accuracy of judgements of learning. Judgements of learning are the assessments that students make about how well they have learned particular information – that is, how likely is it they will remember the material when given an exam question. These assessments influence how much revision students tend to do and which topics they need study further.

It seems likely that there are several processes taking place when students form judgements about what they are learning. We tend to make fairly quick judgements before investing any mental effort in retrieving information from long-term memory based on our familiarity with the material. We may also form a slower, more considered judgement of how readily we can retrieve that information based on actually trying to recall it.

When students try to revise key material in preparation for tests or exams they often overestimate how much they can securely recall. The poor accuracy of these judgements relates back to the rather lazy (or more charitably, effort-efficient) way human beings have evolved to process information – we tend to stop processing information once the analysis relevant to the task has been carried out. For example, it's fairly easy to mistake recognition with recall (see section on retrieval strength in Chapter 5) – so if a page in a textbook looks very familiar, the student may incorrectly judge that they have good recall of the material it contains and stop revising.

Teachers can help students in a couple of ways. Firstly, we can help students identify what they know well, and what needs further study, by providing feedback on what they have learned. This feedback will tend to be more effective if we are fairly specific about where (and how) students can improve. Secondly, we can teach students the importance of making delayed judgements of learning when studying independently so they form a more accurate idea about the content that needs further study. In general, we are more accurate at predicting later performance when there is a delay between studying material and making a judgement about how much we can securely recall. Finally, we can encourage students to test that judgement by attempting tasks or questions from memory. The process of self-testing not only taps into the testing effect, it will also help improve the student's judgement about where they need to focus their efforts.

Into the classroom

When teaching new material, especially when it is abstract or counter-intuitive, we need to ensure that students are not overloaded. The problem of more inductive or discovery methods of teaching is that it requires students to juggle a lot of information in mind at once in order to perceive the relationships or patterns we want them to understand. Providing an element of explicit instruction, using carefully considered explanations, worked examples and accurate analogies, is almost certainly a better bet than providing relatively little guidance using problem-solving or open-inquiry methods.

We want students to develop long-term memory for the key terms, concepts and skills involved in learning a subject, but we also want them to be able to transfer this knowledge to novel problems that may require the application of this knowledge. Careful use of worked examples and problem-solving tasks is one way we use to help manage cognitive load and improve the transfer of learning.

Whilst we tend to readily understand new ideas through worked examples, students don't always pick up on the underlying concepts that unify the different examples. By mixing in problem-solving exercises, so that students alternate between exploring worked solutions and trying to solve problems more independently, we can also help students transfer knowledge to novel examples in future.

We can help students develop reliable long-term recall of material by spacing retrieval practice over time (e.g. over weeks or months). The effort of trying to remember something helps recall more than other studying techniques (especially passive strategies like highlighting or underlining). Using frequent low-stakes quizzes and reviews is also a powerful way to activate relevant schemas when teaching a new topic, assess students' background knowledge and misconceptions, and assist students to form more accurate judgements of learning which will help them when they are revising independently.*

---

* As we go to press, a new study has indicated that the apparent contradiction between the 'worked example effect' (where explicit instruction on new aspects of the curriculum helps reduce cognitive load) and the 'generation effect' (where less guidance can sometimes boost long-term memory) can be resolved by understanding that using worked examples works best with 'high element-interactivity' examples and asking students to generate missing aspects from examples will be more effective when studying 'low element-interactivity' examples. Element-interactivity is a measure of complexity which indicates how likely a new concept is to over burden working memory. See Chen, O., Kalyuga, S, & Sweller, J. (2016) 'Relations between the worked example and generation effects on immediate and delayed tests', *Learning and Instruction,* 45, 21-30.

What every teacher needs to know about effective instruction

- Knowing is essential. Solid background knowledge helps us chunk more material in working memory and helps us link new material to what we already know.
- When introducing new material, explicit instruction – making use of narrative structure, accurate analogies, scaffolded worked examples – combined with probing questioning will help manage the cognitive load imposed by the material.
- All students find it easier to learn when effective visuals compliment text or speech.
- Spaced and (especially for mathematics) interleaved retrieval practice helps long-term memory consolidation.
- Varying the conditions of practice helps the transfer of new knowledge to novel problems.
- Students often mistake familiarity with material for the ability to recall it. We can help students form more accurate judgements of learning by encouraging a delay between studying and self-testing.

References

Chandler, P. & Sweller, J. (1992) 'The Split-Attention Effect as a Factor in the Design of Instruction', *British Journal of Educational Psychology*, 62(2), 233-246.

Clark, R. (2015) *Evidence-Based Training Methods*, Alexandria, VA: ATD Press.

Clark, R., Nguyen, F & Sweller, J. (2006) *Efficiency in Learning: Evidence-Based Guidelines to Manage Cognitive Load*, UK: Pfeiffer.

Deans for Impact (2015) The Science of Learning. Austin, TX: Deans for Impact. http://www.deansforimpact.org/pdfs/The_Science_of_Learning.pdf

Dunlosky, J., Rawson, K. A., Marsh, E. J., Nathan, M. J. & Willingham, D. T. (2013) 'Improving students' learning with effective learning techniques promising directions from cognitive and educational psychology', *Psychological Science in the Public Interest*, 14(1), 4-58.

Dunlosky, J. & Nelson, T. O. (1994) 'Does the sensitivity of Judgements of Learning (JoLs) to the effects of various study activities depend upon when the JoLs occur?', *Journal of Memory and Language*, 33, 545-565.

Hirsch, E.D. (2000) 'You Can Always Look It Up' ...or Can you? *American Educator*, Spring 2000.

Kirschner, P. A., Sweller, J. & Clark, R. E. (2006) 'Why Minimal Guidance During Instruction Does Not Work', *Educational Psychologist*, 41(2), 75-86.

Mayer, R.E. (2009) *Research-Based Principles for Designing Multimedia Instruction*. http://hilt.harvard.edu/files/hilt/files/background_reading.pdf

Mayer, R. & Moreno, R (2003) 'Nine ways to reduce cognitive load in multimedia learning', *Educational Psychologist*, 38, 43-52.

Pashler, H., Bain, P., Bottge, B., Graesser, A., Koedinger, K., McDaniel, M. & Metcalfe, J. (2007) *Organizing Instruction and Study to Improve Student Learning* (NCER 2007-2004). Washington, DC: National Center for Education Research, Institute of Education Sciences, U.S. Department of Education. http://ncer.ed.gov

Pomerance, L., Greenberg, J. & Walsh, K. (2016) *Learning About Learning: What every new teacher needs to know*, National Council on Teacher Quality. Retrieved from http://www.nctq.org/dmsView/Learning_About_Learning_Report

Son, L. K. & Metcalfe, J. (2005) 'Judgements of learning: Evidence for a two-stage process', *Memory & Cognition*. 33(6), 1116-1129

Willingham, D. (2007) 'Critical Thinking: Why is it so hard to teach?' *American Educator*, Summer 2007.

Willingham, D. (2002) 'Inflexible knowledge: The first step to expertise', *American Educator*, Winter 2002.

Part 2
Motivation and behaviour

What motivates students to learn?

A commonly held, implicit belief is that if we can change a person's attitude then we can change their behaviour. However, the psychological research into human motivation shows that this is very often not the case. People have opinions and beliefs about a lot of things, but don't always act in accordance with those attitudes. Back in the 1960s and 70s, psychologists were accruing increasing evidence that measures of attitude had little value for the prediction of overt behaviour; for example, the attitude of people from an ethnic majority towards minority ethnic groups had no significant effect on the rejection of a black ethnic minority individual from a group. People's attitudes towards organ transplants didn't appear to affect their willingness to join a pool of potential bone marrow donors. Attitudes towards child rearing practices did not correspond with how a mother behaved with her own child.

Applied research at the start of the 21st century has found the same problem: for example, naïve attempts at encouraging smoking cessation through direct persuasion fails to change people's smoking behaviour. Another example of the complexity of the relationship between attitudes and behaviour is using fear to change health behaviour. It seems that attempts to change health behaviour through fear appeals can be very effective, but can also quickly backfire where individuals have low self-efficacy in their ability to avert that threat. Worse than having no effect, sometimes poorly-implemented public health interventions based on changing attitudes can have negative effects, for example inadvertently labelling some with a potential illness.

Part of the problem is the measurement of attitude. Firstly, there is the issue of social desirability bias – if we believe there is an expected or socially appropriate answer, then we tend to give it when asked about our beliefs rather than reveal our private (and potentially less acceptable) views. Secondly, there is the issue of the validity of the measurement. Asking broad questions about beliefs may not correspond to a specific behaviour because the researcher hasn't asked about the attitudes immediately relevant to that behaviour. However, even with improved methodology, the relationship between attitudes and beliefs is not a straightforward one. Social norms (unspoken rules and expectations about what constitutes acceptable behaviour in a given context) and the extent to which we perceive control over our actions and the situation also exerts a strong influence on the way we behave.

Changing behaviour is *hard*. Just about everyone is trying to change their behaviour in some way; trying to eat more healthily or take more exercise, cutting down on drinking or quitting smoking, being more environmentally friendly by recycling more or using their car less. However, simply because we hold certain beliefs and attitudes (should eat more vegetables, smoking leads to early death, it's important to protect the environment) doesn't necessarily mean we successfully change our behaviour.

Motivation is not a simple causal arrow between attitudes and behaviour, it turns out to be 'a bit more complicated than that'. Indeed, sometimes the arrow is reversed and the way we behave influences our beliefs!

It's probably true that learning requires motivation, but motivation does not necessarily lead to learning. One reason for this is a conflation between 'engagement' and the motivation to learn. Much of what goes on in classrooms is predicated on the belief that if kids are sufficiently engaged in an activity, they will learn from it. But we can really enjoy something without learning a whole lot from it. For instance, many children will enjoy spending lessons watching cartoons, but they're unlikely to learn much curriculum content this way. Graham Nuthall's research shows that, "students can be busiest and most involved with material they already know. In most of the classrooms we have studied, each student already knows about 40–50% of what the teacher is teaching."[*] We tend to be more motivated to get stuck into tasks we're comfortable with, but that won't necessarily result in us learning much. Many of the behaviours we perceive as motivated are, in the words of Robert Coe, "poor proxies for learning".[†]

---

[*] Nuthall, G. (2007)
[†] Coe, R. (2013: xii)

A teacher interested in the psychology of motivation is faced with a somewhat daunting task: the literature is huge. In order to assess the thousands of psychology papers published on motivation we need first to consider what we actually need in schools. The problem we face is that learning requires effort, attention, concentration, discipline and motivation. What we teach is subject to rapid and substantial forgetting. Because of this, students are unlikely to learn something if they're not sufficiently interested in it. Even when pupils are interested, concentration spans are short and attention is easily disrupted. What's more, the act of concentrating and the effort of maintaining self-control can overload our limited mental resources. Students' self-control strategies are often insecurely learned, relatively unpractised and easily depleted.

Being sufficiently curious about what you're learning can make the effort involved in learning seem worthwhile. However, curiosity benefits from knowing something about a topic already. Motivation is driven not so much by the relevance of the content as the challenge of the task. Students may find undemanding tasks, like completing a word search, fun for a while, but they soon become dull. On the other hand, being asked to perform complex calculations in your head when you're still struggling with the basics is unlikely to have much appeal for most students. If a task is too easy, or too hard, students are likely to give up. We appear motivated by problems that are both challenging *and* attainable – otherwise we get frustrated, bored or complacent. Teaching needs to stretch but not overwhelm pupils.

The science of motivation is complex and, to our eyes, full of contradiction. In many ways the science appears less settled than it is for the aspects of psychology related to memory and learning discussed in Part 1. In order to make sure that busy teachers are armed with what we believe are the theories most likely to impact positively on classroom practice we've winnowed down our discussion to a few well-chosen areas. However, this is offered as a starting point for teachers interested in understanding some of the psychology of this fascinating branch of research rather than a definitive guide. We hope you're inspired to explore some of these areas further, weighing the evidence as you go, to guide you on your journey to becoming the most effective teacher you can be.

We start by exploring the power of teacher expectations on students' motivation and learning, the importance of students' beliefs and perceptions of their intelligence, the role of effective rewards and sanctions, the differences between intrinsic and extrinsic motivation, how to foster effective self-regulation, the why and wherefores of restorative practices, the functioning of groups and their social norms, and the science behind the murky realm of target setting.

References

Ajzen, I. & Fishbein, M. (1977) 'Attitude-behavior relations: A theoretical analysis and review of empirical research', *Psychological bulletin*, 84(5), 888.

Coe, R. (2013) *Improving Education – A triumph of hope over experience*. Centre for Evaluation and Monitoring, Durham University http://www.cem.org/attachments/publications/ImprovingEducation2013.pdf

Glasgow, R. E., Klesges, L. M., Dzewaltowski, D. A., Estabrooks, P. A. & Vogt, T. M. (2006) 'Evaluating the impact of health promotion programs: using the RE-AIM framework to form summary measures for decision making involving complex issues', *Health Education Research*, 21(5), 688-694.

Kim, M. S. & Hunter, J. E. (1993) 'Attitude-behavior relations: A meta-analysis of attitudinal relevance and topic', *Journal of communication*, 43(1), 101-142.

Nutbeam, D. (2000) 'Health literacy as a public health goal: a challenge for contemporary health education and communication strategies into the 21st century', *Health promotion international*, 15(3), 259-267.

Nuthall, G (2007) *The Hidden Lives of Learners*. Wellington, NZ: NZCER Press.

Smith, J. R., Terry, D. J., Manstead, A. S., Louis, W. R., Kotterman, D. & Wolfs, J. (2008) 'The attitude–behavior relationship in consumer conduct: The role of norms, past behavior, and self-identity', *The Journal of Social Psychology*, 148(3), 311-334.

Witte, K. & Allen, M. (2000) 'A meta-analysis of fear appeals: Implications for effective public health campaigns', *Health education & behavior*, 27(5), 591-615.

Chapter 11
Beliefs

Beliefs matter. Generally speaking if you believe you can do something then there's a good chance you will put in the effort required to be successful. Conversely, if you're sure you can't, then you probably won't. Clearly beliefs must conform to reality – merely believing in your ability to read minds or foretell the future is unlikely to pay dividends – but most people agree that anyone can get better at playing the piano or speaking French through practice and that hard work will help anyone, no matter their current level of skill, to improve their ability to ski, put up wallpaper and do cryptic crosswords. But not everyone believes they can become more intelligent than they are currently.

Thanks mainly to Carol Dweck's wildly popular book, *Mindset*, the idea that our perceptions about intelligence affect how we perform is well established. Dweck argues that what students attribute their successes and failures to affects how they respond to the challenges and obstacles they face when learning in schools. Some students possess an 'incremental theory' of intelligence (what has become known as a 'growth mindset'). This means they tend to frame the experience of school in terms of learning goals and see ability as something that can be increased with effort and time. Other students possess an 'entity theory' of intelligence (a 'fixed mindset') and frame school work in terms of performance goals; seeing ability as something that is static and inflexible.

How people attribute the cause of their success or failure seems to influence how much effort they're prepared to apply in the future. If we try a new task and our cognitive evaluation of the experience leads to a positive affect (i.e. a positive emotional outcome) and there's a high expectation of future success, we typically show greater willingness to undertake such tasks in the future. Conversely, if the attribution leads to a negative effect and low expectation of success, we're more likely to act in a more helpless manner when placed in a similar situation.

The idea of learned helplessness has been around for quite a while. In the 1960s, Martin Seligman conducted a series of fairly brutal-sounding experiments on dogs. One group of dogs were given electric shocks, which they could learn to switch off by pressing a lever. A second group were given shocks at the same time as the first group but had no lever to push. When the dogs in the first group pressed the lever their shocks stopped too, but they had no idea why – there seemed no explanation for why the shocks ended and the dogs learned that they had no power to do anything about the experience of being electrocuted. In a second round of experiments, the dogs were put into a room divided by a low fence. Seligman electrified one half of the floor but not the other half. The dogs who had learned the lever trick soon learned to jump over the divide, but the dogs who had experienced arbitrary shocks just lay down on the floor and whined. They had learned that nothing they could do would improve their situation so they stopped trying.

Later researchers confirmed the debilitating effects of being unable to control an aversive stimulus. In one experiment, subjects were asked to perform a series of mental tasks as a distracting tone was played. Those who were able to use a switch to stop the noise rarely bothered to do so, yet performed better than those were unable to turn off the noise. The conclusion was that just being aware of the option was enough to counteract the effect of the noise.[*]

Essentially, this boils down to the belief that if you can control an outcome through your own efforts then you're more likely to put more effort into challenging tasks. Similarly, if you believe you can increase your intelligence through effort then you are more likely to be willing to attempt challenging tasks. When you experience setbacks you are likely to believe that effort and practice will enable you to overcome the obstacle.

But, if you believe nothing you do makes a difference and that your ability is never going to improve, then setbacks are more serious: they tell you that you're incapable of a task and that your best bet is to give up. After all, why persist if you don't think you can improve?

Students with an incremental mindset generally focus on learning goals and are more willing to take on challenging tasks in an effort to test and expand (as opposed to defensively prove) their intelligence or ability. Hence, they rebound

---

[*]   Hiroto, D. & Seligman, M.E.P. (1975)

more easily from negative feedback and failure. Accordingly, students who believe that intelligence and ability can be enhanced tend to perform better on a variety of cognitive tasks and in problem-solving situations.

Whenever we fail at something we look for reasons. If those reasons are seen as within our power to change – "I didn't try hard enough" – then we can do something about it, but if we find reasons that are outside of our sphere of control – "I'm not clever enough" – then we're stuffed. It should go without saying that we will be better able to cope when our failure is attributed to a lack of effort rather than to a lack of ability.

This is not entirely uncontroversial. Other studies have been unable to replicate Dweck's original results, finding instead that if students with a growth mindset were overly concerned with academic performance they tended to behave similarly to those students with a fixed mindset.[*] There's also a question as to whether a growth or fixed mindset is a global attribution, i.e. whether we really have the same mindset across all subjects and challenges, or whether we adopt a fixed mindset for some things (many interventions focus on maths) and a growth mindset for others. Most of us cut our losses and give up on some things in order to improve on others. It may be that a fixed mindset about, say, our ability to perform quadratic equations, saves us from a good deal of frustration and wasted time. In essence, the fixed mindset may be an adaptive response, an evolved strategy preventing us from 'wasting' effort where we have experienced frequent failure and the opportunity for future success is low, and encouraging us to invest effort in areas where it may be more likely to pay off for us.

Finally, there's the question of cause and effect. It's possible that the causal arrow between mindset and performance is not a straightforward one. It's natural to assume that changing a person's beliefs will alter their behaviour, but the evidence on this is much more complicated. It could be that students are more likely to adopt a growth mindset based on positive feedback on their performance.[†] Maybe we are more likely to alter beliefs by trying to change behaviour.

The real question is what teachers can do to foster students' beliefs that their intelligence and ability can be developed through effort and experience. Whilst successful interventions have been reported in relatively small-scale experiments, it's possible that the elements of a psychological intervention which led it to be successful will be lost or negated when scaled at a school level.

---

[*] Crocker, J. et al (2009)

[†] Indeed, Blackwell, L. et al (2007) found increases in achievement (though fairly modest) through teaching an incremental theory of intelligence to 7th graders.

Of course, you can *tell* students that their failure at any given task is not due to lack of ability and that with effort they can enhance their performance, but will this make a difference? It sounds lovely, and it may be exactly what some students need to hear, but what if a student is trying as hard as they are able? What if they've already tried a range of approaches and still failed? Is telling them their performance can be enhanced with even greater effort likely to be motivational? Having a growth mindset does not confer magical powers; Dweck herself admits a growth mindset alone is insufficient to affect pupils' performance at school.[*] Maybe we *can* all be cleverer, but surely there must be a limit. Whatever beliefs we might have, clearly ability matters.

Dweck talks about the development of growth mindsets as a *journey*. She says it really isn't enough to simply be told about mindset theory, you have to believe it. At first glance, this sounds a little like religious faith – it only 'works' if you're a true believer. Dweck has identified a phenomenon she calls the 'false growth mindset': because there is a consensus that having a fixed mindset is egregious and a growth mindset makes you a better all-round human being, no one wants to admit to being 'fixed'. When asked, we tend to say, "Yes of course I have a growth mindset," because the alternative is to say, "No, I'm afraid I'm a terrible person."

This is one reason why self-report questionnaires are unlikely to provide a valid way of measuring changes in student mindsets. Students will quickly cotton on to the idea that 'four legs growth, two legs fixed' and likely report apparent changes in attitude which do not reflect their private beliefs. But how else can you measure what someone believes other than by asking them?

It seems reasonable to suggest teachers are at least as prone to the false growth mindset as students; we tend to know more about the perceived benefits of growth mindset than most other people and so there's a huge social pressure to fall into line. But just saying you have a growth mindset does not (*quelle surprise!*) mean you actually have one. Maybe what you actually have is a *false growth mindset*. This goes some way to explaining why schools are so bad at allowing teachers to behave in ways consistent with the growth mindset.

However, the idea of a false growth mindset creates a potential problem for the science, as it risks making the theory harder to falsify. For example, if you run a mindset intervention and find that, although children's mindsets appeared to have changed, there was no increase in performance, then it's possible to dismiss this result by claiming the children had a false growth mindset. This may well

---

[*] David Glenn, 'Carol Dweck's Attitude' *The Chronicle of Higher Education* http://chronicle.com/article/Carol-Dwecks-Attitude/65405/

explain some of the rather flimsy findings in the Education Endowment Foundation's recent report, 'Changing Mindsets'. This study explored two separate inventions. The first, which focused on informing students about the malleability of their intelligence through a series of six workshops, seemed to have a small effect on their progress in English and maths, but the other, which focused on addressing teachers' beliefs about intelligence though a two-and-a-half day course, seemed to produce a small negative effect on students' progress!

So what should we do? Dweck suggests the first step is to validate and explore the fixed mindset and admit that we probably all have fixed and inflexible beliefs about *something*. By honestly exploring our prejudices and biases we're much more likely to embark on the kind of journey necessary to genuinely changing our beliefs about intelligence and ability.

There are two ways to take this. One could be to shrug cynically and point out that all snake-oil peddlers say we need to be true believers before we'll feel the benefit. Or we could, if we were open minded enough, really try to interrogate our prejudices and reservations to find out why we don't believe developing a growth mindset might work with 'kids like these'.

The other point that seems worth making is that there's almost certainly an element of 'adaptive value' in reducing effort when we experience frequent failure. Perhaps rather than trying to increase motivation by manipulating children's attributions about intellect, we'd be better off focusing on helping them achieve some measure of success and let their mindsets look after themselves. Maybe, the more you experience struggle and receive a sense of success at the end of the endeavour, the better you get at coping with the risk of failure?

Into the classroom

Messages about effort

Some students give up because they don't believe they're clever enough. If you're never going to succeed, what's the point in trying? Other students seek to protect their fragile egos by not trying as hard as they might. After all, if you try your best and fail then you must really be dumb; at least if you haven't tried there's a ready-made excuse for failure. Of course, no teacher would deliberately attribute students' failure to their ability, but we may well communicate this inadvertently.

We should focus on what students can control, such as the effort they have invested in a task and the strategies they use. It can be useful to suggest that there are two types of work: excellent work and work which has not yet been finished. Ask students if their work is excellent – if not, suggest they crack on and finish it.

However, attributing failure to lack of effort is potentially problematic. If you've worked your socks off and believe you've done your best, having this questioned by a well-intentioned teacher may well reinforce a belief that you have limited ability. Failure then seems like a character flaw. Simply urging students to work harder is not the answer. The student may simply have wasted a lot of time and effort trying to implement an ineffective strategy. Students also need to be taught a range of potentially useful strategies. Sometimes we don't need to work harder, we just need to work differently.

The overriding component in all of this is that students must *believe* they can improve though their own efforts. Probably the best way of achieving this is for students to experience some success as a consequence of applying greater effort.

Praise

Students' beliefs can be affected by the way teachers communicate with students. For example, it's probably better to avoid personal praise and phrase feedback in terms of the product, the effort involved or the process used instead. However, this rule of thumb has limitations. If we praise students for completing unchallenging tasks we may end up convincing them that success should be effortless. This might present problems when they face more challenging tasks in the future.

Another risk with praising students for completing routine tasks is that they might just conclude teachers have low expectations. It may be tempting to give a sympathetic or enthusiastic response to a student's piece of work. The problem is, if the student knows that it's not very good, or certainly not their best work, they may well interpret that praise as meaning that the teacher doesn't expect very much of them. It is probably better to be 'tactically grumpy": hard to please, sceptical of excuses and exceptionally sparing with praise, thereby conveying the highest of expectations.

Avoiding unearned praise, offering support and expressing disappointment will not, of course, magically result in the creation of resilient students. Teachers must exercise their judgement when deciding how to interact with the students in their classes. But we should always be aware that sometimes well-intentioned actions may have unexpected, or even negative, effects on students' beliefs about their own abilities.

---

*   Rose, N. (2014) https://evidenceintopractice.wordpress.com/2014/03/28/killing-with-kindness-and-the-dangers-of-differentiation/

Scaffolding

If we're serious about changing students' perceptions about intelligence and ability, then it's worth knowing that students are more likely to change their mindset if they first experience success. Interventions which focus on changing attitudes will have less impact than those which focus on increasing performance. The principle here is to encode success rather than failure: first provide support to help students experience success, then, as students become more successful, we should make them aware of how their thinking and behaviour are changing.

Thinking about where the scaffolding metaphor comes from is instructive. Builders use scaffolding to enable them to attempt projects which would be otherwise impossible – or at least very unsafe. And then, when they've erected their shining skyscrapers, they take the scaffolding away. Unless scaffolding is removed we are unable to fully appreciate an architect's vision.

However, builders do not use scaffolding to help them knock together a dwarf wall in your back garden or leave the skyscraper covered in scaffolding. In teaching, we tend to use scaffolding to make work easier. In order to prevent students feeling stuck, or to overcome difficulty, we give them a writing frame. Then, when they've finished, we leave it there.

There are two principles for the effective use of scaffolding. First, we should never use scaffolding to make easy work easier. We should only ever use it to make the impossible possible. We need to simplify the task sufficiently to allow pupils to attempt it, but make it hard enough so that everyone has to do something challenging. Everyone should struggle (and with effort, succeed), no matter their ability.

Second, never put up scaffolding unless you have a plan for taking it down. If we leave it there, students will become dependent on it. They'll never be able to perform without support, and this often ends up stifling their ideas and expression. Clunky straitjackets like PEE (Point Evidence Explain) and its many variants can be useful as a starting point, but as soon as students have mastered using them they need to be taken away. Taking away the scaffolding forces students to struggle. The act of dredging memory for ideas helps the process to become internalised. If students are struggling too much, put the scaffold (or at least some of it) back. And then take it away again. As soon as possible.

Teachers' beliefs and school culture

We should also challenge our own beliefs about intelligence; if we don't think intelligence is malleable then it's less likely that our students will. Do all we believe that all children can be successful, even 'those kids'? Teachers should be encouraged to adopt the belief that all students should struggle (and with effort, succeed), no matter their ability.

Sadly, many schools actively prevent teachers from adopting a growth mindset. Teaching has become increasingly high-stakes and the consequences for having a poor lesson observation or a bad set of exam results can be pretty awful. Teachers are incentivised to cover their backs and find excuses for any mistakes. And let's be clear: we *all* make mistakes. If we want to engender a growth mindset in education we need to remove the high stakes for failure. We need to make it OK for teachers to admit their mistakes and, in so doing, learn from them; to move from teaching as an 'outstanding' performance, to an incremental view of improvement.

School culture plays a huge role in how students behave in school. As well as focusing on making it 'cool to be clever', we should think carefully about whether systems like setting target grades communicate the message that intelligence is fixed. Simply handing out a worksheet on growth mindsets and sticking up some motivational posters isn't enough. Whatever we attempt, we should evaluate what has actually changed in the way students behave; what are they *doing* differently?

Maybe because teachers are, on the whole, academically successful, we've experienced less in the way of academic struggle and therefore it's harder for some of us to take on new beliefs? Perhaps we don't have the same capacity for suspending doubt as others? Or maybe you just don't have a growth mindset... yet.

What every teacher needs to know about beliefs

- Students are more motivated if they believe that intelligence and ability can be improved through hard work.
- We can contribute to students' beliefs about their ability to improve their intelligence by praising productive student effort and strategies (and other processes under student control) rather than their ability.
- Avoid giving students the impression that a fixed mindset is a character flaw; acknowledging a fixed mindset is a fairly natural reaction when people have experienced repeated failure in the past.
- Students need to know that just making more effort won't always work, you also have to know *how* to apply effort effectively.

> - Students should be supported to experience success *before* we attempt to change their beliefs about intelligence.
> - Just as teachers can support students to risk failure by removing high-stakes consequences, school leaders can support teachers to learn from mistakes by fostering a culture where mistakes and struggle are not punished.

References

Aronson, J., Fried, C. & Good, C. (2002) 'Reducing the effects of stereotype threat on African American college students by shaping theories of intelligence', *Journal of Experimental Social Psychology*, 38(2), 113-125.

Aronson, J. & Juarez, L. (2012) 'Growth mindsets in the laboratory and the real world', in Subotnik, R. F., Robinson, A., Callahan, C. M. & Gubbins, E. J. (eds.), *Malleable minds: Translating insights from psychology and neuroscience to gifted education*, Storrs, CT: National Research Center on the Gifted and Talented, pp. 19–36.

Blackwell, L. S., Trzesniewski, K. H. & Dweck, C. S. (2007) 'Implicit theories of intelligence predict achievement across an adolescent transition: A longitudinal study and an intervention', *Child Development*, 78(1), 246-263.

Burnette, J. L., O'Boyle, E. H., VanEpps, E. M., Pollack, J. M. & Finkel, E. J. (2013) 'Mind-sets matter: A meta-analytics review of implicit theories and self- regulation', *Psychological Bulletin*, 139(3), 655-701.

Crocker, J., Olivier, M. A. & Nuer, N. (2009) 'Self-image goals and compassionate goals: Costs and benefits', *Self and Identity*, 8, 251–269.

Dweck, C. S. (2006) *Mindset: The new psychology of success*, New York, NY: Random House.

Dweck, C. S (2000) *Self-theories: Their Role in Motivation, Personality, and Development (Essays in Social Psychology)*, New York: Psychology Press; New Ed edition.

Education Endowment Foundation (2015) 'Changing Mindsets' https://educationendowmentfoundation.org.uk/uploads/pdf/Changing_Mindsets.pdf

Elliott, E. S. & Dweck, C. S. (1988) 'Goals: An approach to motivation and achievement', *Journal of Personality and Social Psychology*, 54(1), 5-12.

Good, C., Aronson, J. & Inzlicht, M. (2003) 'Improving adolescents' standardized test performance: An intervention to reduce the effects of stereotype threat', *Journal of Applied Developmental Psychology*, 24(6), 645-662.

Hiroto, D. S. & Seligman, M. E. P. (1975) 'Generality of learned helplessness in man', *Journal of Personality and Social Psychology*, 31, 311–27.

Kamins, M. L. & Dweck, C. S. (1999) 'Person versus process praise and criticism: implications for contingent self-worth and coping', *Developmental Psychology*, 35(3), 835-847.

Mueller, C. M. & Dweck, C. S. (1998) 'Praise for intelligence can undermine children's motivation and performance', *Journal of Personality and Social Psychology*, 75(1), 33-52.

Seligman, M. E. P. (1975) *Helplessness: On Depression, Development, and Death.* San Francisco: W. H. Freeman.

Seligman, M. E. P. (1972) 'Learned helplessness', *Annual Review of Medicine* 23(1), 407–412.

Smiley, P. A. & Dweck, C. S. (1994) 'Individual differences in achievement goals among young children', *Child Development*, 65(6), 1723-1743.

Walton, G. (2014) 'The new science of wise psychological interventions', *Current Directions in Psychological Science*, 23(1), 73-82

Woodcock, S. & Vialle, W. (2011) 'Are we exacerbating students' learning disabilities? An investigation of preservice teachers' attributions of the educational outcomes of students with learning disabilities', *Annals of dyslexia*, 61(2), 223-241.

Yeager, D., Walton, G. & Cohen, G. (2013) 'Addressing achievement gaps with psychological interventions', *Phi Delta Kappan*, February 2013.

Yeager, D. & Walton, G. (2011) 'Social-Psychological Interventions in Education: They're Not Magic', *Review Of Educational Research* 81(267), originally published online 19 April 2011, DOI: 10.3102/0034654311405999

Chapter 12
Expectations

It's no surprise that we usually experience what we expect to experience. You'll probably already be aware of the placebo effect – the phenomenon that an inert tablet triggers a psychological response, which in turn impacts, usually positively, on a patient's health. Research on the placebo effect has focused on the relationship between mind and body. One of the most common theories is that physical responses may be due to our expectations: if we expect a pill to do something, then it's possible that our body's chemistry can trigger effects similar to those actual medication might have caused. It seems reasonable to suggest that a pupil's belief about their learning could be influenced in a similar way.

Less well known is the Hawthorne effect. This is the name given to the tendency to work harder and perform better when we know we're taking part in an experiment. It seems we may change our behaviour due to the attention we receive from researchers rather than because of any manipulation of independent variables. Henry A. Landsberger first described the effect in the 1950s in his analysis of experiments conducted during the 1920s and 1930s at the Hawthorne Works electric company to determine if there was a relationship between productivity and work environment. The focus of the studies was to determine if the amount of light workers received had an effect on their productivity. Productivity seemed to increase due to the changes, but then decreased when the experiment was over. Researchers suggested that the increases were due to attention from the research team, not the changes to the experimental variables. Landsberger defined the Hawthorne effect as a short-term improvement in performance caused by the observation of researchers.*

We should also be aware of the Pygmalion effect. According to ancient Greek legend, Pygmalion invested so much love and care in sculpting a statue of the most beautiful and inspiring woman he could imagine that he fell in love with it. Too ashamed to admit he'd fallen for a statue, he prayed for a bride who would be a living likeness of his impossibly beautiful sculpture. The gods granted his wish and the statue became flesh.

Pygmalion's impossibly high expectations for the woman of his desires resulted in him getting what he wanted. Likewise, teachers' expectations can be a self-fulfilling prophecy. Our beliefs about pupils have a tremendous impact on their progress and attainment. The self-defeating corollary of the Pygmalion effect is the Golem effect – the idea that negative expectations lead to decreases in performance. Rosenthal and Jacobson's landmark 1968 experiment demonstrated that if teachers were led to expect enhanced performance from certain students, then these students' performance was indeed enhanced. Pupils were given a disguised IQ test at the beginning of the study and teachers were told that some of their students (about 20% of the cohort chosen at random) would likely be 'spurters' that year, doing better than expected in comparison to their classmates. At the end of the study, all pupils were retested and the results showed statistically significant gains favouring the experimental group. This led to the conclusion that teachers' expectations can have a strong influence on students' achievement.

And so they do, but maybe not as much as is commonly believed. Jussim and Harber argue that teacher expectancy effects may be overstated: "Self-fulfilling prophecies in the classroom do occur, but these effects are typically small, they do not accumulate greatly across perceivers or over time, and they may be more likely to dissipate than accumulate"†. They conclude that there appears to be a high degree of correlation between teacher expectations and reality; maybe the reason our expectations come true is because they're accurate?

In some cases though, particularly when students come from less advantaged socio-economic backgrounds, teachers do often seem to expect less of students than they can actually achieve. If we signal, intentionally or otherwise that 'kids like these' are less capable, then they may well begin to perform in ways that conform to our expectations. For instance, if we give certain students less

---

* Though, this interpretation is contested, for example see Olson, R., Hogan, L. & Santos, L. (2006) 'Illuminating the history of psychology: Tips for teaching students about the Hawthorne studies', *Psychology Learning & Teaching*, 5(2), 110-118. doi: 10.2304/plat.2005.5.2.110

† Jussim, L. & Harber, K. (2005: 131)

challenging material to study we guarantee that they will achieve less than those given the opportunity to study more challenging material. This *might* be due to accurate predictions about ability, but in the case of students from less affluent or ethnic minority backgrounds this tends not to be the case.

Erroneous expectations are more likely to occur when children first start school, at the beginning of a new school year, and during transitions between phases of schooling. It turns out that predictions about students' ability are least accurate when we are most uncertain. This uncertainty causes us to come up with answers based not on evidence but on bias.

Despite our ignorance we make decisions based on irrelevant and available information. The halo effect is a form of confirmation bias, which prevents us from becoming aware of the uncertainty we really ought to feel. The term was first coined by educational psychologist Edward Thorndike back in the 1920s, and has since been thoroughly established as a real and powerful cognitive bias.

In 1974, Barry Staw designed a study to test how people reacted when given information that made no apparent sense. Business school students were grouped into threes and each group was asked to estimate the sales and earnings per share for a company based on its financial reports from the previous five years. Researchers told the students they had previously analysed the performance of groups of five people on this task, and were now keen to see how smaller groups would perform. When the students were told they had performed very well, they attributed that success to things like skilful communication, group cohesion, openness to change, competence, a lack of conflict and so on. Groups told that they'd performed poorly did the opposite. They explained their results as a lack of communication, differences in ability, closed-mindedness, dysfunctional groups and a variety of other confounding variables. In truth, neither group was able to explain their performance as the results had been rigged. Regardless of how well they had actually performed, each group were randomly told either that they had done extremely well or spectacularly badly. In an effort to explain the unexplainable, they resorted to plucking causes from the air.

Into the classroom

How often might this desperate hunt for reasons be enacted to explain unexpected exam performance? When we are uncertain, our brains use a heuristic and then cover up the evidence so we won't notice that we had no idea what we were doing. 'Communication skills' are too vague to quantify, so when the business school students were asked to rate their communication skills, they looked for something more concrete to go on. In Staw's experiment it was the randomly assigned rating. That rating became a halo whose light affected the way they were able to understand their experiences. This might have worked except that the rating was a lie, and consequently, so were the explanations. When target grades are applied to individual students, instead of cohorts, they can no longer provide meaningful predictions and can become a self-fulfilling prophecy (see Chapter 13).

The economist and psychologist Daniel Kahneman relates how the halo effect led him to systematically misgrade students' essays. Quite reasonably, if a student's first essay was awarded a high score, mistakes in later essays were ignored or excused. But Kahneman noticed a problem:

> *If a student had written two essays, one strong one weak, I would end up with a different final grade depending on which essay I read first. I had told students that the two essays had equal weight but this was not true: the first one had a much great impact on the final grade than the second.**

You might think we could pick up these sorts of mistakes through a process of introspectively retracing our mental steps back to the original mistake, but you'd be wrong. Research into the halo effect suggests this sort of thing happens all the time. In Nisbett and Wilson's study into the way students make judgements about their university lecturers, students were told the experimenters were interested in whether judgements varied depending on the amount of exposure students had to a particular lecturer. This was another of those pesky lies psychology researchers tell their participants. The American students were divided into two groups to watch two different videos of the same lecturer, who happened to have a thick accent. In one video the professor was cold and distant, in the other he was warm and approachable. Both groups of students were asked to rate his appearance, mannerisms and accent. As you're no doubt expecting, the students who'd seen a warm, friendly professor rated him as more attractive and his accent as more pleasant, while those who'd seen an unfriendly professor rated him as unattractive and his accent as distracting.

It's also worth being aware of the pratfall effect. Originally described in 1966 by Elliot Aronson, there is tendency for our ratings of others' attractiveness to increase or decrease after they make a mistake, depending on our perception of how well we think they should perform. A teacher might find a student they perceived as able more likable after committing a blunder, while the opposite would occur if student perceived as middle or low ability made a mistake.

It probably comes as no surprise to know we make decisions about people's intelligence and competence based on our perception of their attractiveness, but

---

*   Kahneman, D. (2012: 83)

the extent to which we do this is terrifying. In studies where teachers were told that a student had a learning disability, they rated that student's performance as weaker than did other teachers who were told nothing at all about the student before the assessment began. The fact that we treat students according to the halo cast by superficial traits is well known. We assume that well-behaved students are also bright, diligent, and engaged.

> **What every teacher needs to know about expectations**
>
> The best course of action is to make sure we communicate high expectations to all students and maintain appropriately high standards for everyone – no matter our perceptions of their ability – in order to avoid negative self-fulfilling prophecies. We should make it a habit to look at more than one source of information when making judgements about students' ability, especially for students from ethnic minorities and those who come from lower income families.
>
> Because teachers will be unaware of treating students differently based on often-unconscious judgements of ability, we should ask ourselves the following questions:
>
> - Who is seated at the front of the class?
> - Who is being asked the majority of questions?
> - Who is getting the most feedback?
> - Did I look at the name of the student before giving a grade?
> - Did I base this grade on what I gave the student in previous assessments?
>
> If it turns out 'high-expectancy' students are being favoured, maybe some positive discrimination is in order. Probably the best antidote to the effects of low expectations is to insist on holding the same high standards and expectations for all students, and never give up on a student.

References

Abikoff, H., Courtney, M., Pelham, W. E. & Koplewicz, H. S. (1993) 'Teachers' Ratings of Disruptive Behaviors: The Influence of Halo Effects', *Journal of Abnormal Child Psychology* 21(5).

Aronson, E., Willerman, B. & Floyd, J. (1966) 'The effect of a pratfall on increasing interpersonal attractiveness', *Psychonomic Science*, 4(6), 227-228.

Jussim, L., Eccles, J. & Madon, S. (1996) 'Social perception, social stereotypes, and teacher expectations: Accuracy and the quest for the powerful self-fullling prophecy' in Zanna, M. P. (ed.), *Advances in experimental social psychology* (Vol. 28), San Diego, CA Academic Press, pp. 281–388.

Jussim, L. & Harber, K. D. (2005) 'Teacher expectations and self-fulfilling prophecies: Knowns and unknowns, resolved and unresolved controversies', *Personality and Social Psychology Review,* 9(2), 131–155. doi:10.1207/s15327957pspr0902_3

Jussim. L., Robustelli, S. & Cain, T. (2009) 'Teacher expectations and self-fulfilling prophecies'. in Wigfield, A. & Wentzel, K. (eds.) *Handbook of motivation at school,* Mahwah, NJ: Erlbaum, pp. 349–380.

Kahneman, D. (2012) *Thinking, Fast and Slow.* London: Penguin.

Nisbett, R. E. & Wilson, T. D. (1977) 'The halo effect: Evidence for unconscious alteration of judgments', *Journal of Personality and Social Psychology,* 35(4), 250.

Rosenthal, R. & Jacobson, L. (1968) *Pygmalion in the Classroom,* New York: Holt, Reinhart and Winston.

Salkind, N. J. & Rasmussen, K. (eds.) (2008) *Encyclopedia of Educational Psychology, Vol. 1,* Sage Publications.

Schunk, D. H., Meece, J. L. & Pintrich, P. R. (2014) *Motivation in education: Theory, research, and applications,* Boston, MA: Pearson.

Staw, B. M. (1975) Attribution of the 'Causes' of Performance: A General Alternative Interpretation of Cross-Sectional Research on Organizations, *Organisational Behaviour and Human Performance,* 13(3), 414-432.

Stipek, D. J. (2002) *Motivation to learn: Integrating theory and practice* (4th ed.), New York, NY: Allyn & Bacon.

Thorndike, E. L. (1920) 'A constant error in psychological ratings', *Journal of Applied Psychology* 4(1): 25–29, doi:10.1037/h0071663.

Chapter 13
Goal setting

Goal setting, we're told, is "important for motivation because students with a goal and adequate self-efficacy are likely to engage in the activities that lead to attainment of that goal. Self-efficacy is also increased as students monitor the progress they are making toward their goals, especially when they are acquiring new skills in the process."* When goals or targets are set for students, a process much along the following lines is usually followed:

- Write down the goals
- Make goals specific and clear
- Indicate how you'll measure goal accomplishment
- Have goal timelines and deadlines
- State goals in terms of specific outcomes or results
- Attach incentives for attainment and consequences for failure

Look familiar? The trouble is, the evidence on goal setting appears to be vastly overstated. Some sources of advice suggest that if goals are to be motivating they should be:

- Short term (proximal)
- Specific (because this makes them easier to quantify and monitor)
- Moderately difficult (challenging but attainable)

King and Burton (2003) argue that setting goals only works in the narrowest of circumstances: "The optimally striving individual ought to endeavor to achieve

---

* Top 20 Principles From Psychology for preK–12 Teaching and Learning. p. 20

and approach goals that only slightly implicate the self; that are only moderately important, fairly easy, and moderately abstract; that do not conflict with each other, and that concern the accomplishment of something other than financial gain"[*] Otherwise, research indicates the structure, content and use of goals may all lead to negative outcomes.

So what does it actually mean? For a start it undermines the popular idea of SMART targets. The acronym is used to mean a variety of different things – take your pick:

S – specific, significant, stretching

M – measurable, meaningful, motivational

A – agreed upon, attainable, achievable, acceptable, action-oriented

R – realistic, relevant, reasonable, rewarding, results-oriented

T – time-based, time-bound, timely, tangible, trackable

SMART goals are performance goals: *"I will increase my grade in maths from a C to a B by the end of the term."* It sounds good, but it's 'magical thinking'; it reveals nothing about how the goal would actually be accomplished. You might as well have written *"I will work hard in maths this term"* as at least this implies the mechanism by which an improved performance might come about! It might be better to set learning goals instead: *"I will practise more maths questions."* This kind of vague statement is the antithesis of most goal setting but learning goals at least encourages focus on behaviour which might (eventually) make a difference to performance. Learning goals can also be less susceptible to change and are more likely to be a useful strategy in a changing environment, over the longer term.

What particularly rankles is the notion that a target must be realistic, reasonable, attainable or achievable. If we conceive of targets in terms of their realism, aren't we setting our sights rather low? How do we know what we can achieve until we've had a bloody good go? This sort of goal setting falls foul of the anchoring effect. In their landmark study, 'Judgment under Uncertainty', psychologists Amos Tversky and Daniel Kahneman demonstrated that the answers given to questions where the subject had no idea what the correct answer might be was anchored by the statistic given on a rigged wheel of fortune, which stopped only at the numbers 10 and 65. If the wheel landed on 10, subjects made a low estimate; if it landed on 65 the estimate was much higher. When we don't have enough information to make a clear judgement, or when we make decisions concerning something too complex to fully grasp, instead of backing off and

---

[*]   King, L. A. & Burton, C. M. (2003)

admitting our ignorance, we rush to any available information to make our decision. Targets, especially if they're numerical, can have exactly this effect on our thinking.

Consider the case of Australian sheep farmer Cliff Young. In 1983, the 61-year-old won the inaugural Westfield Sydney to Melbourne Ultramarathon, a distance of 544 miles. For most of the first day he trailed way behind the leaders. After that first day's running, most of the athletes underwent a strict regime of physiotherapy and nutrition, before going to sleep on special orthopaedic beds. But no one told Cliff to stop. By running while the others slept, he took the lead on the first night and maintained it for the remainder of the race, eventually winning by 10 hours. He told the press that before running the race he had previously run for two to three days straight in wellies rounding up sheep. The Westfield run took him five days, 15 hours and four minutes, almost two days faster than the previous record for any run between Sydney and Melbourne. Most of us are anchored by what has gone before. The idea of running for five days straight simply hadn't occurred to anyone else. Would such a time have seemed realistic to other runners? Probably not. Maybe we should deliberately set goals that initially appear unachievable or unrealistic and equip students to work towards them.

Into the classroom

Eller, Schweitzer, Galinsky and Bazerman (2009), in looking at goal setting in the workplace, suggest that, "the beneficial effects of goal setting have been overstated and that systematic harm caused by goal setting has been largely ignored." It seems probable that this is equally true of education. Here are three of the problems they identify:

1. When goals are specific they cause inattention blindness which prevents us from focusing on areas outside the goal. If for instance a student is given the target of improving their writing by using more interesting vocabulary, this could prevent them from focusing on the structure and content of what they're writing about.

2. When goals are challenging they can create perverse incentives which make us more likely to take unnecessary risks, more likely to cheat or lie to ourselves and more likely to become demotivated if insufficient progress is made.

3. Goals which improve performance tend to inhibit learning. It's common to hear students who are highly motivated to do well in an exam ask, "Why are we studying this? Is it in the test?"

What every teacher needs to know about goal setting

When setting goals and targets, teachers should consider each of the following questions:

- **Are the goals too specific?** We have limited resources. By maximising in one area we may reduce effort or time spent on another. Narrow goals can blind people to important aspects of a problem.
- **Are the goals too challenging?** What will happen if goals are not met? How will individuals and outcomes be evaluated? Will failure harm motivation and self-efficacy? How high-stakes is the goal? Are the measures of success or failure valid (fair?) – or pretty arbitrary?
- **Who sets the goals?** People will become more committed to goals they help to set. At the same time, people may be tempted to set easy-to-reach goals. This might suggest that students and teachers ought to discuss whether a target is appropriate before it is presented as a *fait accompli*.
- **Is the time horizon appropriate?** Short-term goals may harm long-term performance. If students are focused on immediate improvements this can lead to the illusion of knowledge – just because they remember having achieved something they may be fooled into believing they can still do it and therefore fail to practice or revise.
- **How might goals influence risk taking?** Unmet goals may induce risk taking whereas high-stakes goals are likely to reduce risk taking.
- **How might goals motivate unethical behaviour?** Goals – especially where there are high stakes for the individual – narrow focus. Individuals with goals are less likely to recognise ethical issues, and more likely to rationalise their unethical behaviour. Targets related to achieving particular exam grades seem particularly likely to result in undesirable behaviour.
- **Can goals be idiosyncratically tailored for individual abilities and circumstances while preserving fairness?** Individual differences may make standardised goals inappropriate, yet students may perceive unequal goals as unfair. Teachers could explain that while treating everyone the same, no matter their individual differences, is less fair than adapting to and accommodating individual needs, it would be equally unfair to have lower expectations of some students

(see Chapter 12). The solution might be to have the same high standard for every student but provide different levels of scaffolding depending on needs (see page 130).

- **How will goals influence culture?** Individual goals may harm cooperation and corrode culture. If students see themselves as being in competition with their peers this might increase extrinsic motivation for some but, equally, could reduce motivation for others. Goals which allow students to compete with their own personal best may be more beneficial.

- **What type of goal (performance or learning) is most appropriate given our ultimate objectives?** By focusing on performance goals, we may fail to identify suitable strategies or search for better strategies, and fail to learn (see Chapter 14).

- **Are individuals intrinsically motivated?** Goals are essentially an extrinsic method for managing behaviour. Goal setting may, in some instances, harm intrinsic motivation (see Chapter 16). If teachers can in some way assess students' intrinsic motivation they can avoid setting goals when intrinsic motivation is already high.

References

American Psychological Association, Coalition for Psychology in Schools and Education (2015) *Top 20 principles from psychology for preK–12 teaching and learning*. Retrieved from http:// www.apa.org/ed/schools/cpse/top-twenty-principles.pdf

Anderman, E. M. & Wolters, C. (2006) 'Goals, values, and affect: Influences on student motivation', in Alexander, P. A. & Winne, P. (eds.), *Handbook of educational psychology* (2nd ed), Mahwah, NJ: Erlbaum, pp. 369–389.

Eller, Schweitzer, Galinsky & Bazerman (2009) 'Goals Gone Wild: The Systematic Side Effects of Over-Prescribing Goal Setting', Harvard Business School http://www.hbs.edu/faculty/Publication%20Files/09-083.pdf

King, L. A. & Burton, C. M. (2003) 'The hazards of goal pursuit', in Chang, E. C. & Sanna, L. J. (eds.) *Virtue, vice, and personality: The complexity of behavior*, Washington, DC, US: American Psychological Association, pp. 53–69.

Locke, E. A. & Latham, G. P. (2002) 'Building a practically useful theory of goal setting and task motivation: A 35-year odyssey', *American Psychologist, 57*, 705–717. doi:10.1037/0003- 066X.57.9.705d

Martin, A. J. (2013) 'Goal setting and personal best (PB) goals', in Hattie, J. & Anderman, E. M. (eds.), *International guide to student achievement*, New York, NY: Routledge, pp. 356–358.

Schunk, D. H. (1989) 'Self-efficacy and achievement behaviors', *Educational Psychology Review*, 1, 173–208. doi:10.1007/BF01320134

Schunk, D. H. & Zimmerman, B. J. (2006) 'Competence and control beliefs: Distinguishing means and ends', in Alexander, P. A. & Winne, P. H. (eds.), *Handbook of educational psychology* (2nd ed), Mahwah, NJ: Erlbaum, pp. 349–367.

Tversky, A. & Kahneman, D. (1974) 'Judgment under Uncertainty: Heuristics and Biases', *Science*, New Series, 185(4157), pp. 1124-1131.

Chapter 14
Mastery

The term 'mastery' gets bandied around a lot at the moment, but it seems to mean something different every time it's used. In layman's terms, mastery just means the possession of consummate skill that makes one the master of a subject. Clearly this definition is a bit self-referential, so what do psychologists have to say of the matter?

Psychologists describe mastery learning as, "the process of internalizing and understanding a complete area of study."* 'Mastery motivation' is defined by Morgan et al as, "a psychological force that stimulates an individual to attempt independently, in a focused and persistent manner, to solve a problem or master a skill or task which is at least moderately challenging for him or her." Hsieh defines 'mastery orientation' as, "having the goal of learning and mastering the task according to self-set standards. [The] learner is focused on developing new skills, improving, and acquiring additional knowledge." Students who have a mastery orientation will tend to attribute their failures to effort, rather than skill. Using this definition we can see there's a close link with the attitudes to learning discussed in Chapter 11 as well as the qualities of intrinsic motivation examined in Chapter 16.

Generally speaking, teachers are interested in students doing more than 'merely' acquiring new skills and knowledge within the domains of the subjects we teach. We also have an interest in fostering a 'love of learning' and turning students into 'life-long learners'. But how should we go about this laudable aim? Psychologists see the need for achievement as a basic human need – we are all

---

* http://psychologydictionary.org/mastery-learning-1/

driven to achieve, but we may be driven differently. Goal theory identifies two main methods for motivating people to achieve their goals: mastery-oriented goals and performance-oriented goals. As you can probably guess, mastery goals are all about getting really good at something. Performance goals, on the other hand, are all about looking good and impressing others. When students adopt performance goals they may just seek to show they are good enough or to avoid certain tasks in an effort to avoid looking stupid.

Which type of goal orientation would be more useful in the following situations?

- enjoying lessons
- persisting in the face of difficulties
- seeking help when confused
- managing tough decisions
- seeing the point of a task
- performing well in tests

A performance orientation is only likely to be useful in the last case, but doing well in tests might well depend on all the other aspects of learning. Who is most likely to retain information after it's been used to prove competence? Ability appears to be the consequence, not the cause of the differences in what students learn in school.

Schools and teachers must share some of the responsibility for students adopting performance goals. If we continue to value increases in short-term performance (e.g. measuring 'progress' in a lesson – or even 20 minutes of a lesson), then it follows that many pupils will continue to see learning as a set of short-term performance goals. Maybe if we really want students to develop a mastery orientation (that may also equip them with grit, resourcefulness and resilience), we need to stop focusing on what they can do in the here and now and concentrate on what they need to do well elsewhere and later. This strikes at the heart of the division between performance and learning (see page 14).

So, what's stopping us? One obstacle is that we intuitively believe that increasing performance is a good thing. It feels good to perform well and it's uncomfortable to struggle. Pupils are happier with lessons in which they appear to perform well; teachers feel happier designing schemes of learning which allow pupils to jump from one feel-good performance to the next; and school leaders feel happier with a curriculum that ticks boxes, covers content and (with a fair trailing wind, crammed revision sessions after school, tons of last minute intervention and determined teaching to the test) will result in fairly decent exam performance. Anything that confirms this bias is welcomed and anything that contradicts it is dismissed.

Into the classroom

First we should always try to emphasise students' individual effort and focus on their current progress rather than their past performance. When we evaluate students' work we should dwell on their improvements rather than comparing them either with other students or normative standards. As we will discuss on page 167, grading work can encourage comparison whereas more formative feedback is more likely to help students to think in terms of improving previous performance. We should also be cautious in our use of praise and encourage students to see mistakes or wrong answers as opportunities to learn rather than as evidence of lack of ability.

Another idea is to adjust the pacing of instruction for individual needs as much as possible. Perhaps the biggest difference in our perceptions of ability is the rate at which students master new skills and concepts. Students who are often perceived as being 'weaker' often just need more time than others. Allowing students to set their own deadlines and monitor their own progress in order to help them focus on the process as well as the outcome sounds reasonable, but could easily become unworkable in a large class (not to mention that many students may procrastinate with deadlines and may lack the expertise to make reliable judgements about their learning). We might do better to make scaffolding available to help students achieve mastery and to withdraw the support more quickly with some students, and take a more gradual, incremental approach where it's needed. See page 130 for more details.

We should also consider school structures and classroom settings. The institutionalised nature of schools can be a major barrier to encouraging mastery. As we saw in Chapter 11, schools often prevent teachers from having a mastery orientation about education. Everything about schools is set up to value performance over mastery. It would be a brave school indeed that sought to unpick the fabric of classrooms and curriculums and introduce a structure that supported sustained progress instead of the appearance of rapid progress.

Schools should also consider what messages are communicated by such practices as ability grouping and target grades. Any attempt to filter students according to perceptions of their ability will always be flawed. (Some estimates suggest that most measures result in at best 50% of students being in the wrong set!*) While it can be possible for ability groups to work, more often students in lower sets become subject to lower expectations; if students are given less challenging material to match their lower-perceived ability, it risks a self-fulfilling prophecy. Likewise, target grades often cement fixed, performance-orientated attitudes. If

---

*   Wiliam, D. (2001: 19)

you really must use targets, at least think about how they can be subverted to support a mastery orientation. For instance, instead of just telling a student they have a target grade of a C, show them the chance statistics from which the target was derived and discuss how other students with identical prior attainment might have achieved higher grades.

It's all very well to tell students that we want them to get cleverer through taking risks and making mistakes, but nothing in the way most schools operate supports this message. We are deeply suspicious, for instance, of teachers struggling and would much prefer to cultivate competence than run the risks required for real mastery. We may *say* we value mastery but we have a systemically performance-orientated view about what schools should be doing. If we want change, perhaps we need to stop making the same old mistakes and start making some new ones.

What every teacher needs to know about mastery

- Mastery means giving students the opportunity to get good at something; the chance to experience 'hard won' success through the application of effort.
- A mastery orientation is one where success and failure is attributed to effort or to selecting strategies rather than fixed ideas about ability.
- One barrier to developing this orientation in schools is the culture of seeing learning as a series of short-term performances (e.g. rapid progress within a lesson). Better to think of learning over the longer-term and seek 'sustained' progress over time.
- Another issue is ability setting. Whilst this can be done successfully, it can also foster a performance-orientated view of learning and undermine expectations for students in 'bottom sets'.
- Lastly, we may be able to foster a mastery orientation to learning by avoiding unnecessary grading (which often encourages comparison with others or is uncritically compared to an arbitrary target). Use assessment as a guide to the amount of scaffolding a student may need and give feedback in a way which encourages incremental steps towards mastery of the knowledge or skill being learnt.

References

Ames, C. (1992) 'Classrooms: Goals, structures, and student motivation', *Journal of Educational Psychology*, 84, 261–271. doi:10.1037/0022-0663.84.3.261

Anderman, L. H. & Anderman, E. M. (2009) 'Oriented towards mastery: Promoting positive motivational goals for students', in Gilman, R., Huebner, E. S. & Furlong, M. (eds.), *Handbook of positive psychology in the schools*, New York, NY: Routledge, pp. 161–173.

Deci, E. L. & Ryan, R. M. (2002) 'The paradox of achievement: The harder you push, the worse it gets', in Aronson, J. (ed.) *Improving academic achievement: Impact of psychological factors in education*, San Diego, CA: Academic Press, pp. 62–90.

Graham, S. (1990) 'On communicating low ability in the classroom: Bad things good teachers sometimes do', In Graham, S. & Folkes, V. (eds.) *Attribution theory: Applications to achievement*, mental health, and interpersonal conflict, Hillsdale, NJ: Erlbaum, pp. 17–36.

Hsieh, P. (2011) 'Mastery Orientation', in Goldstein, S. & Naglieri, J. A. (eds.) *Encyclopedia of Child Behavior and Development*, Springer.

Meece, J. L., Anderman, E. M. & Anderman L. H. (2006) 'Classroom goal structure, student motivation, and academic achievement', *Annual Review of Psychology*, 57, 487–503, doi:10.1146 /annurev.psych.56.091103.070258

Morgan, G. A., Harmon, R. J. & Maslin-Cole, C. A. (1990) 'Mastery Motivation: Definition and Measurement', *Early Education and Development*, 1(5), 318-339,

Wiliam, D. (2001) Reliability, validity, and all that jazz, *Education 3-13*, 29(3), 17-21.

Chapter 15
Rewards and sanctions

The topic of behaviour management and the problems teachers face in dealing with disruption to lessons continues to evoke strong argument within the profession. The extent of the problem was explored in a 2014 paper by Terry Haydn which argued that whilst 'official' reports like Ofsted inspections appeared to rate behaviour as at least 'satisfactory' in the majority of schools, there was evidence that deficits in classroom climate continue to be a serious and widespread problem.

Systems of rewards and sanctions have long been the norm in schools but perhaps because of a growing feeling that behaviour has become increasingly difficult to manage, behaviour management has become the focus of experimentation. Some schools have reportedly 'banned' punishment altogether, whereas others believe that proportionate sanctions need to be available to teachers as a deterrent. 'Behaviourist' is sometimes (unfairly) used pejoratively when describing behaviour management systems, but schools using some sort of system for rewarding or sanctioning behaviour are implicitly using a behaviourist approach.

Behaviourism was a term coined by John Watson in an article published in 1913, but its roots go back to the famous studies by Ivan Pavlov (who discovered classical conditioning as an accidental sideline to his Nobel Prize winning research on digestion). However, the behaviourist most associated with education is B. F. Skinner. Much misunderstood, and often unfairly maligned, his theory of operant conditioning continues to influence schools to this day.

Drawing on the earlier work of Edward Thorndike, Skinner developed his theory of operant conditioning by exposing animals like rats and pigeons to carefully controlled stimuli and recording their responses (what's often referred to as a 'Skinner box"). Skinner identified a variety of techniques which could be used to shape animal behaviour and wrote about how these might be applied to human behaviour (and education specifically).

The core idea within operant conditioning is reinforcement and punishment. Very simply, when an animal receives reinforcement after performing a behaviour they are more likely to repeat that behaviour. Conversely, receiving a punishment after performing a behaviour leads the animal to be less likely to repeat that behaviour in future. Skinner further described reinforcements and punishments as being 'positive' or 'negative' in character.

	Reinforcement	Punishment
Positive	A behaviour is followed by a rewarding stimulus – like giving a student merit or some sweets	A behaviour is followed by an aversive stimulus – like telling a student off or giving them a 'teacher stare' to express disapproval
Negative	A behaviour is followed by taking away an aversive stimulus – like allowing a kid to jump to skip the dinner queue	A behaviour is followed by taking away a rewarding stimulus – like confiscating a mobile phone or a detention

Figure 1: Positive and negative reinforcements and punishments

Punishments

Despite Skinner's harsh reputation, he was very much against the use of punishment in schools. Skinner believed a major disadvantage of punishment is that, even where it is consistently applied, it merely temporarily suppresses undesirable behaviour.

However, considerations of the effectiveness of punishment are rather more complex than Skinner believed. For example, a fascinating meta-analysis by Balliet and Van Lange examined whether punishment was more effective at promoting cooperation in high- or low-trust societies. They reviewed 83 studies involving 7,361 participants across 18 societies and found a rather surprising conclusion: punishment appears to effectively promote cooperation in societies with high trust. In essence, they argue that where there is a great deal of trust, members of a society adhere to norms that encourage both cooperation and the punishment of those who defy cooperative social norms. Punishment is less effective in societies where there is a lack of trust. They argue that social

---

*   We were delighted to hear from Dylan Wiliam the rather wonderful description of Skinner's work as "pulling habits out of a rat".

norms may be less strongly shared and enforced and so punishment may be less effective in these societies.

An important question for future research is whether 'benevolent punishment' is as effective at an organisational level (e.g. a school) as it appears to be at a society level. However, the implication would be that in benevolent, high-trust environments the proportionate use of sanctions to support cooperative social norms can be effective.

Another reason why sanctions may be effective is the phenomenon of 'loss aversion'. The work of Tversky and Kahneman suggests that there is an asymmetry between the effects of positive reinforcement and negative punishment – in that where people weigh up similar gains and losses, they tend to prefer avoiding losses to making gains. For example, Hackenberg reports an experiment where the value of a loss was worth approximately three times more than a gain. It seems likely that this effect might also apply to the sorts of token reward systems employed in schools, suggesting that negative sanctions (e.g. loss of merits) may be more motivating than opportunities to gain merits.

Rewards

Skinner believed that rewards were the most effective way of shaping behaviour and focused a great deal of his research attempting to find out the most effective patterns of reinforcement. In his 'Skinner box' experiments, he was able to carefully control the 'schedule of reinforcement' and measure the concomitant changes in the desired behaviour.

Schedule of reinforcement	Example
Fixed Ratio	A student receives a reward after a fixed number of times they perform a desired behaviour (e.g. a merit every time they attempt an extension question)
Variable Ratio	A student receives a reward after a variable number of times they perform a desired behaviour
Fixed Interval	A student receives a reward after a fixed period of time in which they perform the desired behaviour (e.g. a merit for working hard for 5 minutes)
Variable Interval	A student receives a reward after a variable period of time in which they perform the desired behaviour

Figure 2: Schedule of reinforcements – examples

Intuitively, teachers see the need for consistency where punishments are applied and I've sometimes heard teachers argue that rewards should be given with equal consistency. However, Skinner's work on 'schedules of reinforcement' appears to show that such systems tend to be relatively ineffective. The problem with systems seeking high consistency in rewarding students is that whilst the student's behaviour may be swiftly modified, the desirable behaviour may become highly contingent upon the presence of the reward. The odd thing about rewards is that they appear to work better when they are slightly unpredictable. A simple summary of these differences:

Schedule of reinforcement	Advantages and disadvantages
Fixed Ratio	Behaviour changes quickly Extinction occurs quite rapidly when rewards cease
Variable Ratio	Behaviour changes quickly Extinction occurs slowly when rewards cease
Fixed Interval	Behaviour changes more slowly Extinction occurs quite rapidly when rewards cease
Variable Interval	Behaviour changes more slowly Extinction occurs quite slowly when rewards cease

Figure 3: Schedule of reinforcements – advantages and disadvantages

In Skinner's experiments, the extinction rates (the rate at which the desired behaviour stopped being performed) were quickest where there was continuous reinforcement (i.e. a reward given for every time the behaviour was performed). However, where there was variability in the time interval or ratio, then the behaviour persisted for longer in the absence of reinforcement. Skinner believed this represented the 'power' of the slot machine. The fact that playing it is unpredictably rewarded by a pay-out encourages the person to continue playing – even when they hit a long streak of losing.

In schools, sometimes these reward systems take on the structure of a 'token economy' (systems also used in prisons and psychiatric units – where individuals earn tokens for good behaviour which can be used to purchase privileges). However, whilst explicit reward schedules have been used with students with special educational needs (e.g. children with attention deficit or autism), these systems have a number of problems which often undermine their use in schools.

Some problems with rewards

One issue is 'satiation' – particularly that students may rapidly lose interest in the rewards (e.g. merit stickers) on offer. I recall a student teacher handing out sweets to reward year 10 students for answering questions in class. Many of the students took part, but I noticed one lad sat there scowling with his arms crossed. Chatting to him, it was clear he knew many of the answers so I asked why he wasn't putting his hand up – he said, "What's the point? I can just buy my own sweets if I want them." Students rapidly learn when they are being manipulated by a reward system and sometimes manage to turn the tables on the teacher by learning to manipulate the criteria used to elicit a reward. This problem often leads into what might be called 'reward inflation' as teachers either have to constantly find novel rewards or end up handing out more and more tokens to elicit the same desirable behaviour.

A second issue is 'extinction' – if the desirable behaviour becomes contingent upon rewards those behaviours may disappear in their absence. We want students to behave appropriately in lessons and around school (and outside school), even when there is no tangible reward on offer. We also don't want students to adopt a 'what's in it for me?' attitude to pro-social behaviour.

However, perhaps the biggest issue is that rewards can sometimes have negative effects on motivation. A famous study carried out by Mark Lepper back in the 1970s illustrates this issue. This study looked at nursery school students and examined the influence of rewarding an activity upon student motivation. The activity they chose for students was the opportunity to draw freely using 'magic markers' (not normally available in the classrooms). Students were divided into three conditions: some students received no reward for engaging in the activity. Others were told they could win a prize (a 'Good Player Award' – a small certificate with space for the child's name and school on the front next to a large gold star and a red ribbon). The last group were not told about the prize in advance, so the reward was an unexpected surprise at the end.

The experimenters observed all the students playing with the pens. The pens were reintroduced after a two-week gap (when the pens were not available) in order to see whether the presence of a reward made the children more or less motivated to draw with them. The students told about the reward spent less time drawing than either of the groups not offered a reward in advance. Indeed, this reduced motivation was apparent in the post-experimental observations of the students, suggesting that the offer of a reward had a negative influence on the students' motivation.

Subsequent research has shown this to be a 'clear and consistent' effect. Offering tangible rewards (e.g. money or marshmallows) dependent on task behaviour has a negative effect on previously high motivation, especially for younger students. Only where motivation is low, for instance when the task is perceived as quite dull, offering tangible rewards appears to have little effect (positive or negative) on motivation.

Some cautions about praise

Unlike tangible rewards (like stickers or sweets), verbal rewards can have a positive effect on students' motivation. Perhaps it is the implicit recognition of this that leads new teachers to be given the advice to praise at least three times more frequently than you admonish. However, the 'how' and 'when' of effective praise is worth careful consideration – as some forms of praise can have some potentially detrimental effects.

Firstly, it seems likely that, like tangible rewards, unexpected praise has a more motivating effect than where praise is expected. For example, if students always get positive feedback for doing a particular task or with a particular teacher, they might well come to expect such rewards. If students start engaging in activities specifically because they expect to get praise, then it seems likely that there will be a negative effect on motivation. To be effective, praise should be spontaneous and genuine.

It's also important that the praise isn't used to try to manipulate or control the student. So, for example, praise which uses a format like 'if you continue working well, then …' or 'that was a good piece of work, but next time …' will likely be interpreted as controlling and risks undermining motivation. It seems that praise given informationally (e.g. 'that was a good piece of work') has a less negative (and potentially more positive) influence on motivation. Given the current preoccupation with giving verbal and written feedback which indicates how a student may make improvements (e.g. two stars and a wish), this may seem counter-intuitive. However, praise appears to work better when given as an honest compliment about the work and can be undermined when accompanied by a 'wish' related to future work.

Teachers are often told to give praise for effort, but that can create another potential problem. Giving praise for work which actually required little effort may inadvertently imply that you have low expectations of that student. Realistically, it's extremely hard in a class of 30 students to accurately assess how much effort students have genuinely put into their class or homework (given a teacher's working memory capacity has the same limitations as everyone else!). Students (especially older students) tend to expect criticism for low effort rather than a poor standard of work and therefore giving praise for high effort when the work is of a poor standard can give a very unhelpful message. Misjudged praise for 'hard work' may unintentionally be understood by a student as effectively saying 'this is all I expect from someone of your ability'.

Lastly, as we discussed in Chapter 11, teachers should consider targeting praise upon an attribute of a student's work or behaviour rather than an attribute of the student. Praise in the form of 'this is a good piece of writing because ...' appears to be more effective than praise in the form of 'you are such a good writer'.

Zero-tolerance

A zero-tolerance approach to behaviour takes the view that any infringements of school rules must be met with non-negotiable sanctions and often permanent exclusion. In the US, the rationale for adopting this approach has been that school violence was so widespread and pervasive that something drastic needed to be done in response.

The American Psychological Association's review of the top 20 principles from psychology for teaching and learning makes the point that while there really isn't all that much evidence available – certainly, far less than you might expect – what there is seems to contradict the effectiveness of zero-tolerance policies. Therefore any conclusions we draw must be cautious.

The goal of an effective disciplinary system should seek to ensure a safe school climate while avoiding policies and practices that may reduce students' opportunity to learn. Intuitively, we might believe that if badly-behaved students were immediately removed from the classroom then other students would be able to learn better, but this belief does not appear to supported by the available evidence.

There's some evidence to suggest schools with higher rates of exclusion appear to have less satisfactory ratings of school climate (Bickel & Qualls, 1980), poorer governance structures (Wu et al, 1982), and spend a lot more time on disciplinary matters (Scott & Barrett, 2004) but none of it really adds up to much. More importantly, some research indicates higher exclusion rates are negatively correlated with academic achievement, even when controlling for demographics such as socio-economic status (Davis & Jordan, 1994; Raffaele-Mendez, 2003; Skiba & Rausch, 2006). Although all the studies available rely on fairly weak correlational data and possibly draw unwarranted conclusions, taken together they should certainly give us pause for thought. Why is it that strictly adhering to rigid behaviour policies appears so damaging?

It may be that strictly adhering to a zero-tolerance policy ignores the normal adolescent psychological and biological development. As we develop, synaptic connections between parts of the brain are myelinated in a gradual process, which moves gradually from the brain stem to the frontal lobes. This might go some way toward explaining teenage stereotypes: mood swings, irritability and impulsiveness; an inability to focus, follow through, and connect with adults; and their temptations to use drugs and alcohol and to engage in other risky behaviour.

This immaturity is also psychological. As any secondary school teacher will know, your average teenager is subject to peer pressure, takes unnecessary risks, doesn't think about consequences and finds self-control tricky. But if this just part of normal development then does this make punitive behaviour policies unreasonable? According to psychologists, certain characteristics of secondary schools are often at odds with the developmental challenges of adolescence, including the need for "close peer relationships, autonomy, support from adults other than one's parents, identity negotiation, and academic self-efficacy."*

Arguably the context is quite different in the UK where the 'no excuses' approach has been far more about intolerance of so-called 'low-level disruption'. There's a distinction between US style 'zero-tolerance' schools and the 'no excuses' movement in the UK. There's no reason why 'no excuses' has to equate with being punitive and making children suffer. Instead it can be seen as holding children to account for their effort, attitude and behaviour. If 'no excuses' results in relatively minor but consistently applied consequences, maybe those being 'punished' might feel differently (see page 152). Maybe they wouldn't rage at the injustice, but take their medicine with good grace. Maybe they wouldn't, but there would be 'no excuse' for choosing to take it with bad grace. How we behave is a matter of choice. Students need to be helped to make good choices sometimes, and will benefit from being reminded of the consequences for poor choices.

This being the case, the rather thin evidence on the efficacy of US style 'zero-tolerance' may not apply at all to the UK version. Various schools in the UK have adopted 'no excuses' approaches to classroom disruption, and reported that the atmosphere in their classrooms has been transformed. Students are happier and teachers can teach. Poor behaviour choices result in after-school detentions and a hard-core of students have been removed from the mainstream, assessed to see if there are underlying reasons for their behaviour and then put through a programme designed to help them make better choices. As yet there is no evidence beyond the anecdotal to suggest that these approaches are effective, but teachers and students self-report that the climate for learning has improved in schools that have embarked on this kind of approach[†].

Some behaviour – violent or extremely disruptive behaviour which prevents

---

*   Top 20 Principles from Psychology for preK-12 Teaching And Learning, p.25

†   Nova Hreod school in Swindon and Hans Price Academy in Weston-super-Mare are two schools that have successfully implemented 'no excuses' behaviour systems. Michaela Community School in Brent, a Free School which opened in 2014, has become well known for its high expectations of student behaviour. Michaela operates an open door policy and encourages anyone interested to visit to see the system in operation.

other students from being able to learn – is intolerable in school settings under any circumstances; schools need to be able to exclude students where their behaviour endangers others in any way. If we specify that offences such as classroom disruption, attendance-related behaviors, or even minor fights among students are met with less severe consequences, that's not to say students should be let off for these 'minor' issues, just that they shouldn't be expelled. Graduated, proportionate discipline policies are likely to increase the efficiency of school discipline.

Into the classroom

Whilst the term 'behaviourist' is used in a pejorative way by some teachers, Skinner hoped his research would be used to create societies where reinforcement rather than punishment was used to encourage people to do the right thing. Schools implicitly apply principles of operant conditioning and run token economies (in the form of reward systems), but understanding some of the nuances of such systems is key to their effectiveness.

There are some interesting reasons why some of Skinner's ideas about punishment may need updating. 'Benevolent' sanctions (i.e. directed towards encouraging pro-social norms in an environment of high trust) and negative sanctions (which may tap into our innate loss-aversion bias) may in some cases be effective.

It is also the case that Skinner's belief in the capacity of rewards to shape behaviour may have been optimistic. Teachers often observe that the students who receive the most 'merits' or 'reward points' tend to be the most academically motivated and the students with the worst behaviour records. It's simple to explain this phenomenon:

Firstly, teachers tend to give rewards to students who produce genuinely exceptional work. These forms of reward are benign enough so long as they come as a bit of a surprise to the student. Secondly, where students lack motivation, teachers instinctively reach for rewards as a way to obtain basic cooperation in the classroom. This is often more problematic, especially where the student comes to expect a reward. Whilst rewards can lead to fairly rapid changes in behaviour, they are at best an interim solution and should probably only be applied where there is a specific short-term goal. Lastly, the majority of students – those who behave well enough in the classroom but rarely produce work that sincerely impresses the teacher – rarely obtain such rewards.

Where reward systems are used to encourage basic cooperation in the classroom there will always be an element of unfairness in how they are applied. To avoid the apparent unfairness of reward systems, We've heard teachers suggest that reward policies should be as consistently applied as sanctions; however the psychology would indicate that this might be a mistake. If we routinely reward students for things they were motivated to do anyway, we risk undermining that motivation. Daniel Willingham suggests what we should only rely upon the influence of rewards to modify behaviour where the potentially negative effects on motivation are outweighed by the benefits of the student achieving a short-term goal – for example, encouraging a student who is no longer willing to try academic work so that they experience success and change their perception about their ability.

Praise, on the other hand, can have a positive effect on motivation. However, here too teachers need to be careful about how they apply praise. Praise should be spontaneous rather than calculated, and focused on some element of the work rather than the student.

What every teacher needs to know about rewards and sanctions

- Sanctions tend to temporarily suppress unwanted behaviour rather than encourage desirable behaviour.
- However, it seems likely that they can be effective when used to promote positive social norms within an environment of high trust. Where used, negative sanctions (e.g. the loss of a privilege) may be more effective than positive punishments.
- Rewards are problematic in that they risk reducing a student's enthusiasm where they already possess motivation.
- Unexpected rewards appear to have no detrimental effect on motivation, but teachers often use them as a way to shape behaviour where motivation appears lacking. As a consequence, reward systems tend to be applied 'unfairly' in schools.
- Spontaneous praise, directed towards some attribute of the student's work, may have a beneficial influence on student motivation.
- However, caution is probably advised when praising students for effort – as over-praising in this regard may inadvertently communicate low expectations of the student.
- Schools should adopt policies that, while not excusing poor behaviour, are flexible enough to anticipate and cope with the normal range of

> teenage behaviour and provide an appropriate response which helps students to learn from their mistakes.
> - Whilst it's true that students will often have compelling reasons for their behaviour, these reasons should not be seen as excusing poor behaviour.
> - Consequences for rule breaking should be certain but, where possible, not severe – as long as students know that certain choices always result in the same consequence, they are more likely to accept these consequences.

References

American Psychological Association, Zero Tolerance Task Force (2008) 'Are zero tolerance policies effective in the schools? An evidentiary review and recommendations', *American Psychologist*, 63, 852–862, doi:10.1037/0003-066X.63.9.852

American Psychological Association, Coalition for Psychology in Schools and Education. (2015) *Top 20 principles from psychology for preK–12 teaching and learning*. Retrieved from http:// www.apa.org/ed/schools/cpse/top-twenty-principles.pdf

Arnett, J. (1992) 'Reckless Behavior in Adolescence: A Developmental Perspective', *Developmental Review*, 12, 339-37, University of Missouri-Columbia.

Balliet, D. & Van Lange, P. A. (2013) 'Trust, punishment, and cooperation across 18 societies A Meta-Analysis', *Perspectives on Psychological Science*, 8(4), 363-379.

Bickel, F. & Qualls, R. (1980) 'The impact of school climate on suspension rates in the Jefferson County Public Schools', *Urban Review*, 12, 79–86.

Cauffman, E. & Steinberg, L. (2000) '(Im)maturity of judgment in adolescence: Why adolescents may be less culpable than adults', *Behavioral Sciences and the Law*, 18(6), 741-760. doi: 10.1002/bsl.416.

Davis, J. E. & Jordan, W. J. (1994) 'The effects of school context, structure, and experiences on African American males in middle and high schools', *Journal of Negro Education*, 63, 570–587.

Deci, E. L., Koestner, R. & Ryan, R. M. (1999) 'A meta-analytic review of experiments examining the effects of extrinsic rewards on intrinsic motivation', *Psychological bulletin*, 125(6), 627.

Dweck, C. S. (2007) 'The perils and promises of praise', *Kaleidoscope, Contemporary and Classic Readings in Education*, 12.

Evertson, C. M. & Emmer, E. T. (2009) *Classroom management for elementary teachers* (8th ed.), Upper Saddle River, NJ: Pearson.

Gardner, M. & Steinberg, L. (2005) 'Peer Influence on Risk Taking, Risk Preference, and Risky Decision Making in Adolescence and Adulthood: An Experimental Study', *Developmental Psychology*, 2005, 41(4), 625-635.

Grisso, T., Steinberg, T., Woolard, J., Cauffman, E., Scott, E., Graham, S. Lexcen, F. Dickon Reppucci, N. & Schwartz, R. (2003) 'Juveniles' Competence to Stand Trial: A Comparison of Adolescents' and Adults' Capacities as Trial Defendants', *Law and Human Behavior*, Vol. 27(4).

Hackenberg, T. D. (2009) 'Token reinforcement: A review and analysis', *Journal of the Experimental Analysis of Behavior*, 91(2), 257-286.

Hooper, C. J., Luciana, M., Conklin, H. M. & Yarger, R. S. (2004) 'Adolescents' Performance on the Iowa Gambling Task: Implications for the Development of Decision Making and Ventromedial Prefrontal Cortex', *Developmental Psychology*, 2004, 40(6), 1148-1158.

Haydn, T. (2014) 'To what extent is behaviour a problem in English schools? Exploring the scale and prevalence of deficits in classroom climate' *Review of Education*, 2(1), 31-64

Jensen, F. E. (2014) *The Teenage Brain*, US: Harper.

Lepper, M. R., Greene, D. & Nisbett, R. E. (1973) 'Undermining children's intrinsic interest with extrinsic reward: A test of the "overjustification" hypothesis', *Journal of Personality and social Psychology*, 28(1), 129.

Luna, B., Garver, K.E., Urban, T.A., Lazar, N.A. & Sweeney, J.A. (2004) 'Maturation of cognitive processes from late childhood to adulthood', *Child Development*, 75(5), 1357-1372.

Raffaele-Mendez, L. M. (2003) 'Predictors of suspension and negative school outcomes: A longitudinal investigation', in Wald, J. & Losen, D (eds.) *New directions for youth development: Vol. 99. Deconstructing the school-to-prison pipeline*, San Francisco, CA: Jossey-Bass.

Scott, T. M. & Barrett, S. B. (2004). Using staff and student time engaged in disciplinary procedures to evaluate the impact of school-wide PBS. *Journal of Positive Behavior Interventions*, 6, 21-27.

Skiba, R. & Peterson, R. (2003) 'Teaching the social curriculum: School discipline as instruction', *Preventing School Failure*, 47(2), 66-73.

Skiba, R. J. & Rausch, M. K. (2006) 'Zero tolerance, suspension, and expulsion: Questions of equity and effectiveness', in Evertson, & Weinstein, (eds.) *Handbook of classroom management: Research, practice and Contemporary Issues*, New York: Routledge

Skinner, B. F. (2005) 'Science and human behavior', The BF Skinner Foundation, 458, 2005.

Slavin, R. E. (ed.) (2014) *Classroom management and assessment*, Thousand Oaks, CA: Corwin Press.

Sprick, R. (2006) *Discipline in the secondary classroom: A positive approach to behavior management* (2nd ed.), San Francisco, CA: Jossey-Bass.

Sugai, G. & Simonsen, B. (2015) 'Supporting general classroom management: Tier 2/3 practices and systems', in Emmer, E. & Sabornie, E. (eds.) *Handbook of classroom management*, New York, NY: Taylor & Francis, pp. 60–75.

Tversky, A. & Kahneman, D. (1991) 'Loss aversion in riskless choice: A reference-dependent model', *The quarterly journal of economics*, 1039-1061.

Willingham, D. T. (2006) 'How Praise Can Motivate – or Stifle', *American Educator*, 29(4), 23-27.

Willingham, D. T. (2007) 'Should Learning Be Its Own Reward?' *American Educator*, 31(4), 29.

Wu, S. C., Pink, W. T., Crain, R. L. & Moles, O. (1982) 'Student suspension: A critical reappraisal', *Urban Review*, 14, 245–303.

Zimring, F. E. (2015) *American Youth Violence: A Cautionary Tale*, https://www.law.berkeley.edu/php-programs/faculty/facultyPubsPDF.php?facID=127&pubID=1

Chapter 16
Intrinsic and extrinsic motivation

It goes without saying that motivation is important, although, "Learning requires motivation, but motivation does not necessarily lead to learning."* So do some kinds of motivation matter more than others?

If we're intrinsically motivated we do a thing for its own sake, whereas the carrot and stick of extrinsic motivation stem from external pressures. Intrinsic goals are seen as more likely to lead to enduring learning whereas extrinsic goals are considered more likely to result in anxiety. Anxiety isn't altogether bad – as we'll see in Chapter 23, we need a modicum of stress to help us perform at our best – but the idea of students learning 'for its own sake' will appeal to most teachers.

A word of caution: it may be that the correlations between intrinsic motivation and better educational outcomes might be putting the cart before the horse. It tends to be that we're intrinsically motivated to do the things we're already good at, and we all need a spot of extrinsic motivation to get on with the stuff we struggle with. It's worth pointing out that intrinsic and extrinsic factors are not mutually exclusive – most of us possess a judicious mix of both. Even a student who passionately loves learning for its own sake may well also be keen to get good grades.

Others, such as Daniel Pink, warn that extrinsic rewards can lead to short-term thinking and act to snuff out intrinsic motivation, diminish performance, crush

---
* Nuthall, G. (2007)

creativity, and encourage cheating, short cuts and unethical behaviour. There is evidence that in some cases where children are already quite intrinsically motivated that offering extrinsic rewards can undermine that motivation (see Chapter 15). Why might an extrinsic reward reduce motivation? Well, there's at least one fairly straightforward reason: if we feel that the only reason for doing something is some sort of reward at the end, what happens when the rewards are no longer offered? However, extrinsic rewards, when properly used, are important in producing positive educational outcomes.

So is intrinsic motivation something you're just born with, or can it be developed? As we explored in Chapter 11, students' beliefs matter hugely, but we can teach in such a way that even the most closed-minded students are more likely to feel a measure of internal motivation.

Pink reckons that the best way to motivate anyone is to give them mastery, autonomy and purpose. Mastery is about getting better at something that matters but students may not always see the value of what they need to learn. As we become proficient in the basics, tasks require less effort and become more enjoyable.

When students repeat tasks and purposefully practice (see Chapter 7) basic skills they get better at whatever it is they're practising. Many parents will be familiar with the experience of having to nag children to practise playing a musical instrument. In the beginning it can be hard work. Many students give up because the effort required to continue doesn't seem worth it, but some continue – maybe because of the extrinsic motivations of nagging, bribery and threats – and, at a certain point, begin the find the practice more rewarding. When you can get a pleasant sound out of an instrument and actually play recognisable tunes, it becomes more fun. Practice can then become intrinsically motivating. Maybe this suggests that we need a little bit of extrinsic motivation to get started before 'mastery' helps us harness intrinsic motivation?

We also need to offer lots of feedback and encouragement to nurture students' burgeoning intrinsic motivation, but if we're patient and if we have consistently high expectations practising the basics like phonics, grammar, number bonds and times tables lays down the foundation required to make future learning significantly easier and more enjoyable. At times, the work students need to do is not inherently fun; success generally requires persistence, determination, hard work and resilience in the face of setbacks.

Autonomy is trickier. If students are given autonomy before they've mastered the basics there's a good chance they'll make poor choices. The key to successful autonomy is effective accountability. The political scientist Philip Tetlock

argues that there are three conditions under which social pressure would encourage people to want to be right rather than look right. They are:
1. The knowledge that we will be accountable to an audience.
2. The audience's views must be unknown.
3. The belief that the audience is well informed and interested in accuracy.

If those conditions are met, people tend to do the right thing.

Purpose is what keeps us going. Paul Dolan tells us in *Happiness by Design* that we need purpose as well as pleasure to feel fulfilled. But if we're only interested in short-term goals like passing exams, what happens when the goal is achieved? Teaching students who seem only motivated by threats and rewards and give every appearance of hating everything to do with school can be a joyless exercise. If it's not in the exam, they're not interested; they take short cuts and balk at the merest whiff of difficulty. Teaching students whose purpose is to learn for its own sake is an altogether different proposition. They listen attentively, work conscientiously and strive to relate new concepts and information to what they already know. Having a purpose gives us the desire to master tricky content just because it's there.

For some teachers this is an argument for 'relevant' or 'authentic' curriculum choices, which appear to be at odds with how we learn. Instead, we should do more to consider the potential benefits of extrinsic motivation. The psychologists Richard Ryan and Edward Deci have proposed what they call Self Determination Theory (STD) as an overarching framework within which to think about motivation. Although a thorough explanation of all the aspects of STD falls outside the scope of this book, it does make some interesting points about extrinsic motivation. Extrinsic motivations can provide a sense of purpose for many students. Ryan and Deci classified four different kinds of extrinsic motivation: external regulation, introjection, identification and integration.

External regulation is the least autonomous form of extrinsic motivation: the classic carrot and stick of rewards and sanctions discussed in the previous chapter. Introjection describes a type of internal regulation that still requires an awareness and response to the demands of others. Whilst we may not be directly rewarded or sanctioned, we are still acting to please someone else – a parent maybe, or a teacher. This may well involve feelings of guilt and anxiety as we strive to maintain our sense of self-esteem. A more autonomous form of extrinsic motivation is regulation through identification. Here, we begin to value a way of behaving as relevant and as likely to be personally important.

We choose to work because we recognise that it's likely to be good for us or provide us with a desirable outcome – a chance to go to university or get a better job. The most autonomous form of extrinsic motivation is integrated regulation. Integration occurs when those things we value become self-determined. A student who has integrated external motivations may want to work hard because they see hard work as a positive trait; they are able to delay gratification because they know that it is the right thing to do. This only differs from intrinsic motivation in that we act for a hoped-for outcome, not simply for the pleasure of doing a thing. Turning these extrinsic motivations into projects which students work towards completing can provide a sense of purpose, as can effective goal setting (see Chapter 13).

Into the classroom

While the message on the importance of intrinsic motivation is hard to dispute, advice offered to teachers is less clear-cut. The American Psychological Association makes a number of suggestions, but some of these are potentially problematic. Teachers should certainly support students' fundamental need to feel valued, competent and in control, the question is how to achieve this. It's probably unhelpful to seek to introduce surprises or gimmicks in an effort to motivate students. The quest for novelty is unsustainable, but also often a distraction, which can reduce the likelihood that students will work hard to achieve difficult mastery goals. Likewise, suggesting that teachers simply allow students to choose their own activities and pursue their own interests is likely to be counterproductive. This approach gives the illusion of autonomy at the expense of mastery and long-term purpose. It's useful to acknowledge that tasks are difficult and that struggle is not just normal but indispensable.

Another nugget of advice is on the issue of grading students' work. In the 1980s, Ruth Butler ran a series of small-scale studies demonstrating the nugatory effects of grading, but these might not count for much on their own. More interesting is the research conducted in Sweden by Alli Klapp. Between 1969 and 1982, Swedish municipalities were given the decision about whether they would grade the students in their schools. This made for a wonderful natural experiment in which some students were given grades and others weren't, and made it possible to examine the longitudinal effects of grading on a huge sample of students. Even here the results were still somewhat equivocal, but it seems pretty clear that although grades might be useful (or even essential) for some purposes, on the whole they seem to undermine many children's academic performance. That said, for some students – particularly girls and higher achieving students – being awarded grades did seem to be motivational.

It seems obvious that a poor grade is likely to be demotivating whereas being awarded a high grade will be more likely to motivate students to work harder.

The reasons why grades might harm educational outcomes is unclear, but one speculation is that when students receive a grade, their first instinct is to compare their performance with that of others. If students are not given a grade but instead have to read through feedback on how they might improve their performance they are more likely to focus on mastery goals rather than performance goals (see Chapter 13).

If students are extrinsically motivated they may not find school work inherently interesting and will need external prompts. The main reason they are willing to work is because doing so is valued by those around them. A school or classroom culture where it is 'cool to be clever' and where effort is valued is likely to be motivating. Another important issue is whether students perceive themselves as competent in a particular subject. The more success students have experienced, the more likely they are to be motivated to work harder. Rather than motivation resulting in improved performance, it seems that improved performance leads to increased motivation.

For students to commit to investing effort in school they must have a stake in it. They must see the point and believe that the fruits of education are worth working for. This is by no means an argument for making subjects 'relevant' by appealing to students' interests, rather it is the observation that if students believe that effort will result in better grades and that better grades offer some form of meaningful incentive, then they are more likely to commit to trying harder and aiming higher.

Motivation to work hard requires self-control. Some studies suggest self-control is a limited resource which depletes as we expend it.* Expecting students to continually make the right choice when there are so many distracting options is possibly unreasonable. If we work hard to reduce distractions and limit the choices available, then maybe we'll make it easier for students to make the choice to work hard. We can set up classrooms and run schools so that choosing effort and risking failure becomes the default option so that it's easier to learn and socially awkward and undesirable to muck about. We need to apply gentle but firm pressure to encourage pupils to avoid the behaviours that run counter

---

* Bauminster, R. et al (1998) argued that self-control was a limited resource, which could be depleted with use, making us less able to exert willpower. However more recent attempts to replicate the effects of ego-depletion seem to have failed, casting doubt on the theory (see Lurquin et al, 2016), whereas others (see Sripada et al, 2014) are convinced the effects are real. For now the jury's still out and any conclusions we draw about ego-depletion must necessarily be cautious.

to their best interests and then provide rewarding release when they make choices that result in them being best able to learn.

> **What every teacher needs to know intrinsic and extrinsic motivation**
> - Be aware that grading students' work can have a negative effect on intrinsic motivation. If you have to grade particular pieces of work, it's probably not worth also providing feedback. Conversely, if you want students to act on feedback, awarding grades can backfire.
> - However, grades can be a spur to work harder for some students as long as they believe that increasing effort will result in improvements (see Chapter 11).
> - Avoid strategies that seek to directly build students' intrinsic motivation – these tend to be short-lived and potentially distracting. Instead explicitly teach students that they must master the basics in order to find enjoyment in a subject.
> - Reduce distractions so that students can concentrate on mastering challenging goals. Some activities teachers plan into lessons for the sake of variety or engagement can be a distraction, as students will tend to remember what they think about; if they're thinking about the activities they may well forget the purpose of the lesson.
> - Extrinsic motivation can be very effective and, rather than expecting all students to learn to love studying, it may be more realistic to focus on instilling a good work ethic and teaching students the value of delaying gratification.
> - Students are likely to be better able to motivate themselves to work hard if we satisfy students' needs to feel valued, competent and in control.

References

Anderman, E. M. & Anderman, L. H. (2014) *Classroom motivation* (2nd ed.), Boston, MA: Pearson.

Baumeister, R.E., Bratslavsky, E., Muraven, M. & Tice, D. M. (1998) 'Ego Depletion: Is the Active Self a Limited Resource?', *Journal of Personality and Social Psychology*, Vol 74(5), 1252-1265. https://faculty.washington.edu/jdb/345/345%20Articles/Baumeister%20et%20al.%20(1998).pdf

Brophy, J. (2004) *Motivating students to learn*, Mahwah, NJ: Erlbaum.

Brophy, J., Wiseman, D. G. & Hunt, G. H. (2008) *Best practice in motivation and management in the classroom* (2nd ed.), Spring eld, IL: Charles C Thomas.

Butler, R. (1987) 'Task-involving and ego-involving properties of evaluation: Effects of different feedback conditions on motivational perceptions, interest and performance', *Journal of Educational Psychology*, 79, pp. 474–482.

Butler, R. (1988) 'Enhancing and undermining intrinsic motivation: The effects of task-involving and ego-involving evaluation on interest and performance', *British Journal of Educational Psychology*, 58, 1–14.

Deci, E. L. & Ryan, R. M. (1985) *Intrinsic motivation and self-determination in human behavior*, New York, NY: Plenum.

Deci, E. L. & Ryan, R. M. (2000) 'The "what" and "why" of goal pursuits: Human needs and the self-determination of behavior', *Psychological Inquiry*, 11, 227-268.

Deci, E. L. & Ryan, R. M. (2000) 'Intrinsic and Extrinsic Motivations: Classic Definitions and New Directions', *Contemporary Educational Psychology*, 25, 54–67

Dolan, P., *Happiness by Design* (2014), London: Penguin.

Klapp, A. (2015) 'Does grading affect educational attainment? A longitudinal study', *Assessment in Education: Principles, Policy and Practice*, 22(3), 302-323.

Lepper, M. R., Greene, D. & Nisbett, R. E. (1973) 'Undermining children's intrinsic interest with extrinsic reward: A test of the" overjustification" hypothesis', *Journal of Personality and social Psychology*, 28(1), 129.

Lurquin, J.H., Michaelson, L.H., Barker, J.E, Gustavson, D. E., von Bastian, C. C., Carruth, N. P. & Miyake, A. (2016) 'No Evidence of the Ego-Depletion Effect across Task Characteristics and Individual Differences: A Pre-Registered Study' http://journals.plos.org/plosone/article/asset?id=10.1371%2Fjournal.pone.0147770.PDF

Nuthall, G. (2007), *The Hidden Lives of Learners*. Wellington, NZ: NZCER Press.

Pink, D. (2009) *Drive: The surprising Truth About What Motivates Us*, New York: Canongate Books.

Sripada, C., Kessler, D. & Jonides, J. (2014) 'Methylphenidate Blocks Effort-Induced Depletion of Regulatory Control in Healthy Volunteers', *Psychological Science*, 25(6) 1227–1234.

Tetlock, P. E. (1983) 'Accountability and complexity of thought', *Journal of Personality and Social Psychology*, 45(1), 74-83.

Thorkildsen, T. A., Golant, C. J. & Cambray-Engstrom, E. (2008) 'Essential solidarities for understanding Latino adolescents' moral and academic engagement', in Hudley, C. & Gottfried, (eds.) *Academic motivation and the culture of schooling in childhood and adolescence*, Oxford, England: Oxford University Press, pp. 73–89.

Willingham, D. T. (2007) 'Should Learning Be Its Own Reward?' *American Educator*, 31(4), 29.

Chapter 17
Self-regulation

Before getting into the thorny matter of whether self-regulation can be taught, we need to be clear about what we actually mean by the term. Psychologists define self-regulation as the ability to control our behaviour and impulses in order to meet standards, achieve goals, or reach ideals. Self-regulation involves being able to set goals, monitor our behaviour, and have the willpower to persist in a course of action until our goals are achieved and includes attention, organisation, self-control, planning, and memory strategies.

It seems obvious that helping students to become more independent in their learning and better able to regulate their emotions and interactions with others in a positive way will benefit those students in terms of their educational experience and achievement as well as their long-term well-being. What is less obvious is the way in which teachers can successfully foster these capabilities in their students.

As adults, we tend to possess a strong feeling of voluntary control over our behaviour. There is a powerful subjective impression that we have conscious control of mental events (conscious thought) and behaviour (deliberate actions) in our daily lives and we readily contrast these with involuntary or unconscious thoughts and actions. This ability to apparently take control of our thoughts and actions – to self-regulate – is related to what psychologists often call executive functioning. Executive functioning is, in some ways, difficult to precisely define as it's implicated in so many different tasks. Broadly, it represents our capacity for things like problem solving, reasoning, planning and organisation, inhibiting action or speech within context of appropriate norms, managing attention control and various other abilities.

Executive functioning develops rapidly in early childhood, then slowly throughout adolescence and early adulthood – reaching a peak in our mid-twenties before gradually beginning to decline. In many ways, it represents a key cognitive difference between young children and adults and arguably forms a better basis for understanding cognitive development across childhood than Piaget's stage theory (see Chapter 21 on cognitive development). The figure below gives a rough outline of how executive functioning develops over the years:

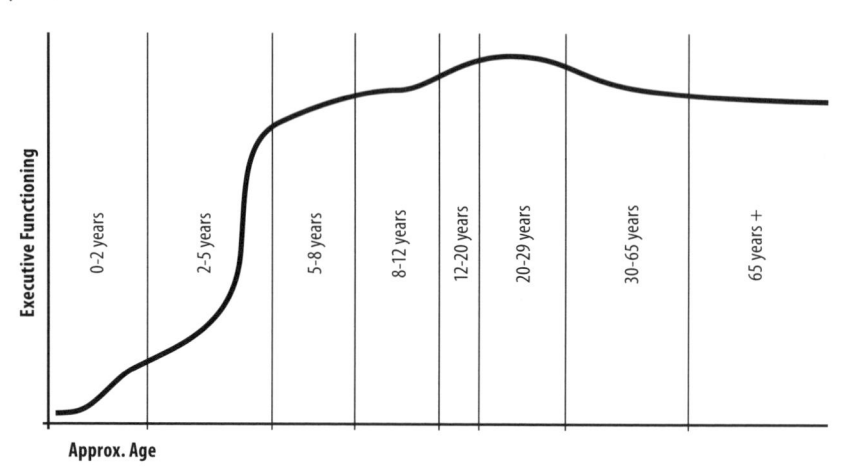

Figure 1: Development of executive functioning

Deficits in executive function are associated with a number of conditions which teachers encounter, for example ADHD (attention deficit hyperactivity disorder). For example, one study conducted by the clinical psychologist Joseph Biederman found that deficits in executive functioning had a significant detrimental effect on academic outcomes for children with ADHD even when socio-economic factors, IQ and other learning disabilities were taken into account.

Perhaps the most famous test of executive functioning with respect to self-regulation is the 'Marshmallow Test' by Walter Mischel. In these studies a child is offered a choice: a small immediate reward (e.g. a marshmallow) or double the reward if they can wait for 15 minutes. What Mischel found across a range of studies examining children's ability to exert self-control was that the children who deferred gratification (i.e. waited for the bigger reward) rather than going for immediate gratification (i.e. couldn't wait) showed different characteristics even years later. Children who deferred gratification were rated as better able to handle stress, engage in planning, and exhibit self-control when adolescents

10 years later and went on to obtain higher SAT scores. They found that these differences appeared to be apparent even when participants were in their 40s.

Sometimes this ability to set aside temptation and act in accordance to longer-term goals is called 'impulse control', though that's probably not a very helpful term. The psychologist Roy Baumeister makes the point that impulses (like reflexes) arise outside of conscious control. Self-regulation, therefore, is not about preventing those impulses, but about not acting upon them. Baumeister reviewed examples of failures of self-regulation and suggested there were three components needed for an individual to be successful. These components form a 'feedback loop':

Standards: Children need clear and consistent ideals and goals pitched at the appropriate level (i.e. not unambitiously low or unattainably high). Unclear or inconsistent standards lead to an internal dilemma as the child tries to resolve an incompatible or conflicting set of expectations. This impairs the ability to self-regulate. Albert Bandura noted that whilst the power of socially transmitting standards through modelling was well evidenced, we don't just passively absorb these standards from what we see modelled or what we are taught. There is significant diversity and inconsistency in the norms we observe. For example, the same individual may promote different standards in different settings, or some of the standards promoted by teachers, parents and peers may be in competition with one another.

Monitoring: Assuming the goals are clear, students needs to be able to compare their actual state or behaviour to the desired state or behaviour. Monitoring one's own actions or states is a vital ingredient of self-regulation, and when people lose control (e.g. binge eating or excessive alcohol consumption, or by having a meltdown in the classroom) it tends to be when they stop monitoring themselves. This isn't a mechanical process of judging performance; it's influenced by our beliefs and expectations. For example, what aspect of our performance we're paying attention to, what we believe about our competence, how well we remember previous successes and failures, even our mood, can all influence how effectively we monitor our current performance.

Operate: Where monitoring shows that the current state falls short of the standards, some strategy or process must come into play to change the current state. If a child recognises that their current behaviour is falling short of expectations, they need be in a position to do something about it. Even where standards are clear and students are successfully monitoring themselves, they may fail to self-regulate simply because they don't know what to do to change their behaviour.

This provides some insight into why some children failed the 'Marshmallow Test'. It may have been some ambiguity in the *standards* of the task – for example, the child may not have trusted the experimenter to really come through with the second marshmallow if they waited. It might also have been a failure of *monitoring* – the child may not have recognised that they were fuelling their temptation to eat the marshmallow by looking at it or thinking about eating it. Lastly, it may have been a failure to *operate* upon that monitoring – children who succeeded the test often covered their eyes or turned away from the marshmallow, or distracted themselves by deliberately thinking about something else.

Can we train children to have more self-control?

Given the importance of executive function in school achievement, there's been considerable interest in whether such abilities can be taught. The idea of executive functioning is related to the central executive component of the Working Memory Model (see Chapter 3) and one approach has been to try to train children's working memory in the hope that it might help them achieve more in school.

For example, a recent meta-analysis by Melby-Lervåg and Hulme examined the claims of training programmes (which typically involve numerous computerised memory trials) designed to boost working memory function. They reported that some of these working memory training packages made confident claims about helping children with ADHD, dyspraxia and autistic spectrum disorders to improve school grades and could boost children's IQ. Sadly, the outcomes of the meta-analysis were not supportive of these impressive claims. Whilst there appeared to be short-term improvements on both verbal and non-verbal working memory tasks, these gains did not last very long, nor did they generalise to things like the ability to do arithmetic or decode words. For attentional control, which we'd expect to be related to self-regulation, the effects were small to moderate immediately after training, but reduced to nothing in the follow-up.

One problem they identified is that these training programmes rely on a rather naïve model of how our brains work. Many of these memory training packages appear based on the idea that repeatedly loading working memory will lead to it increasing in capacity (like strengthening a muscle by repeated use). Unfortunately, the brain is simply not like a muscle.

One reason for the failure of this 'exercise approach' to developing self-regulation may be due to the fact that continuous efforts to exert self-control may actually lead future attempts at self-control to fail. For example, a review of research by Mark Muraven and Roy Baumeister found evidence to suggest that our capacity to exert self-control is somewhat limited. They argue that this capacity for self-control sometimes appears to be depleted after a period of intense or continuous use. Thus, when people are forced to exert strong or unexpected demands for self-control or when people 'waste' their self-control efforts in activities which prove to be unproductive, they may find that their self-control becomes vulnerable to failing in other, unrelated situations. It seems that controlling one's self can be costly and draining in the short run, even if it is beneficial in the long run.*

It may be unsurprising that generic 'brain training' programmes fail to have lasting or generalisable effects on working memory, but what about school-based interventions – specifically aimed at improving executive functioning? There's certainly been a recent surge of interest for the idea of developing self-control and executive functioning in our pupils – often linked with the whole notion of 'character education'. Do these interventions work to raise attainment? After all, interventions to increase executive functioning probably have little value unless they are also helping children achieve greater success within school. A systematic review of attempts to target students' executive functioning through school-based interventions was recently carried out by Robin Jacob and Julia Parkinson.

Although there is substantial evidence that academic achievement and measures of executive function are correlated – across a variety of age groups – there is surprisingly little evidence that a causal relationship exists. Interestingly, they found that there was no significant difference between self-control and working memory measures in their correlation with student achievement. Both appeared to have a relatively weak correlation with student outcomes. However, they argue this doesn't necessarily mean that improving executive functioning or working memory will improve achievement. Thus they focused their meta-analysis on whether interventions designed to improve executive functioning *caused* improvements to outcomes.

The intervention programmes they reviewed varied in content, but tended to be taught as stand-alone, 'skills-based' approaches. For example, one of the curricula reviewed was called the REDI programme. This was taught to pre-school children in weekly lessons and extension activities where children were taught language skills, social skills, emotional understanding, self-regulation and aggression control by teachers given specific training. Overall, the review found that most of the studies they reviewed appeared to show that despite the

---

* On the other hand, support for the long-standing idea that self-control is a limited resource has recently been challenged. A recent meta-analysis by Evan Carter and Lilly Kofler (2015) found little evidence to support for this 'depletion effect' arguing that self-control in general does not decrease as a function of previous use.

positive impact on measures of executive function, there was little to support the claim that improving executive function leads to increases in academic achievement. In short, these generic intervention programmes don't appear to directly improve student outcomes.

So, what might be the factor underlying both executive functioning and school achievement? The authors explore a range of possible factors. Once social and economic background characteristics and IQ were accounted for, the association between executive function and achievement dropped close to zero. In terms of the school-based interventions, the results were equally disappointing. The authors found that even the most effective school-based interventions designed to improve executive function would only have the potential to increase future achievement by less than a tenth of a standard deviation. This suggests that school-based interventions focused on improving executive functioning will have a disappointing impact on achievement.

Into the classroom

Our ability to self-regulate represents a key cognitive difference between young children and adults – developing rapidly in early childhood and reaching a peak in early adulthood. The ability to adapt our behaviour in accordance to social norms and expectations, regulate attention and avoid distractions, and engage in reasoning and planning are well correlated with success in school. However, it's far from clear how best we might help students experience that success. We need to remember that interventions based on improving identified psychological differences may not necessarily lead to benefits for students.

Of course, when schools have invested a great deal of time, effort and training in an intervention scheme, it becomes easy for teachers to convince themselves that they are seeing a genuine difference. We can't rely on anecdotal evidence or professional experience alone. It seems that the evidence to date suggests that teachers should be highly sceptical of intervention programmes which claim to have success in raising achievement through generic exercises or training intended to develop self-regulation or executive functioning.

However, whilst fairly generic attempts to train students' executive functioning has, thus far, delivered disappointing results, there may be some value in teachers helping students develop subject-specific strategies related to self-regulation and metacognition. Studies looking at the student outcomes for English and mathematics, and to a more limited degree other subject areas like science, have found evidence indicating that *teaching self-regulation strategies can be effective at raising attainment for low-achieving and older pupils.*

---

*   The Sutton Trust-EEF (2013) Teaching and Learning Toolkit.

If we refer back to the reasons why self-regulation fails, we can see why implementing these strategies can difficult to achieve:
1. Students require a shared and consistent understanding of *standards* – the ideals and goals they are working towards. Part of this involves students taking more responsibility for their learning but it also requires a secure understanding of what is required to succeed.
2. Students will also need to be able to *monitor* their progress towards the desired goals. Students might consider where the task could go wrong or identify the key steps involved in working towards a goal, and be able to evaluate the strategies they have used in order to complete a task.
3. Students will also need to able to apply a variety of strategies in order to *operate*. These may involve teaching subject-specific and explicit strategies on how to plan, monitor and evaluate specific aspects of their learning. Students will also likely need some practice and support before being able to apply these independently. Some element of scaffolding will probably be required – with the teacher providing fairly intense and explicit support at first, before reducing that support to ensure the student doesn't become too reliant upon the prompts provided by the teacher.

Some of the ways we could consider helping students develop an ability to self-regulate might include:

- Helping students identify and evaluate the short- and long-term consequences of their decisions. As novices, students are unlikely to understand the consequences of the decisions they make and so teacher input might be valuable and result in an improved awareness of what it means to self-regulate.
- Present the goals of lessons and tasks very clearly and break down tasks into smaller, 'bite-size', meaningful components, clearly spelling out the criteria for successful task performance.
- Organise classroom time by balancing focused time, interactive periods, and so forth, in order that students are able to practice intense focusing followed by more socially interactive methods of learning.
- Providing opportunities for students to discuss and collaborate is probably an effective way to see whether students have the ability to self-regulate. Will they choose to get on with their work, or will they chat to their mates? This will largely depend on the classroom culture the teacher has established and the wider school culture enforced by the leadership team.

If either of these permit students to make poor choices with little or no consequence, self-regulation will be largely left to the motivation and personality of individual students.

> **What every teacher needs to know about self-regulation**
> - The ability to self-regulate is related to a capacity called 'executive functioning' in psychology. This capacity develops rapidly in early childhood, though there may be significant individual differences in the rate at which it matures.
> - There is reason to believe that at least some children with SEND may have deficits in executive functioning (e.g. ADHD). Additionally, the relationship between executive functioning and school achievement is very strong.
> - Given this relationship, there's been a growing interest in training programmes and interventions based on improving students' executive functioning. The evidence supporting many of these 'generic' programmes appears quite weak. Even where they appear to improve executive functioning, the effects don't seem to be long-lasting or help improve student outcomes very much.
> - On the other hand, further studies have found that metacognition and self-regulation interventions have helped raise student achievement. However, it's worth being aware that successful implementation of these interventions is not necessarily straightforward.
> - A good bet might involve quite explicitly taught strategies specific to a subject domain, delivered in a 'scaffolded' way which gradually reduces support.
>
> In conclusion, the ability to regulate ourselves is essential to success in pretty much any area. But the jury's still out on whether these skills can be taught. Certainly they can be encouraged, modelled and rewarded, but this may not result in students learning them. We absolutely recommend spending time getting students to think about the need to self-regulate within subjects, showing them how to self-regulate as a mathematician, historian or linguist and acknowledging their successes, but we would advise against committing curriculum time to a programme designed to teach a set of generic skills. Maybe we can sum up by say that while we might be able to teach the concept of self-regulation, teaching the process is much more challenging.

References

Bandura, A. (1991) 'Social cognitive theory of self-regulation', *Organizational behavior and human decision processes*, 50(2), 248-287.

Baumeister, R. F. & Heatherton, T. F. (1996) 'Self-regulation failure: An overview', *Psychological inquiry*, 7(1), 1-15.

Biederman, J., Monuteaux, M. C., Doyle, A. E., Seidman, L. J., Wilens, T. E., Ferrero, F., Morgan, C.L. & Faraone, S. V. (2004) 'Impact of executive function deficits and attention-deficit/hyperactivity disorder (ADHD) on academic outcomes in children', *Journal of consulting and clinical psychology*, 72(5), 757.

Carter, E. C., Kofler, L. M., Forster, D. E. & McCullough, M. E. (2015) 'A series of meta-analytic tests of the depletion effect: Self-control does not seem to rely on a limited resource', *Journal of Experimental Psychology: General*, 144(4), 796.

Diamond, A., Barnett, W. S., Thomas, J. & Munro, S. (2007) 'Preschool program improves cognitive control', *Science*, 318(5855), 1387–1388. doi:10.1126/science.1151148

Galinsky, E. (2010) *Mind in the making: The seven essential life skills every child needs*, New York, NY: HarperCollins.

Hadwin, A. F. & Jarvela, S. (2011) *Introduction to a Special Issue on Social Aspects of Self-Regulated Learning: Where Social and Self Meet in the Strategic Regulation of Learning* https://www.researchgate.net/publication/230555582_Introduction_to_a_Special_Issue_on_Social_Aspects_of_Self-Regulated_Learning_Where_Social_and_Self_Meet_in_the_Strategic_Regulation_of_Learning

Jacob, R. & Parkinson, J. (2015) 'The Potential for School-Based Interventions That Target Executive Function to Improve Academic Achievement – A Review', *Review of Educational Research*, 85(4), 512-552.

Melby-Lervåg, M. & Hulme, C. (2013) 'Is working memory training effective? A meta-analytic review', *Developmental psychology*, 49(2), 270.

Merino, A. & Aucock, M. (2014) *The role-modelling of self-regulated learning strategies and skills through enrichment tutorials* https://ctl.curtin.edu.au/events/conferences/tlf/tlf2014/refereed/merino.pdf

Mischel, W. (2015) *The Marshmallow Test: Understanding Self-Control and How to Master It*, UK: Random House.

Mischel, W., Ebbesen, E. B. & Raskoff Zeiss, A. (1972) 'Cognitive and attentional mechanisms in delay of gratification', *Journal of personality and social psychology*, 21(2), 204.

Muraven, M. & Baumeister, R. F. (2000) 'Self-regulation and depletion of limited resources: Does self-control resemble a muscle?', *Psychological bulletin*, 126(2), 247.

Muraven, M., Baumeister, R. F. & Tice, D. M. (1999) 'Longitudinal improvement of self-regulation through practice: Building self-control strength through repeated exercise', *The Journal of social psychology*, 139(4), 446-457.

Posner, M. I. & Rothbart, M. K. (2000) 'Developing mechanisms of self-regulation', *Development and psychopathology*, 12(3), 427-441.

The Sutton Trust-EEF, (2013) Teaching and Learning Toolkit. Also available from: https://educationendowmentfoundation.org.uk/evidence/teaching-learning-toolkit/meta-cognition-and-self-regulation/ accessed 1 March 2016

Wolters, C. A. (2011) 'Regulation of motivation: Contextual and social aspects', *Teachers College Record, 113*(2), 265–283.

Zimmerman, B. J. (2002) 'Becoming a self-regulated learner: An overview', *Theory Into Practice,* 41(2), 64–70.

Zumbrunn, S., Tadlock, J. & Roberts, E. D. (2011) *Encouraging self-regulated learning in the classroom: A review of the literature.* Retrieved from http://www.mehritcentre.com/assets/documents/Self%20Regulated%20Learning.pdf

Chapter 18
Restorative approaches

It's frequently observed in schools that the same children tend to end up in detention over and over again. The belief that 'punitive' approaches to school discipline were proving ineffective or even counterproductive has led to an interest in 'restorative' practice approaches. These approaches appear strongly influenced by 'positive psychology' and frequently also import ideas from a variety of therapeutic disciplines like cognitive behavioural therapy.

The roots of this behaviour management strategy are 'restorative justice' programmes arising from criminology. Difficult to define and frequently implemented under a variety of different names, restorative justice is sometimes typified as a compromise position in the 'rehabilitation vs retribution' debate. Broadly, they might be defined as processes where the parties with a stake in a particular crime are brought together to resolve how to deal with the aftermath of the offence and what implications it has for the future. In essence, the focus of these approaches is to repair the harm caused by the criminal act, so that the victim and the offender have an opportunity to discuss the event and decide appropriate reparations for the offence.

Research into restorative justice suggests that victims and offenders tend to have higher satisfaction with the justice system using this approach compared the traditional approach, and offenders are more likely to complete restitution agreements and less likely to reoffend. The reported success of these programmes has led to similar systems, often influenced by therapeutic models, being imported into schools as 'restorative practice'.

Once again, the principles behind restorative practice are difficult to define and tend to operate under a wide variety of names. Typically they offer a compromise position between authoritarian and more *laissez-faire* disciplinary systems.

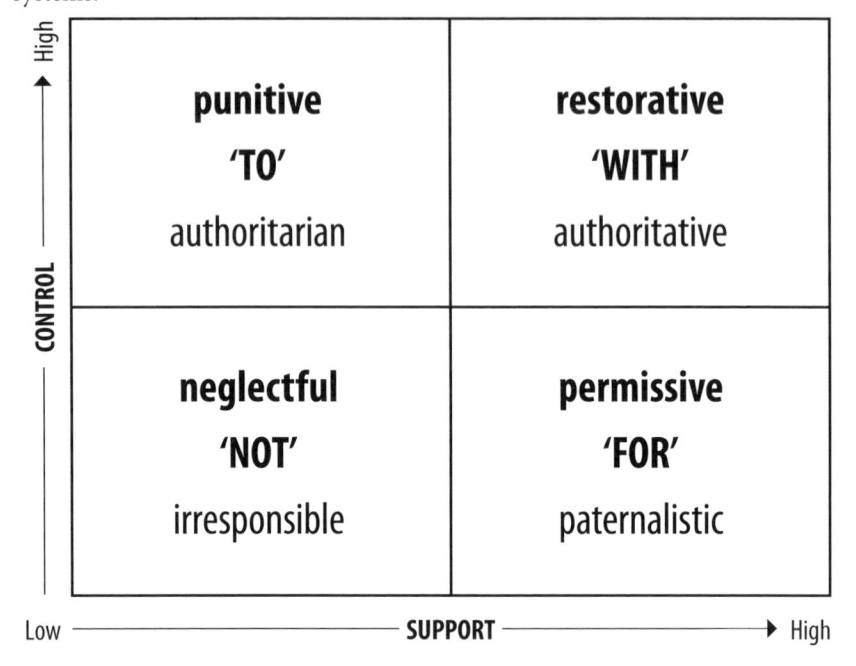

	Low SUPPORT → High
High CONTROL	**punitive 'TO'** authoritarian / **restorative 'WITH'** authoritative
Low	**neglectful 'NOT'** irresponsible / **permissive 'FOR'** paternalistic

Figure 1: Adapted from McCold and Wachtel (2003)

Restorative practice isn't intended as a permissive or 'soft option' in terms of school discipline – but neither is it a 'zero-tolerance' approach (see pages 157-159). The idea is that students will be more likely to make positive changes in behaviour (i.e. be more cooperative and work better in lessons) when teachers exert authority in a process which includes the student. What this often means in practice is that teachers and students discuss the events which took place with a view to resolving conflict and repairing the relationship. The intended outcome is that the student recognises the impact of their behaviour and takes responsibility for it, making some form of reparation.

Positive psychology

We see the influence of positive psychology in all sorts of areas of education: for example, the idea of 'teaching for happiness' or 'teaching mindfulness' and many of the ideas underpinning 'character education'.

Positive psychology arose out of the 'Humanistic approach' developed by psychologists like Abraham Maslow (most well known for the 'hierarchy of needs') and Carl Rogers, who developed theories around human happiness and helping people to thrive or reach their potential. Positive psychology was a term probably coined by Maslow, but has become strongly associated with the work of Martin Seligman – its philosophy essentially the same as humanistic approaches: to understand the nature of human happiness and well-being.

Applied within education, this approach tends to focus upon how schools can promote positive emotions and relationships, engagement and a meaningful sense of purpose, and positive goals leading to accomplishment. Seligman suggests these form five distinct elements – summarised by the acronym PERMA:

P   Positive Emotion

E   Engagement

R   Positive Relationships

M Meaning and Purpose

A   Accomplishment

There appears to be a clear influence of positive psychology in opposition to more 'behaviourist' ideas within restorative practices applied in schools. For example, the behaviourist approach is often typified as an impersonal process focused on the punishment of rule-breaking, leading to the individual needs of students being ignored. However, as we saw in Chapter 15, this may be an unfair caricature.

Explicit application of positive psychology in schools often includes references to restorative approaches. For example, Toni Noble and Helen McGrath use Seligman's five pillars of positive psychology in their Positive Educational Practices (PEPs) framework and suggest that the adoption of restorative practices promotes empathy, conflict management skills and social responsibility as well as repairing damaged relationships. They see this as part of a whole-school approach based on positive psychology which includes building resilience and emotional literacy skills, ensuring students experience positive emotions like a feeling of belonging and optimism, making students aware of and giving them opportunities to develop their cognitive and character strengths, and developing a sense of meaning and purpose.

More generally, positive psychology is often cited in support of the claim that schools should consciously direct the majority of their efforts on building and maintaining relationships between teachers and students by encouraging empathy and creating a sense of safety and trust where both parties can express their thoughts, feelings and needs; encouraging self-actualisation and optimistic beliefs about personal development; and supporting individual and shared responsibility.

Despite the natural appeal of applying positive psychology in education, the theory has faced significant criticism. Firstly, there's a concern that much positive psychology is based on circular reasoning and poorly-defined terms. Instead of demonstrating how positive attitudes explain things like achievement or well-being (and rigorously defining these outcomes), positive psychology merely describes a correlation between mental health and having a sociable, cheerful, goal-driven and status-seeking approach to life. We should also note that there's a difference between describing something as 'good' and prescribing it as 'good'. Whilst optimism is generally associated with good mental health and well-being, this does not necessarily mean that the prescription to 'think optimistically' will necessarily ensure you feel any better. In addition, Borton and Casey have shown that trying to suppress negative feelings actually makes you think about them more and, contrary to our intuitions, discussing our problems with someone else often makes them worse.* Finally, there's the accusation that positive psychology tends to pathologise normal emotions and behaviour, labelling ordinary feelings of sadness or anxiety as 'bad', and underestimating their adaptive function (e.g. defensive pessimism – predicting negative events so that you can take action to avoid or prepare for them).

Cognitive-behavioural therapy

An alternative psychological foundation for restorative practice has been cognitive behavioural therapy (CBT). The focus in CBT is to identify and change patterns of thinking or beliefs which underlie behaviours which are unhelpful to the individual. It's often typified as a problem-solving, therapeutic approach – finding ways to better cope with 'here and now' practical problems (rather than by analysing childhood experiences).

Albert Ellis developed some of the core principles involved in CBT back in the 1950s and 60s. He developed Rational Emotive Behavioural Therapy (REBT) which emphasises the role of 'faulty thinking' (an individual's interpretation or view of an event or situation) which gives rise to emotional distress and subsequent unhelpful behaviours (e.g. avoidance coping). This might seem intuitive to many teachers. For example, a student faced with an impending exam may believe that they will fail regardless of what they do, so they find ways to distract themselves from this anxiety (e.g. procrastination) and fail to revise for the exam.

---

*   Zech, E. & Rimé, B. (2005)

In restorative practice, these elements of CBT tend to involve encouraging the student to relate their offending behaviours to the thoughts and feelings which caused them. By exploring alternatives to the way the student interpreted an event and emotionally reacted to it, the idea is that the student finds better ways to respond to these events in future.

Whilst optimistic claims were initially made for the efficacy of CBT as a treatment for mental illness, much of the empirical evidence supporting these has come into question – not least because, along with other forms of psychotherapy, there's no easy way to create a 'double-blind' arrangement (where the recipient and the person giving the treatment are unaware of whether they are in the experimental or the control condition of the study) within randomly controlled trials. This means that the positive results for CBT may be influenced by the beliefs and expectations of the people involved. A recent meta-analysis suggests that effect sizes for CBT outcomes for treating depression have been steadily declining since the 1970s, implying that sources of bias may have given a distorted view of its efficacy. After all, if CBT was genuinely working, we'd expect its apparent effectiveness to remain the same or even improve over time (as therapists refine better ways to apply it). Instead, its apparent effectiveness appears to be declining over time – possibly as researchers refine the methodology used to test its effectiveness.

Do restorative approaches work?

It's almost impossible to give an empirical answer to this question. Case studies appear to provide very positive evaluations for programmes. For example, Littlechild and Sender (2010) conducted interviews with students and staff at four residential homes for young people with developmental and physical disabilities and provided very positive evaluations of restorative justice. However, data from police call-outs was more mixed. The researchers gave a broadly positive evaluation of the restorative approach used, but noted that one unit had an increase in call-outs! It's possible that the decrease in call-outs at the three other units wasn't necessarily due to the introduction of restorative justice programme.

An area where more systematic evidence is available is the success of anti-bullying programmes, many of which use restorative justice principles. For example, restorative approaches are commonly used in conjunction with sanctions within secondary schools to tackle bullying.

A report for the DfE[*] examined the range of practices used in schools and attempted some evaluation of their effectiveness. They found that over two-

---

[*] Thompson, F. & Smith, P. K. (2011)

thirds of schools used some form of restorative practice in tackling bullying and that these approaches were recommended by the majority of local authorities above the use of sanctions. The survey reported that 97% of both primary and secondary schools rated restorative approaches as effective in reducing bullying, with high proportions of both school types rating them as cost-effective and easy to implement. Small group discussions (circles) were the most common approach in primary schools (96%) whereas some form of restorative discussion was the most common in secondary schools (90%).

So, while these kinds of anti-bullying programmes are popular and perceived to be effective, there's little evidence to support their adoption beyond case studies. The fact that most schools mix restorative programmes with sanctions makes it difficult to pick apart whether these programmes are effective as practised in schools. Historically, the evidence supporting the general effectiveness of anti-bullying programmes is mixed. For example, in one meta-analysis which examined the effectiveness of school-based anti-bullying programmes, researchers found what appeared to be a 'significant effect', but the effect size was very small and the researchers were concerned that this might be due to publication bias. Thus, they concluded that the school-based anti-bullying programmes they reviewed were not particularly effective in reducing bullying or violent behaviour in schools.

Other studies have reported more positive outcomes. Another meta-analysis suggested that significant reductions in bullying tended to be associated with more intensive programmes; programmes including parent meetings, firm disciplinary methods, and improved playground supervision. However, work with peers (including things like peer mediation, peer mentoring, and encouraging bystander intervention) was associated with an increase in victimisation. They recommend that work with peers (arguably a central feature of restorative practice approaches to reducing bullying) should *not* be used.

Despite mixed and sometimes disappointing evidence of effectiveness with regard to bullying, the popular perception of restorative practice has led some schools to implement these sorts of programmes as whole-school behaviour management systems. There is a great deal of variation in how these models are applied, but typically they involve facilitated discussion between the teacher and student about low-level disruption in lessons in place of – though sometimes in addition to – a direct sanction. Again, there are many case studies reporting positive effects for these programmes, but systematic quantitative evidence is thin on the ground.

Evidently there are all sorts of difficulties in trying to implement restorative practice programmes in schools. Perhaps the biggest problem is that it is used as a blunt tool and sometimes places the culprit's needs over those of the victim. This becomes even more of an issue when such programmes are used for issues of low-level disruption. It's possible that where the student genuinely accepts they were in the wrong and is keen to make amends, the approach may be quite successful. However, we might expect much less success where the student isn't prepared to accept any responsibility or tries to manipulate the discussion to appear a victim.

Restorative approaches are a response to the perception that the same students end up in detentions over and over again. If these same students who simply end up in endless 'conflict resolution discussions' instead, then it's not clear how they offer much benefit. Ultimately, if a student merely goes through the motions and isn't interested in taking responsibility for their actions, there's the risk that such systems may inadvertently undermine teachers and fail to promote good behaviour in schools.

Into the classroom

Restorative practice is intended as compromise between permissive and 'zero-tolerance' approaches to school discipline. In practice the teacher and the student are brought together to discuss the impact of the behaviour on the lesson and find ways forward so that the behaviour isn't repeated. Positive psychology places this process within a broader context related to promoting positive emotions and relationships, creating engagement and a meaningful sense of purpose, and identifying positive goals. However, whilst this is an attractive proposition, it's not easy to evaluate whether the inclusion of concepts from positive psychology enhances the original restorative justice model. Many teachers are unaware that some of the claims of positive psychology are contested and controversial.

Likewise, therapeutic approaches like CBT have influenced restorative practices; typically by encouraging students to understand the relationship between their behaviour and the thoughts and feelings which caused them. The idea is to help the student adopt more helpful ways of thinking about the situation in the classroom and encourage more appropriate emotional and behavioural responses to that situation in future. However, once again, it is difficult to evaluate whether this therapeutic approach has advantages over the original model. Whilst CBT is considered an evidence-based approach to psychotherapy, there are questions about its efficacy.

Finally, there are important questions about both positive psychology and CBT being applied to schools. Do these approaches encourage teachers to 'pathologise' poor behaviour in the classroom? Do they encourage an anxious pre-occupation with the 'self' and stigmatise feelings of sadness or worry which are a normal part of the human condition?

Restorative approaches to tackling bullying have become very popular in schools, but once again the evidence of their effectiveness is quite mixed. Where anti-bullying programmes have been effective, they appear to involve quite intensive programmes involving parent meetings, firm disciplinary methods, and improved playground supervision. However, things like peer mediation and peer mentoring seem to have a negative effect – potentially increasing victimization.

What every teacher needs to know about restorative practices

- Restorative approaches to behaviour management are intended as a way of resolving conflict and repairing the relationship between student and teacher (and sometimes between students).
- The outcome is that the student recognises the impact of their behaviour and takes responsibility for it (e.g. through making some sort of reparation).
- Teachers should be aware that therapeutic approaches arising from fields like positive psychology and cognitive behavioural therapy are not without criticism.
- Whilst they have intuitive appeal and an evidence base outside of education, it may be wise to approach educational claims based on these disciplines with a degree of professional scepticism.
- Reviews of anti-bullying programmes provide mixed support. Where these programmes appear to be effective, they involve parent meetings, firm disciplinary methods, and improved playground supervision rather than peer-mediated processes.

References

Borton, J. L. S. & Casey, E. C. (2006) 'Suppression of Negative Self-Referential Thoughts: A Field Study', *Self and Identity*, 5, 230-246.

Didau, D. (2015, June 28) *20 psychological principles for teachers #17 Classroom management*. Retrieved from: www.learningspy.co.uk

Ferguson, C. J., San Miguel, C., Kilburn, J. C. & Sanchez, P. (2007) 'The effectiveness of school-based anti-bullying programs: A meta-analytic review', *Criminal Justice Review*, 32(4), 401-414.

Fernández-Ríos, L. & Novo, M. (2012) 'Positive Pychology: Zeigeist (or spirit of the times) or ignorance (or disinformation) of history?' *International Journal of Clinical and Health Psychology*, 12(2), 333.

Gable, S. L. & Haidt, J. (2005) 'What (and why) is positive psychology?' *Review of general psychology*, 9(2), 103.

Johnsen, T. J. & Friborg, O. (2015) The effects of cognitive behavioral therapy as an anti-depressive treatment is falling: A meta-analysis, *Psychological Bulletin*, Vol 141(4), 747-768.

Latimer, J., Dowden, C. & Muise, D. (2005) 'The effectiveness of restorative justice practices: A meta-analysis', *The prison journal*, 85(2), 127-144.

Littlechild, B. & Sender, H. (2010) *The introduction of restorative justice approaches in young people's residential units: A critical evaluation.* NSPCC.

McCold, P. & Wachtel, T. (2003) 'In pursuit of paradigm: A theory of restorative justice'. Paper presented to the 13th World Congress of Criminology, Rio de Janeiro, Brazil, *International Institute for Restorative Practices,* 10, p. 15.

Miller, A. (2008) 'A critique of positive psychology – or 'the new science of happiness', *Journal of Philosophy of Education*, 42(3-4), 591-608.

Noble, T. & McGrath, H. (2008) 'The positive educational practices framework: A tool for facilitating the work of educational psychologists in promoting pupil wellbeing', *Educational and child psychology*, 25(2), 119-134.

Thompson, F. & Smith, P. K. (2011) *The use and effectiveness of anti-bullying strategies in schools.* Research Brief DFE-RR098. Department for Education.

Ttofi, M. M. & Farrington, D. P. (2011) 'Effectiveness of school-based programs to reduce bullying: A systematic and meta-analytic review', *Journal of Experimental Criminology*, 7(1), 27-56.

Zech. E. & Rimé, B. (2005) 'Is Talking About an Emotional Experience Helpful? Effects on Emotional Recovery and perceived Benefits', *Clinical Psychology and Psychotherapy*, 12, 27-87.

Chapter 19
Social norms

Another approach to improving behaviour in lessons is encouraging adherence to social norms. Social norms are the (often unwritten) rules about how we behave in a social context. One of the functions of social norms is to distinguish who is part of our group and who is an outsider (which will be explored further in Chapter 20). Behaving in accordance to the norms of our group, especially when there is a 'cost' attached, signals our membership of that group. Breaking social norms carries with it a risk of exclusion from the group.

Humans are social animals and benefit enormously from shared resources, protection, and the ability to engage in acts of reciprocal altruism with reduced risks of exploitation within social groups. Conversely, exclusion from a group tends to have a highly detrimental effect on an individual's capacity to survive and reproduce. Therefore, we've evolved a complex range of strategies for maintaining our membership and status within social groups.

It's hard to see how society could function at all if we didn't conform to some fairly predictable set of rules about how we behave. Some of these norms become enshrined as formal laws, like driving on the left in the UK. However, many involve unspoken arrangements, merely triggering disapproval from others if we break them, e.g. the rules of queuing, or saying 'please' and 'thank you'. Like all cultural institutions, schools possess social norms regarding the behaviour of students. Some of these are explicitly communicated through school rules, but many are based on the unspoken expectations of the teachers and students who make up the school.

Normative influence

The power of this desire to fit in with a group was demonstrated by Solomon Asch in a famous series of experiments conducted in the 1950s. He asked groups of students to make a series of comparative judgement about the length of a line:

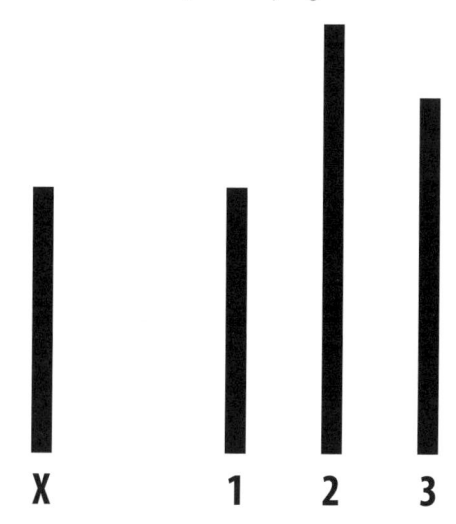

Figure 1. Which of the lines (1, 2 or 3) matches the length of the target line 'X'?
Would you pick '3' if everyone else in your group apparently thought that was the right answer?

What the participant didn't know is that the other people in the group were actually 'confederates' of the experimenter, instructed to deliberately give wrong answers on certain critical trials. Asch was investigating the extent to which the participant would conform to the rest of the group by also giving the wrong answer. He found that 25% of participants would disregard the wrong answer given by the rest of the group and give the correct answer every time. However, 75% of the participants gave at least one wrong answer and 5% of the participants followed the group in giving the wrong answer on every occasion. For Asch, this demonstrated a strong human instinct to fit in, even with a group of strangers and when the task involved unambiguously wrong answers.

Asch went on to use this experimental technique to examine the key variables which strengthen and weaken normative influence. He found that when participants could give their answers in private (by writing them down) they were less likely to conform to the group. He also found that the strength of normative influence was greatly diminished by a lack of unanimity; the presence of a 'fellow dissenter' making it much easier to act against the behaviour of the rest of the group.

Further insight into the factors which appear to underlie normative influence comes from the research of Robert Cialdini. For example, Cialdini and Goldstein (2004) identify three major components to social influence: accuracy, affiliation and maintaining a positive self-concept.

The Goal of Accuracy represents an individual's motivation to be right thinking or possess the correct information when making a decision. They make the point that individuals often look to social norms to gain an accurate understanding of and effectively respond to social situations, especially during times of uncertainty. For example if you were to go a highly formal meal for the first time you might be confronted by more cutlery than you knew what to do with. For guidance you might look to see which knife, or fork, or spoon other people were using for each course.

The Goal of Affiliation represents an individual's motivation to create and maintain good relationships with others. In essence we tend to adopt the behaviour of others so they will be more likely to like us. Quite superficial characteristics tend to trigger this kind of behaviour; for example physical attractiveness, perceived similarity (e.g. a shared birthday or the same name), ingratiation (e.g. remembering a person's name or mild flattery – though it's worth noting that whilst the target tends to develop more positive feelings towards the person, onlookers tend not to), and reciprocation (the obligation to repay others for what we have received from them).

An interesting aside to this influence of bolstering affiliation through reciprocation is the Franklin effect. The Franklin effect exploits cognitive dissonance by getting someone who doesn't like you to do a small favour for you. As a result, that person often develops more positive feelings towards you. For example, asking a challenging student to carry some books to another classroom for you.

The Goal of Maintaining a Positive Self-Concept represents our tendency to maintain our concept of self through behaving consistently with past "actions, statements, commitments, beliefs, and self-ascribed traits". When we have behaved in a particular way in the past, or expressed strong views about a situation, there is a motivation to behave in a way consistent to that in the future. Cognitive dissonance plays a strong role in this process of maintaining a self-concept. Cognitive dissonance refers to the uncomfortable state of having thoughts, beliefs, or attitudes which are inconsistent with our behaviours. In essence, if we have done something a certain way for a long time, then we tend to believe that those behaviours are correct.

The danger for students is that should they develop patterns of disruptive behaviour, their attitudes to that subject or school generally will tend to try to justify that behaviour. For example, the student adopts beliefs like 'school is pointless' or 'I can't be bothered with maths' so that their attitudes appear consistent with the disruptive behaviour.

Applying normative influence

Psychologists have attempted to apply normative influence in order to promote pro-social behaviour. For example, a study by P. W. Schultz used normative messages in order to encourage hotel guests to conserve energy. In this study, hotel guests were randomly allocated to a number of different messages relating to energy conservation. The control group only received information about the hotel's energy conservation policy e.g. 'Washing towels every day uses a lot of energy, so using towels is one way you can conserve energy'. Whereas another group additionally received normative information about energy conservation involving descriptive norms e.g. 'Nearly 75% of hotel guests choose to reuse their towels each day' and injunctive norms 'Many of our guests have expressed to us their approval of conserving energy'.

This study is interesting as it appears to show that merely trying to change attitudes (by providing information about the importance of energy conservation) appeared to have little effect on behaviour. The presence of a 'normative message' along with this information appeared to have a much stronger effect on the behaviour of guests.

Normative messages have also been used to try to reduce alcohol consumption amongst US students. For example, a study by Brian Borsari reviewed various social influence strategies used to encourage moderation in drinking and reported that in some cases normative messages about drinking led to reduced self-reported alcohol consumption. This study suggested there were a range of cognitive factors related to perceived norms which influenced behaviour:

- Descriptive and injunctive norms: 'a student will match the drinking they perceive other students doing (descriptive norm) and approving of (injunctive norm)'.
- Pluralistic ignorance: 'individuals assume that their own private attitudes are more conservative than are those of other students, even though their public behaviour is identical'.
- Attribution theory: 'the student observes others drinking heavily, it is assumed that such excessive use is typical, resulting in elevated norms'.

A combination of these processes leads to exaggerated norms for drinking, which then perpetuated themselves when new students observed others drinking heavily. This led to researchers attempting to use messages based on descriptive and/or injunctive norms to try to correct this exaggerated view of acceptable drinking. In the review, Borsari points to a number of successful attempts to reduce self-reported alcohol consumption using descriptive and injunctive normative messages.

Applying normative influence in schools

It's not difficult to imagine the various normative influences which might affect student behaviour in the classroom. Students hold ideas about the typical behaviour of their peers in lessons and the popularity or approval of those peers amongst their fellow students. It seems likely that students who misbehave in lessons will think the behaviour of other students is worse than their own (despite being equally disruptive). It also seems plausible that students who observe other students behaving poorly in the classroom will assume that such behaviour is typical, thus elevating the norm of disruptive behaviour.

To a great extent, schools have always tried to create social norms within their institutions to support a positive classroom climate. Either through explicit messages like school rules or through implicit mechanisms like ethos or traditions, schools attempt to separate their institutions from the 'mundane world' outside their gates.

Long established schools, whether in the state or independent sector, are often remarkable for their extensive lineage of school traditions and small rites and practices which mark the 'other worldliness' of their institutions. Some private schools provide an almost 'cloistered' atmosphere (quite literally in some cases given their historical origins) which helps create the impression that you are entering a world that in some ways is very separate from everyday life. Schools use a wide variety of techniques to create a strong sense of social norms specific to their institution: school uniforms are perhaps the most common and most visible strategy.

In social learning theory, Albert Bandura suggests that whilst we learn through vicarious reinforcement (e.g. observing others being rewarded and imitating that behaviour) we also form a set of 'mental representations' of acceptable behaviour specific to a social environment which regulates how we act. It seems likely that these traditions, small rituals and changes in dress all act as cues which facilitate behaving within a set of pro-social normative influences within the environment of the school.

One of the difficulties for many schools is how to create this strong sense of pro-social norms within the institution so that anti-social behaviours (e.g. bullying) are not imitated. There's not much empirical evidence looking specifically at this question, but there is some support from a recent study of a successful anti-bullying programme.

Elizabeth Paluck and her team attempted to test the idea that students attend to the behaviour of their peers to build a sense of what is socially normative and modify their own behaviour in response. They randomly allocated an anti-conflict intervention across 56 schools with 24,191 students – but what's really interesting is that they measured every school's social network ("whom did you choose to spend time with, face to face or online?"), before randomly selecting 'seed groups' of students and assigning them to an intervention that encouraged a public stance against conflict at school. They found that treatment schools reported fewer disciplinary problems compared to the control group. Furthermore the effect was stronger where these 'seed groups' contained more socially connected students.

They concluded that students pay particular attention to the behaviour of certain individuals in their community as they infer which behaviours are socially normative and adjust their own behaviours accordingly. This offers some interesting ways forward with research examining how behavioural climates are produced and changed.

Classroom routines

Indeed, it seems likely that incidences of low-level disruption in lessons are similarly occasions where students make socially normative judgements and adjust their own behaviour in line with these norms. One example of where normative influence has been exploited to improve behaviour comes from Doug Lemov's observations of effective teachers. In *Teach like a Champion*, Lemov identifies a set of classroom routines which, he suggests, work together to create a positive classroom culture.

Schools often try to sell education through trying to change attitudes, for example inspirational talks or aspirational values, but whilst these messages may be effective for some students, many will merely 'talk the talk' rather than 'walk the walk'. One reason Lemov's approach may be successful is that rather than trying to promote a positive culture through psychological or social manipulation of attitudes or beliefs (c.f. growth mindset, see Chapter 11), the routines effectively create a strong set of social norms based on simple, visible behaviour routines.

The success of Lemov's system probably stems from its behavioural focus and uniformity. However, therein also lays the controversy. For some critics, it denies practitioners the chance to discover effective systems for themselves which reflect their unique personality and approach to teaching. Proponents of these systems might reasonably argue that the purpose of these routines is not to suppress creative or imaginative teaching, but to allow teachers to focus that creativity on their actual teaching rather than battling for control of the classroom.

It seems likely that using uniform behavioural routines promotes a strong normative influence to support a positive classroom culture. In light of this, there are interesting questions which teachers might ask themselves.

We know that conformity benefits from unanimity; therefore the uniformity of Lemov's routines likely underlies their effectiveness. However, does the creation of positive classroom norms require strict uniformity in routines used across a school, or merely an element of consistency? For example, all teachers have an entry routine, but what that routine happens to be may be different for a science lesson compared to a PE lesson.

Do some routines do more 'work' than others? For example, are entrance and settling routines a more important factor in promoting positive classroom behaviour than the transition routines a teacher uses? There may be some routines worth adopting as a whole-school approach and others which might be left to the professional judgement of the teacher.

Into the classroom

As social animals, humans are highly sensitive to the unspoken rules – the social norms – which govern social interaction and group membership. Schools have long attempted to foster pro-social norms through school rules, and the ethos and values they promote, but there may be some benefits to applying these ideas more explicitly to classroom behaviour.

Students develop beliefs about the social norms of behaviour in the classroom through observing their peers (especially peers who enjoy popularity or approval amongst other students). Students who often observe other students disrupting lessons will assume that such behaviour is socially normal and acceptable. They may form negative attributions related to the teacher or the subject based on these negative social norms, which act to reinforce the disruptive behaviour in future lessons.

Schools might consider trying to exploit the positive power of normative influence. For example, using messages based on descriptive and/or injunctive norms to correct an exaggerated view of disruptive behaviour in lessons (e.g.

Injunctive messages: Many students have told us that they approve of the new behaviour expectations in lessons. Descriptive norms: 75% of students received no sanctions or warnings for behaviour last half-term).

There may also be a benefit in schools being aware of the social networks that students possess. Students are particularly influenced by the behaviour of socially connected students, and this has been used to improve the effectiveness of anti-bullying campaigns. It seems likely that these same students may also have a disproportionately large influence on social behaviour in the classroom. By recruiting socially connected students to help promote a positive classroom climate, schools may see a reduction in disruptions to lessons.

Another approach to reducing disruption has been the adoption of standardised classroom routines. These routines, like meeting and greeting students at the door before directing them to a seat, probably work because students quickly form socially normative judgements about acceptable behaviour and adjust their own behaviour in line with these norms. There is, however, an open question as to which routines might need to become a whole-school policy* (uniformity) and which merely require an element of consistency (e.g. teachers have a routine, but that routine might look a bit different in each classroom) in order to be effective.

What every teacher needs to know about social norms

- Students hold ideas about the normality and acceptability of disruptive behaviour in the classroom. They develop these norms more through observing the behaviour of their peers.
- Schools may be able to exploit normative messages to correct exaggerated beliefs about the extent or acceptability of disruptive behaviour.
- Students who are highly socially connected appear to have a disproportionate influence on the social norms of fellow students. Involving socially connected students in reinforcing pro-social normative messages may help reduce disruptive behaviour in lessons.
- Classroom routines can be a powerful way to explicitly communicate

---

*   There are likely particular advantages for students who struggle with behaviour not to have to change the rules every hour as they move from class to class.

> normative messages about behaviour expectations. Encouraging the adoption of standardised routines across a whole school may reduce disruptive behaviour, but potentially merely asking teachers to develop their own routines around a consistent set of expectations may be effective.
> - For some students, adapting to new rules each time they change classroom can be challenging so minimising inconsistency across a school is probably advantageous.

References

Bandura, A. (1977) *Social learning theory*, New York: General Teaching Press.

Bond, R. & Smith, P. B. (1996) 'Culture and conformity: A meta-analysis of studies using Asch's (1952b, 1956) line judgment task', *Psychological bulletin*, 119(1), 111.

Borsari, B. & Carey, K. B. (2001) 'Peer influences on college drinking: A review of the research', *Journal of substance abuse*, 13(4), 391-424.

Cialdini, R. B. & Goldstein, N. J. (2004) 'Social influence: Compliance and conformity', *Annual Review of Psychology*, 55, 591-621.

Lemov, D. (2011) *Teach Like a Champion, Enhanced Edition: 49 Techniques that Put Students on the Path to College (K-12)*, San Francisco, CA: Jossey-Bass.

Paluck, E. L., Shepherd, H. & Aronow, P. M. (2016) 'Changing climates of conflict: A social network experiment in 56 schools', *Proceedings of the National Academy of Sciences*, 113(3), 566-571.

Schultz, W. P., Khazian, A. M. & Zaleski, A. C. (2008) 'Using normative social influence to promote conservation among hotel guests', *Social influence*, 3(1), 4-23.

Chapter 20
In-group and out-group

As social animals, humans obtain a large number of advantages belonging to a group. As discussed in the chapter on social norms (see page 190) the advantages of freely sharing resources within a group comes with the disadvantage of potential exploitation. One adaptation to counter this disadvantage is to punish those who deviate from the social norms of the group. Another, in common with many other social animals, is our readiness to identify individuals as outside our social group and discriminate against them.

Schools try to create a sense of social identity and belonging through a wide variety of methods. Social norms like the school uniform and rules of conduct are intended to propagate pro-social norms within the school community. Organising students into forms and houses, and creating competitive events between these groups, is intended to foster a sense of membership to these groups and help students form positive relationships with their peers.

However, there is also a darker side to social identity. As friendship groups shift, some students find themselves suddenly ostracised or bullied by former members of their in-group. Our sense of social identity is a double-edged blade: identification with a group can cultivate esteem and confidence, but it can also promote hostility towards those identified as outside of that group.

Inter-group discrimination

Perhaps the most famous study of inter-group dynamics was the 'Robber's Cave' experiment conducted by Muzafer Sherif and his team in the summer of 1954. The researchers organised a camp for 24 white, middle-class boys at a

200-acre site within the Robber's Cave State Park in Oklahoma. The boys were divided into two teams and, at first, had no contact with one another. Over the course of five or six days, each group formed a strong in-group identity; they spontaneously adopted the names 'The Rattlers' and 'The Eagles'. As the groups became aware of the existence of the other, this reinforced their in-group identity and they became defensive that the out-group might be 'abusing' the camp facilities. The researchers organised competitive events between the two groups with desirable prizes for the winners and no consolation prizes for second place. These were intended to create some inter-group frustration and it appears to have been highly successful. Within a few days the groups started name-calling and singing derogatory songs about the other group, one group raided the others' camp and took any prizes they could locate, and almost came to blows when the theft was discovered. The researchers found that this was accompanied by the attribution of unfavourable characteristics to the out-group and favourable characteristics to the in-group.

Of course, it's impossible to fully control all the extraneous variables in a field study like the Robber's Cave experiment. However, laboratory studies appear to show quite similar processes at work. Henri Tajfel conducted a range of experimental studies aimed at identifying in-group and out-group bias. Comprehensive school students involved in the studies believed they were assigned to groups based on some characteristic. These characteristics were pretty superficial; for example, in one experiment, students were shown pairs of paintings and picked their preference. Afterwards, they were told they had been put into groups based on whether they had preferred paintings by Klee or Kandinsky. However, what the students didn't know was that they were randomly assigned into groups regardless of the pictures they had picked.

Despite the fact that these groups were based on trivial differences, Tajfel discovered that it influenced the decisions students made when playing an economic game. It seemed that, regardless of how the contrived groups had been put together, students made decisions that unambiguously favoured members of their in-group. However, this favour wasn't simply an attempt to maximise outcomes for the student's own group, but to maximise the advantage over the out-group. In other words, where a rational choice might have led to the in-group scoring more points this was rejected in favour of a choice which discriminated against the out-group.

What Sherif's and Tajfel's famous studies appear to show is that social groups readily form around even the most trivial (and sometimes non-existent) differences. We quickly form a social identity based on any identifiable objective or subjective criteria. When we interact based on these social group identities we tend to 'like' members of our in-group more (e.g. rate them as having more pleasant personalities) and act to maximise the difference in resources between our in-group versus the out-group. This positive impression of individuals within our in-group almost certainly benefits the self-esteem of the members of that group. The downside is that we tend to show discriminatory bias in favour of individuals identified as part of our in-group and against those we see as outsiders.

There's some evidence to suggest that there's a pattern to the cognitive development of in-group and out-group bias. Research by Dominic Abrams suggests that intergroup biases (e.g. bias in favour of a member of an in-group) tend to form earlier than intragroup biases (e.g. bias against in-group members who deviate from expected social norms). They studied 5 to 11-year-olds and found that as children get older, they cease to only make judgements based on group membership alone and start to combine these with social judgements on the basis of the individual's adherence or deviance from the social norms of their group. In adults, there is still strong evidence for in-group bias, however when deviant members of a group are considered, in-group deviants are rated lower than out-group deviants (this is sometimes called the black sheep effect).

This implies that the nature of bullying may alter as students get older. Younger students may target individuals they identify as outside of their social group, especially where that in-group has a social norm related to hostility towards an out-group and individuals believe their status within the group will be enhanced by hostile acts towards members of that out-group. In older students this may combine with hostility towards perceived deviants within their in-group. Certainly in my experience as a form tutor, it's not uncommon for bullying to emerge from volatile friendship groups – where the individual being victimised was formerly friends with the group that is doing the bullying, but has deviated from some expected attitude or behaviour of that group.

Overcoming inter-group discrimination

In the Robber's Cave experiment, Sherif's team tried to overcome the inter-group tensions and encourage friendly interaction between the two groups of boys. Initially, the boys were very resistant to this. The organised 'getting to know you' events like a bean collecting contest or showing a film produced no appreciable lessening of tension between The Rattlers and The Eagles. The researchers decided to create a series of contrived scenarios involving superordinate goals – tasks which would require significant cooperation between the two groups. For example, one scenario involved resolving a problem with the drinking water supply and another involved extricating a food truck which had become stuck in a ditch. Over time, these superordinate activities appeared to successfully reduce the inter-group tensions – to the extent that on the bus home the boys did not sit along group lines and The Rattlers used prize money to buy malted milks for both groups of boys.

Another well-known classroom intervention intended to break down inter-group prejudice is the 'jigsaw technique' developed by Elliot Aronson. In order to tackle racial prejudice amongst students, Aronson organised the teaching of a topic so that students worked in small but ethnically diverse interdependent groups. Each student in a group was given part of the topic to study, before all students in that group would bring their 'pieces' together to form the whole picture. Thus, all members of the group were brought together by a superordinate goal – having to work together to combine the separate information each student possessed. Aronson found that this method of classroom teaching appeared to reduce prejudice towards group members belonging to an ethnic minority. What's unclear is whether the reduction in prejudice was generalised beyond the individual member of a minority group taking part in the classroom exercise. It seems possible that attitudes towards the individual working within the group are improved, but that generally held prejudicial views towards that member's ethnic group may not be altered, at least in the long term.

As an aside, it's worth noting that reviews of academic outcomes appear to show the original jigsaw technique wasn't especially effective at helping students actually learn the material. One issue with group work is 'social loafing'. Social loafing is a phenomenon studied in a range of social contexts and refers to the fact that as you increase the number of individuals involved in a task, the effort of individuals tends to decline. A collaborative learning task needs to be organised so that all students have an important part to play (and a sense of being personally accountable) in helping the group to complete the activity. If you've taught a science practical with insufficient equipment for a class, then you've probably seen this problem in action: one or two students in the group get on with the practical, whilst any others tend to sit around with little to do. There's also some evidence that lower-achieving pupils may contribute less to collaborative activities unless encouraged to take part and articulate their thinking. Well planned group work may, on the other hand, reduce the cognitive load involved in a complex task (see Chapter 4 for a discussion about cognitive load). By dividing a complex task into components, each student may be better able to accommodate the elements they are given in working memory.

Stereotype threat

Another aspect of inter-group dynamics are the problems created for individuals who don't identify as a member of a majority group. For example, research from the US has looked at reasons why members of socially stigmatised groups such as African Americans or students from lower socio-economic status backgrounds frequently suffer poorer school outcomes. One factor identified has been the presence of 'stereotype threat'. Aware of the negative stereotypes related to their minority group, members of the group may lack a feeling of acceptance or belonging within the school as an institution. This absence of 'social belonging' may act to undermine performance in school.*

This has led to attempts to overcome stereotype threat through subtle interventions (related to 'growth mindset' interventions, see Chapter 11). In the United States Gregory Walton and Geoffrey Cohen tested an intervention designed to help students going through the challenging transition to college. Their view was that students' subjective interpretations of the quality of their relationships strongly influences their academic outcomes and well-being. Many students find the transition to college comes with social and practical difficulties, but interpreting that adversity as evidence of not belonging at the institution may make students much more likely to drop out or under-perform academically. The intervention they designed was intended to encourage a subtle shift in these attributions related to challenges of going to college.

The intervention itself was deliberately brief (rather than prolonged or high profile). The theory behind such interventions is that a subtle shift in attribution compounds into long-term effects through students entering a 'virtuous circle' of thinking. During transition to college, students can experience social setbacks and suffer feelings of isolation. Their well-being and performance, the researchers argue, depend greatly on whether such experiences are interpreted as evidence of 'not belonging here' rather than fairly typical for students making the move to college. They suggest that students who feel more assured of their belonging may initiate more social interactions and form better relationships, which help to support long-term attendance and performance in school.

The intervention provided students with a narrative that framed the challenges of going to college as shared and short-lived, and encouraged students to attribute adversity to common adjustment processes rather than related to personal deficits or their ethnic group. They found quite strong positive effects in terms of GPA scores (Grade-Point Averages) and well-being measures (e.g.

---

* Some researchers have argued that stereotype threat makes claims that are overblown, misrepresented and misinterpreted (e.g. www.psychologytoday.com/blog/rabble-rouser/201606/hard-truths-and-half-truths-about-race-campus-part-ii) subjective measures of happiness) for the students randomly assigned to the intervention group compared to the control, and this effect was strongest for African-American students who the researchers predicted would be most vulnerable to stereotype threat.

It's important to emphasise the brevity and subtlety of this intervention. For example, students involved in the intervention group were unaware of the intervention's effect, which suggests that its efficacy did not depend on conscious awareness of the messages contained in the intervention. There's also an issue of whether such interventions can be successfully scaled from these relatively small-scale studies and generalised to the different context of UK schools. However, there's a possibility that carefully designed and implemented interventions might potentially work to reduce stereotype threat and raise school performance.

Into the classroom

Creating a community with a sense of belonging is the ambition of all schools. Part of this involves creating a sense of being part of an in-group – whether in a local sense of membership of a form group or a house, or a larger scale sense of belonging to the school community. The psychological research shows that we readily identify with a social group, even forming in-groups with individuals with whom we actually have little in common other than perhaps fairly superficial labels. We might reasonably expect that the more meaningful these groups are the stronger or deeper the feelings of belonging will be. Most of the experiments into group identity have utilised competition as the basis of creating a sense of 'shared fate' for members of the group. Schools regularly utilise this in the shape of inter-form or inter-house style competitions and could probably quite straightforwardly find out from students whether these have successfully helped to foster a feeling of membership to those groups.

However, competition can also exacerbate inter-group tension. As the Sherif study suggested, high-stakes competition for limited resources (e.g. prizes) can create tensions which may lead to friction or even outright hostility between groups. On the other hand, it's important not to exaggerate the negative effects of competition – they likely intensify in-group/out-group distinctions – acting to bolster feelings of in-group membership[*] as well as out-group difference. Finding a level of healthy competition which effectively brings students together without overly setting different groups of students at odds with one another is probably a good bet for helping to create a sense of membership within a cohesive school community.

---

[*] For example Linnenbrink, E. (2005)

Beyond competition, however, schools also make use of superordinate goals in order to foster a broader spirit of school community. Charity fundraising events requiring cooperation across different forms, year groups or houses are one example commonly seen in schools. Perhaps the key element for creating a successful superordinate goal is that it requires significant cooperation between members of different groups – merely interacting isn't sufficient, again it requires a strong sense of 'shared fate' to overcome entrenched in-group and out-group distinctions.

This warning also relates to setting up collaborative learning activities in the classroom. There may be some benefit to students having to work together to accomplish a learning task, but the structure of these activities requires significant thought and effort in the planning to be effective. Poorly structured group work may end up being ineffective for learning and for reducing inter-group tensions within the classroom. Avoiding the problems of social loafing or redundancy and creating tasks which can be meaningfully broken up into independent components which are vital to the whole, is not easy.

Lastly, it is worth being aware of the fact that some students may interpret setbacks and challenges in school as evidence that they do not belong within that community. The sorts of subtle psychological interventions used to foster a 'growth mindset' or overcome stereotype threat are not easy for schools to implement effectively – though future research may provide ways to scale up such interventions in the future. In the meantime, it seems reasonable to gently assure students that social setbacks and feelings of isolation are pretty common experiences when transitioning to a new school or starting a new phase of education.

What every teacher needs to know about in-groups and out-groups

- Social identity can be a source of self-esteem and confidence, but the downside is that it tends to also come with greater discrimination or hostility towards individuals who are not part of the group.
- High-stakes competition for scarce resources likely increases inter-group tension. However, it probably also helps facilitate in-group membership. A balance involves finding a level of healthy competition which helps establish a feeling of belonging without creating unnecessarily high levels of friction between different groups.

- Superordinate goals, where different groups are forced to cooperate for the common good, likely reduces inter-group tension. Contriving opportunities for this – whether in the classroom as part of collaborative learning, or within a school community – is a non-trivial task.

- It's possible that some groups of students interpret setbacks and social challenges as evidence that they do not belong within a community. Evidence suggests this may be true for ethnic minority students as well as students from low-income families. Successful interventions to overcome this have involved creating a subtle change in thinking, so that challenges are interpreted as typical for any student rather than evidence of not belonging because of a student's membership to an ethnic or social group.

References

Abrams, D., Rutland, A. & Cameron, L. (2003) 'The development of subjective group dynamics: Children's judgments of normative and deviant in-group and out-group individuals, *Child development*, 74(6), 1840-1856.

Aronson, E. (1978). *The jigsaw classroom*, Sage.

Gini, G. (2006) 'Bullying as a social process: The role of group membership in students' perception of inter-group aggression at school', *Journal of School Psychology*, 44(1), 51-65.

Harvey, O. J., White, B. J., Hood, W. R. & Sherif, C. W. (1961) *Intergroup conflict and cooperation: The Robbers Cave experiment* (Vol. 10), Norman, OK: University Book Exchange, pp. 150-198

Jussim, L. (2016) 'Hard Truths and Half-Truths about Race on Campus, Part II', *Pyschology Today*, June 12th 2016 https://www.psychologytoday.com/blog/rabble-rouser/201606/hard-truths-and-half-truths-about-race-campus-part-ii

Linnenbrink, E. A. (2005) 'The dilemma of performance-approach goals: the use of multiple goal contexts to promote students' motivation and learning', *Journal of Educational Psychology*, 97(2), 197–213.

Mattingly, R. M. & Van Sickle, R. L. (1991) 'Cooperative learning and achievement in social studies: Jigsaw II', *Social Education*, 55(6), 392-395.

Spencer, B. & Castano, E. (2007) 'Social class is dead. Long live social class! Stereotype threat among low socioeconomic status individuals', *Social Justice Research*, 20(4), 418-432.

Tajfel, H., Billig, M. G., Bundy, R. P. & Flament, C. (1971) 'Social categorization and intergroup behaviour', *European Journal of Social Psychology*, 1(2), 149-178.

Walton, G. M. & Cohen, G. L. (2011) 'A brief social-belonging intervention improves academic and health outcomes of minority students', *Science* 331(6023), 1447-1451.

Part 3
Controversies

Professional scepticism

"... at the heart of science is an essential balance between two seemingly contradictory attitudes – an openness to new ideas, no matter how bizarre or counter-intuitive, and the most ruthlessly sceptical scrutiny of all ideas, old and new. This is how deep truths are winnowed from deep nonsense."

Carl Sagan, *The Demon-Haunted World*, p. 287

There's been a resurgence of interest in how evidence-based research and the scientific method can be applied to education, but it's important to acknowledge the limitations of this approach. Science can help us towards a better understanding of what *is*, but tells us little about what *ought* to be. The purpose of education (what education *ought* to be about) – whether it is to pass on the best that has been thought and said, gain qualifications and skills for the workplace, guide individuals towards becoming citizens of a 21st century global community, etc. – is a debate about social and political values (and beyond the scope of this book). All teachers should argue and debate the 'what *ought*' of education.

However, where we are reasonably clear about what education is trying to achieve, science can help with how to achieve it. One reasonably uncontroversial aim might be helping children to learn. Psychology and the scientific method can feasibly help us improve the answers to the questions: how do children learn? and how can we help them learn? Most teachers already have some ideas about the answers to these questions and this creates a natural tension in discussions about evidence-based research. Our beliefs about how the world works are important to us and it is natural to defend them when others say they are incorrect. However, whilst *people* are worthy of respect and consideration, people's *ideas* about how children learn deserve no special protection.

Science poses difficult questions to those who would claim expert authority. As a system of thought, it is a systematic way of asking questions which forces us to test our claims and reject or refine our beliefs over time. The reason we need scientific input into teaching is because without it the profession will simply continue to be vulnerable to bad ideas. We can't rely on charismatic gurus and evangelist 'experts' to point us in the right direction. Education is riddled with pseudoscientific claims about learning, for example: claims that children have visual, auditory or kinaesthetic learning styles, or that pressing lightly on each side of your sternum and your navel improves academic skills, or that we only remember 10% of what we read but 75% of what we do. We can't rely on experience alone to keep the profession free of pseudoscientific ideas.

As important as our ideas may be to us, we're genuinely not very good at evaluating them. Human reasoning is flawed in many ways – we possess numerous examples of what psychologists call cognitive biases. For example, where we feel personal responsibility for an investment of time, effort or money, we tend to overestimate the probability of that investment providing a benefit (called the sunk cost heuristic); where we are presented with evidence which directly contradicts firmly held beliefs, we tend to dismiss or ignore that evidence (called the backfire effect); we have a tendency to overestimate our abilities when we are unskilled and underestimate our abilities when we are highly skilled (called the Dunning-Kruger effect); we tend to overestimate the probability of an event occurring if we have a recent or emotionally charged memory for that event (called the availability heuristic). There are dozens of examples of cognitive biases which distort the way we reason and process information about the world.* As a consequence, reliance upon reflection or experience when evaluating our professional decisions is insufficient.

An important bias in our reasoning is that rather than trying to test our own ideas about the world, we tend to try to confirm them – by searching for and remembering evidence that supports our ideas, rather than evidence that challenges them. This is *confirmation bias* and there appears to be a reasonable explanation from evolutionary psychology for why we possess this major flaw in our logical reasoning. Like most cognitive biases, our propensity to seek to confirm our ideas rather than test them has probably emerged because it was adaptive – in that it helped humans to survive in our evolutionary past.

---

*   These examples and many more are explored in *What If Everything You Knew About Education Was Wrong?*

False positives and false negatives

Wherever we make a measurement, for example trying to discern the success or failure of an approach to teaching, we may make one of two types of error: Type 1 errors and Type 2 errors (summarised in Fig. 1).

		Reality	
		Actually true	Actually False
Observation/ Measurement	Appears true	✓	**Type 1 error** False negative
	Appears false	**Type 2 error** False negative	✓

Figure 1: A contingency table showing Type 1 and Type 2 errors.

For example, let's take the idea of a teacher doing action research in their classroom. They want to see whether making some sort of change to the way they teach helps students to learn. The teacher prepares some new materials for the lessons and then looks at student outcomes.

Imagine that student performance improves in some way – does this mean that the teacher's intervention caused this? Well, maybe! However, it might also be a Type 1 error, a false positive. The improvement in performance might be unrelated to the intervention (perhaps simply practice or natural variation that occurs when you measure performance).

Imagine that student performance stays the same – does this mean that the teacher's intervention didn't work? Again, maybe! However, it might also be a Type 2 error, a false negative. The poor performance might be unrelated to the intervention (perhaps students were tired when performance was assessed, or again it might simply be natural variation in performance).

Humans appear to have a cognitive bias towards making Type 1 errors at the expense of avoiding Type 2 errors – and there are some possible evolutionary explanations as to why. The suggestion is that throughout our evolutionary history making a Type 2 error has been a bit more dangerous than making a Type 1 error.

For example, consider the following scenario: You are walking along when you spot, just where you were about to step, a shape within the long grass. It might simply be a stick or a piece of rope, but there's a possibility that it might be a snake. In an instant we need to make a decision whether to step into the patch of grass or avoid it. Our decision looks like the table below (Figure 2).

		Reality	
		It's a snake	Not a snake
Observation/ Measurement	Appears to be a snake	We avoid stepping on it and we were right to	**Type 1 error** We avoid stepping on it when it was harmless
	Appears not to be a snake	**Type 2 error** We step on it and get bitten by the snake	We step on it and it was harmless

Figure 2: A contingency table showing the outcomes of detecting a snake in the grass.

If I step on the grass and there *is* a snake present (false negative – I wrongly thought there wasn't a snake) then the outcome is potentially much worse than if step around a patch of grass and there wasn't a snake present (false positive – I wrongly thought there was a snake).

Whenever you try to minimise one type of error (e.g. reduce the possibility of a Type 2 error) we increase the probability we make the other type of error (i.e. increase the chance of a Type 1 error). If I make the test of my observation or measurement very strict, I may be able to reduce the chance of a false positive error, but I inevitably increase the chances of making a false negative. In other words, if I'm very alert to the dangers of snakes, I'm more likely to make a false positive error (Type 1) and less likely to make a false negative error (Type 2).

There may be an adaptive advantage to making Type 1 rather than Type 2 errors. I'm less likely to step on poisonous snakes for the small cost of occasionally avoiding things that look a bit like snakes (but aren't). We can apply the same logic to a range of different scenarios: for example, should I eat this funny looking mushroom? Eating a poisonous mushroom is quite dangerous (false negative – I wrongly thought wasn't poisonous). Better to avoid the novel food even though it's actually safe to eat (false positive – I wrongly thought it was poisonous).

This also relates to our ability to perceive causal connections between events that correlate – an important part of conditional learning (see Chapter 15 on Behaviourism). I found water here last time, should I go back? Typically it is better to revisit on the off-chance there was a legitimate cause for the water being there (e.g. a hollow where rain collects) than miss that connection and have to search from scratch to discover a new source of water.

Going back to the teacher doing action research, we can create a similar contingency table:

		Reality	
		Intervention had an effect	Intervention had no effect
Observation/ Measurement	Performance improved	We think the intervention helped and it really did	**Type 1 error** We think the intervention helped when it really didn't
	Performance didn't improve	**Type 2 error** We think the intervention didn't help when it really did	We think the intervention didn't help and it really didn't

Figure 3: A contingency table showing the outcomes of a teacher's action research

Millions of years of evolution appear to have wired us to prefer Type 1 errors and avoid Type 2 errors (to see causal connections where none exist), so it's not surprising that if the action research appears to have a positive effect on performance, the teacher will assume the intervention caused this change in performance. Even assuming the researcher wasn't so wedded to their ideas that they (inadvertently) biased the outcome of the test, the correlation between 'something I tried' and the appearance of a 'positive outcome' convinces us that thing we did *caused* those outcomes. This process probably also underlies a great deal of superstitious and magical thinking – I had my lucky rabbit's foot and I won £10 on the lottery. In education, a lot of what we call 'best practice' is likely no better; I differentiated by learning styles and my students learnt more.

The problem is that there are lots of correlations in the world – and despite strong beliefs many of them are not causal. For example, there's a widespread belief that the weather influences arthritic pain. To test this theory Redelmeir and Tversky studied patients for more than a year but found no association between their arthritis pain and the weather conditions. Given that scientific studies have found no consistent association, they suggested that the popular belief persists because of people's tendency to perceive patterns where none exist. People are likely to remember evidence which appears to confirm their beliefs (e.g. when it rains and their arthritic pain is particularly bad) but quickly forget disconfirming evidence (e.g. when it rains and the pain isn't too bad).

Tyler Vigen is something of a collector when it comes to these sorts of correlations. In *Spurious Correlations,* he describes hundreds of variables which happen to correlate to one another*: for example, US spending on science, space and technology correlates strongly with suicides by hanging, strangulation and suffocation (r=0.9979), or the divorce rate in Maine correlates with per capita consumption of margarine (r=0.9926).

The trade-off (in evolutionary terms) for a system than is primed for pattern recognition and errs on the side of caution is that by reducing false negative errors we increase our capacity for making false positive errors. This readiness to perceive causal connections between unrelated events is compounded by the fact we also prefer people who believe the same things as us: something psychologists call the false consensus effect. We typically prefer to interact with people who validate (rather than challenge) our beliefs, leading us to believe that our beliefs are more common or more valid than they actually are.

As a consequence, we are unlikely to uncover the flaws in individual and even collective untested beliefs about teaching. What we need to do is regularly put our ideas about effective teaching into the crucible of science.

Science as a crucible for ideas

An important principle within science is falsification. The philosopher Karl Popper suggested that every genuine test of a theory is an attempt not to confirm it (which is easy if you only look for confirming evidence) but to falsify it; to refute it.

In this way, the process of science can be seen as an attempt to collectively correct for the essential biases in the way we form beliefs about the way the world works. Experiments are not conducted to simply confirm theories, but to test them to see where they fall down. In essence the scientific process isn't one of discovering the 'truth' – but a way of weeding out the Type 1 errors that tend to accumulate within a culture over time.

Popper thought scientists should be dispassionate about their theories but whilst we may endeavour to be impartial, in practice it's really, really hard to give up on our precious ideas (even when they fail). Individually, we are always likely to be wedded to some ideas more than others. Indeed, if we didn't champion our ideas then no one would ever hear about them! Thus, in practice

---

* You can also discover many more humorously spurious correlations for yourself on Tyler's website: http://tylervigen.com/discover

science evolves through a collaborative 'battle of ideas'; our theories have to survive the scepticism of our peers.

To actually test hypotheses about how children learn, quantitative research can play a powerful role. The controlled conditions and processes like 'blinding' help reduce the biases inherent to observations. However, it's important to remember that the purpose of things like randomised controlled trials (RCTs) is not to confirm theories but to falsify them. That's not to say that qualitative methods of research don't have a role to play in developing better ideas about how children learn. Qualitative research, for example based on case studies and interviews, is great for delving deep and generating hypotheses about learning. However, such methods are poorly suited for the falsification of ideas about learning. That's what laboratory experiments and RCTs in the field are really about: they can't tell us what will work in the classroom, but they can help identify which ideas fail. In this battle, meta-analysis (an examination of many studies in order to identify a general pattern in results) can be a useful tool. A quick way of spotting what has survived the crucible (so far) and what has failed.

On the other hand, the evidence from science is never cut-and-dry and good research adopts a language of uncertainty when it summarises the implications of its findings. A classic example of this problem was the EEF Toolkit reporting on the effectiveness of teaching assistants (TAs). The summary of the evidence on TAs suggested that they were highly expensive and providing very little impact, but the simplicity of the Toolkit belied the nuance of the conclusion. There were concerns that schools would reduce the numbers of TAs working in their schools, but it turns out that, where used effectively, TAs can provide a strong impact on students' attainment. A better conclusion would be that schools should look hard at how best to deploy TAs (which would require digging into the evidence of where TAs added value) – rather than sack them!* If we want pedagogy to ever rise above the level of homeopathy, we need teachers to develop their capacity for professional scepticism. That means asking searching questions when people make claims about teaching. Even if a source appears trustworthy, a professor of something or other or a headteacher from an 'outstanding' school, it's probable they are wedded to many ideas about education which simply have not been subjected to the crucible of science.

---

*   It's hard to know whether schools did reduce numbers of classroom assistants because of the poor rating they had on the toolkit, but there were certainly concerns raised that this was happening e.g. https://thesuttontrust.wordpress.com/2013/04/25/worlds-apart/

Into the classroom

One aspect of confirmation bias is the tendency to see correlations in a set of data as evidence of causes – seeing connections where none exist and ignoring other factors which may underlie the relationship we perceive. For example, as a teacher I adapt my lesson so that some children are taught visually (watching a video), others through a kinaesthetic task (building a model) and others through an auditory task (listening to a story). At the end of the lesson, I ask all the students to rate how much they have learnt – and the ratings are quite high. I conclude that my effort to differentiate by learning style has led to improved learning.*

However, that conclusion isn't warranted. At most I can say there was a correlation between my choosing to differentiate in this way and student ratings of how much they learnt. Of course, the validity of the measurement of learning is suspect (the improved ratings may not reflect how much students actually learnt) – but even beyond that, it would be an error to form a causal conclusion. For example, perhaps the material I was teaching was easier to learn than for other lessons, or perhaps students would have learnt equally well if I'd assigned them to different groups, or perhaps I communicated my expectation that there would be an improvement in learning and the students merely responded to these expectations.

Unfortunately, many ideas about how children learn and how we can help them learn within teaching have not been tested in any kind of rigorous way. Quite frequently, teachers are encouraged to adopt teaching techniques, curriculum changes and 'best practice' based on extremely weak evidence (if any at all). On the flip side, our strong feelings of ownership when it comes to our ideas means that we tend to ignore disconfirming evidence when it is presented to us. 'It works for me' may simply represent that person's bias – even 'it works for us' isn't more convincing given our capacity to form a false consensus with people who share our ideas. Instead, we need to subject ideas about how children learn and how we can help them learn to the crucible of science.

The astronomer and philosopher of science Carl Sagan suggested that we should subject all new ideas and theories to a series of rigorous tests, what he called a 'baloney detection kit'. Although he was writing about science, the kit applies equally well to new ideas and trends in education:

1. Wherever possible there must be independent confirmation of the 'facts'.
2. Encourage substantive debate on the evidence by knowledgeable proponents of all points of view.

---

* We also need to consider regression to the mean – see page 94 for an explanation.

3. Arguments from authority carry little weight – 'authorities' have made mistakes in the past. They will do so again in the future. Perhaps a better way to say it is that in science there are no authorities; at most, there are experts.

4. Spin more than one hypothesis. If there's something to be explained, think of all the different ways in which it could be explained. Then think of tests by which you might systematically disprove each of the alternatives. What survives, the hypothesis that resists disproof in this Darwinian selection among 'multiple working hypotheses', has a much better chance of being the right answer than if you had simply run with the first idea that caught your fancy.

5. Try not to get overly attached to a hypothesis just because it's yours. It's only a way station in the pursuit of knowledge. Ask yourself why you like the idea. Compare it fairly with the alternatives. See if you can find reasons for rejecting it. If you don't, others will.

6. Quantify. If whatever it is you're explaining has some measure, some numerical quantity attached to it, you'll be much better able to discriminate among competing hypotheses. What is vague and qualitative is open to many explanations. Of course there are truths to be sought in the many qualitative issues we are obliged to confront, but finding them is more challenging.

7. If there's a chain of argument, *every* link in the chain must work (including the premise) – not just most of them.

8. Occam's Razor. This convenient rule of thumb urges us when faced with two hypotheses that explain the data equally well to choose the simpler

9. Always ask whether the hypothesis can be, at least in principle, falsified. Propositions that are untestable and unfalsifiable are not worth much. Consider the grand idea that our Universe and everything in it is just an elementary particle – an electron, say – in a much bigger Cosmos. But if we can never acquire information from outside our Universe, is not the idea incapable of disproof? You must be able to check assertions out. Inveterate sceptics must be given the chance to follow your reasoning, to duplicate your experiments and see if they get the same result.'

---

* Sagan, C. (200: 212-214)

What every teacher needs to know about professional scepticism

Scepticism is a professional responsibility. Every teacher owes it to the children they teach to resist poorly thought-out claims and pseudo-scientific mumbo jumbo. The following points might help you on your quest:

- There are strong biases in human reasoning and the scientific method can (over time) help to weed out the bad ideas that tend to accumulate within teaching. However, this requires teachers to develop professional scepticism towards claims made about how children learn and how we can help them learn.
- Be suspicious of 'experts'. Don't accept something just because there's a Dr or Prof in front of their name – especially if they are trying to sell you something. Don't be impressed by a long bibliography – how many of the books and articles did they write themselves? How many do they list which actually tested their claims in any robust way?
- Ask yourself, what would show the claim to be false? Is the claim structured in such a way that it can never be tested? e.g. the claim relates to outcomes that cannot reasonably be measured in any sort of accurate or valid way.
- Find out whether the claim has been tested. Assuming there's a testable claim, why hasn't this been done? e.g. if it claims to raise attainment or improve well-being, is there a well-controlled RCT to test those claims?
- Be wary of cherry picking. A common strategy of charlatans is to only present narrow evidence that appears to support their claim – whilst ignoring any body of work which refutes it. Is the evidence being provided only from a single study or just one researcher? Be a little proactive at least – check online to see what the counter-arguments are for a claim before you decide.
- Are they hostile or dismissive of people who disagree with them? Is the person selling the idea defensive when asked sceptical questions? Do they attack anyone who questions their claims rather than engage with the debate?

- If anyone says, "Well, you can't prove it *doesn't* work," remember that the burden of proof falls on the person making a scientific claim, it is not the sceptic who has to provide evidence that the claim is wrong.

References

Dekker, S., Lee, N. C., Howard-Jones, P. & Jolles, J. (2012) 'Neuromyths in education: Prevalence and predictors of misconceptions among teachers', *Frontiers in Psychology*, 3.

Didau, D. (2015) *What if everything you knew about education was wrong?* Carmarthen, UK: Crown House Publishing Ltd.

Geary, D. (2007) 'Educating the Evolved Mind: Conceptual Foundations for an Evolutionary Educational Psychology', in Carlson, J. S. & Levin, J. R. *Educating the evolved mind: Conceptual foundations for an evolutionary educational psychology*, IAP, pp. 1–100.

Goldacre, B. (2013) *Building evidence into education.* Retrieved from http://dera.ioe.ac.uk/17530/7/ben%20goldacre%20paper_Redacted.pdf on 20 March 2016

Howard-Jones, P. A. (2014) 'Neuroscience and education: myths and messages', *Nature Reviews Neuroscience*, 15(12), 817-824.

Redelmeir, D. A. & Tversky, A (1996) 'On the belief that arthritis pain is related to the weather', *Proceedings of the National Academy of Sciences* 93 (7): 2895–2896.

Sagan, C. (2000) *The Demon-Haunted World: Science as a Candle in the Dark*, US: Ballantine Books Inc.

Vigen, T. (2015) *Spurious correlations*, Hachette Books.

Willingham, D. T. (2012) *When Can You Trust the Experts?: How to Tell Good Science from Bad in Education,* John Wiley & Sons.

Willingham, D. T. (2014) 'People Aren't Stupid; Science Is Just Hard – Why We're Wrong to Quickly Dismiss Ed Research'. *Real Clear Education*, retrieved from http://www.realcleareducation.com/articles/2014/05/06/people_arent_stupid_science_is_just_hard_963.html on March 20th 2016

Chapter 21
Cognitive development

Most teachers' understanding of cognitive development begins and ends with the Swiss developmental psychologist, Jean Piaget. However, whilst teachers are often aware of Piaget's Stages of Cognitive Development, other aspects of his theory tend to be less well known.

Piaget's theory starts with the idea of schemas (discussed in Chapter 1). He suggests that children start with a set of fairly simple inherited behaviours (e.g. reflexes), but over time construct more complex models of the world – schemas – based on their interactions and experiences.

The key process of cognitive development involves what he called 'equilibration'. When a child's schema gives rise to predictable responses from the environment, this results in a state of equilibrium. If a new situation is experienced, the child will attempt to utilise a familiar schema. Where that schema produces the expected response, that new situation is 'assimilated'. Assimilation is where an existing schema can be applied to the new situation. The child simply 'adds' the example of the new object or condition to a schema it has already learnt.

However, when a student comes up with an unexpected response, they enter a state of disequilibrium, with an attendant sense of discomfort, puzzlement or uncertainty sometimes referred to as cognitive conflict. For example, a child may learn that you can bash a table with objects to make a pleasing noise. This works fine for a building block and a toy hammer (easily assimilated), but attempting this with an egg doesn't get the expected response. Piaget believed it was this mismatch between the schema and the response from the environment that drives cognitive development. To restore equilibrium, the child needs to accommodate the new object or situation. Accommodation is where a new schema is learnt or an existing one is modified.

Jean Piaget believed learning occurred when there was a mismatch between a schema held in mind and feedback from the environment. For example, what would happen if you tried to use the restaurant schema to get a drink in a British pub. The mismatch, he argued, created a sense of discomfort – cognitive conflict – which was resolved by the modification of the schema to accommodate the new information. However, subsequent research suggests that schemata are highly resistant to change, and it seems that we are more likely to simply disregard information that doesn't accord with a schema rather than change it. Along with memory, there's evidence that schemata influence our attention, our perceptions and our interpretations of events, and thus can lead us to overlook anything that contradicts our prior beliefs and expectations.

There is also a question about whether schemas are actually modified at all, or whether newly acquired schemas merely sit alongside the old ones. If this were the case, the schema used in a particular situation depends upon which version of it is activated; subtle differences in the context, and the frequency with which a particular schema is used, may cause one schema to come to mind or a similar alternative one. For example, the persistence of science misconceptions and social stereotypes despite disconfirming evidence suggests we maintain prior schema in long-term memory rather than alter them. These simpler schemas appear to be retained and occasionally become active despite having learnt a more accurate conception.

This can make life difficult for teachers and their students. For example, you can teach a student all about photosynthesis, that the carbon which forms the basis of wood comes from carbon dioxide absorbed from the air, but when asked, 'Where does the wood of a tree come from?' the unusual context of the question doesn't activate the new schema and an older 'folk biology' schema may be activated instead which will lead the student to conclude that wood comes from soil. There's some evidence to suggest that scientific concepts do not replace or change earlier folk theories, but instead suppress them. This appears to falsify the Piagetian concept of 'accommodation' and cast doubt on the utility of teaching approaches which rely on cognitive conflict to create conceptual change: it may be that we don't change our ideas at all.

There are many other questions regarding Piaget's theory of cognitive development. For example, he claimed that children developed schema primarily through physical interaction with the world, but there's evidence that falsifies this view; for example, children with even quite severe physical disability can develop normal cognitive abilities. Finally, and perhaps most controversially, Piaget appeared to believe that cognitive development was in some way hampered by explicit teaching – that children learnt best by discovering these mismatches between schemas and the environment for themselves. This appears to be in opposition to Vygotsky, who saw cognitive development arising from social interaction with an expert (a 'more knowledgeable other') – though this contrast often appears glossed over in many discussions of constructivist approaches to teaching.*

However, perhaps the most problematic aspect of Piaget's ideas about how children learn was his 'stage theory' of cognitive development. Piaget claimed that all children pass through a predetermined sequence of four distinct developmental stages. It is this stage theory of cognitive development that has bewitched and bedevilled education for almost a century, guiding how we structure schools and curriculums.

Here's a brief summary of Piaget's four stages:

Sensorimotor (ages 0-2): In the beginning, a child's understanding of the world depends on their direct experience of perceptions and objects. Actions discovered first by accident are repeated and applied to new situations to obtain the same results. Toward the end of the sensorimotor stage, the ability to form primitive mental images develops as the infant acquires 'object permanence'. Until then, children have no idea that objects can exist apart from themselves.

Preoperational (ages 2-7): As children acquire language, they are able to represent the world through mental images and symbols, but these symbols depend on their own perception and intuition. At this stage, children are completely egocentric. Although they are beginning to take interest in objects and people around him, they are unable to see them from a viewpoint other than their own. Their understanding of the world is based on their very limited experiences; if they don't have an explanation for how the world works they will make one up. Centration is the tendency to focus on just one aspect of a complex situation. For example, Piaget observed that if you show a five-year-old identical glasses containing the identical amounts of liquid, she will say that they are the same. But, even if children watch you transfer the contents of one glass into a

---

* Indeed, some researchers have argued that a more complete view of Vygotsky reveals an interpretation of his theory that is potentially at odds with social-constructive theories of learning. This alternative view of Vygotsky is based on the view that his later work led towards seeking to understand the processes by which formal knowledge becomes internalised through education. In essence, they claim, Vygotsky can be interpreted as supporting the role of instruction and transmission of knowledge. See Yvon, L. et al (2013).

taller, narrower glass, they'll say that it now contains more than the other. This error occurs because young children focus on one feature – the height of the juice in the glass – and ignore another, equally important feature – the width.

Concrete Operations (ages 7-11): Mental operations – actions performed in the mind – permit children to think about the past and speculate about the future. The primary characteristic of concrete operational thought is its reversibility; children can mentally reverse the direction of their thought. A child knows that something that he can add, he can also subtract. He can trace his route to school and then follow it back home, or picture where he has left a toy without a haphazard exploration of the entire house. Operations are labelled 'concrete' because they apply only to those objects that are physically present. Conservation – the ability to see that objects or quantities remain the same despite a change in their physical appearance – is the major acquisition of the concrete operational stage.

Formal Operations (ages 11-16): Piaget's final stage coincides with the beginning of adolescence, and marks the start of abstract thought and deductive reasoning. Thought that is more flexible, rational, and systematic. The individual can now conceive all the possible ways they can solve a problem, and can approach a problem from several points of view. The adolescent can think about thoughts and operate on operations, not just concrete objects, and can think about such abstract concepts as space and time. As well as developing an inner value system, adolescents will also develop a sense of moral judgement.

According to Piaget, all children must pass through each stage, and the sequence of stages is fixed and immutable. Later stages evolve from and are built on earlier ones. Whilst all children proceed through the stages in the same order, they may progress through them at different rates. This understanding of child development has been passed on with the certainty of a natural law but is in fact just a metaphor which may or may not be a useful way of viewing the world.

Piaget's theory relies on two erroneous assumptions. Firstly that children's thinking is relatively stable at each stage of development, but then undergoes a radical shift, before stabilising again until the next developmental stage is reached. The second is that the developmental state affects all tasks and abilities consistently.

More recent research on cognitive development has supplanted stage theory accounts of cognitive development. We now know that infants have been found to have early, possibly native, competencies in certain domains. For example, very young children seem to show an almost innate knowledge of principles related to the physical world, biological causality, numbers and morality. As we discussed in Chapter 1, David Geary says these are part of 'biologically primary culture' – aspects of culture which are rapidly and effortlessly learnt because they granted advantages in our evolutionary past and so we have evolved to easily learn them. Futhermore, cognitive development looks more continuous and gradual than stage-like, and the way children perform cognitive tasks varies considerably. Children will not only perform different tasks in different ways, they may go about the same task in two different ways on successive days. This is supported by Siegler's 'overlapping waves' theory of development (see Chapter 2). Certainly children change as they age, but context matters: what children may think, believe or be able to do in one context, they may not be able to replicate in another.

An alternative to stage theories is the contextualist approach to cognitive development and learning. This approach takes the view that reasoning can be facilitated to more advanced levels when students interact with more capable others and with more advanced materials. This is the good old Zone of Proximal Development. Scaffolding to you and me. Mixed in with all this is the notion that cognition is *situated*, that it is to say, what we know is the product of society's knowledge within a specific context (in essence, we think and reason differently in different situations). This sounds a bit mysterious, but essentially all this means that cognitive development does not follow a predetermined linear progression and what children can do is a bit more complicated than Piaget would have us believe. Some aspects of development *are* determined by biology, but familiarity with particular contexts and the guidance of experts can have surprising results on what children are to be able to do. Obviously enough, students who are not familiar with particular knowledge domains, are not challenged by knowledgeable others, or find themselves in unfamiliar contexts, may evince less sophisticated reasoning.

Into the classroom

There is a developmental sequence (if not stages) from birth through adolescence, but trying to pinpoint where a particular child is in that sequence probably isn't very helpful. Simply tuning your teaching to a child's cognitive capabilities is unrealistic. If we decide that certain topics are beyond students or that particular ways of thinking may be unproductive, we condemn children with lower expectations. As we saw in Chapter 9, baseline assessments can be used to assess what children know, and the results can be very informative for instructional design. Teachers' judgement of students' developmental levels is important, but age shouldn't be seen as the main factor in determining what students are capable of learning. Given the huge variation in achievement within any age group, the concept of age-related expectations (ARE) is potentially misleading and dangerous. There are no age-related expectations in the real world; we can either do or not do something. Teachers are better off thinking about what prior knowledge is required to tackle a new topic, rather than worry about whether the topic is 'developmentally appropriate'.

Differences and similarities

Knowing about principles of cognitive development like centration or egocentrism may help us think productively and provide insights into how children are thinking, but it's important to know that these principles are not absolute and should never be applied to all children of a particular age.

Children sometimes understand a principle embedded in one task and fail to understand it in another. This is the problem of 'transfer', the fact that things we learn in one context rarely appear to advantage us even in apparently similar contexts. A description of the principle does not provide a foolproof guide to what children will understand, but knowing which tasks have worked well in the classroom and which have not is obviously useful. Keeping track of how well an activity works will be useful but we will also benefit from sharing this sort of information with other teachers – especially those who teach similarly aged children or the same subject.

Think about *why* students do not understand. Students' performances at any one time are not a reliable indicator of their abilities. If a student – or even the whole class – fails to understand a new concept, we shouldn't assume the task was developmentally inappropriate. It might be that students are missing the necessary background knowledge, or that a different presentation or scaffolding of the same material would make it easier to understand.

If we accept that students' failure to understand is not a matter of content, but either of presentation or a lack of background knowledge, then the natural extension is that no content should be off limits. Jerome Bruner suggested that children can gain an intuitive grasp of a complex concept before they have the background and maturity to deal with the same topic in a formal manner. His advice was to, "begin with the hypothesis that any subject can be taught effectively in some intellectually honest form to any child at any stage of development" (Bruner, 1960: 33).

Scaffolding

If we want students to be academically successful they must be given the language (and conceptual understandings) required for academic success. We need to understand that children are – for the most part – novices and we are experts. As such we think differently. The more students know the more they will be able to think about. We need to systematically build up their understanding of the world maintaining the expectation that they struggle with new and challenging material but with us there to support them in their journey to expertise.

What students know affects further learning. New knowledge will build upon existing schemas and so it's reasonable to build a bridge between a new topic and material with which students are already familiar. This bridge-building – or scaffolding as it's more usually termed – is an important factor in dealing with the unpredictability of children's cognitive development. Pretty much everyone agrees scaffolding students' work is a 'good thing'. Whenever they get stuck we leap in with our trusty writing frames and help them get going. A good writing frame can teach an understanding of text coherence and structure, prompt metacognition and serve as a useful checklist.

For more detail on scaffolding, see page 130.

Ability grouping

It's commonly claimed that mixed ability groupings allow for interaction with higher level thinkers in learning and problem solving. Peers and school culture can have a profound effect on students. Graham Nuthall's discoveries about the power of peer culture make it clear that not only do teachers underestimate the influence of peers, but also that we are largely unaware of it.

In *The Nurture Assumption*, Judith Rich Harris argues that peer culture – or 'groupness' as she calls it – is indeed the most powerful influence on how children behave and think, and teachers have a formidable effect "because they are in control of an entire group of children. They can influence the attitudes and behaviors of the entire group. And they exert this influence where it is likely to have long-term effects: in the world outside the home, the world where children will spend their adult lives." She goes on to illustrate that the choices we make as teachers have wide-ranging and surprising repercussions. For instance:

> When teachers divide up children into good readers and not-so-good ones, the good readers tend to get better and the not-so-good ones to get worse. A group contrast effect at work. The two groups develop different group norms – different behaviors, different attitudes. (p. 261)

We've only focused on a narrow aspect of this ongoing debate, but this might imply that mixed ability groupings are better for the totality of children although not for the most able. Maybe the peer effects Harris discusses really do account for the way in which children's brains develop.*

> **What every teacher needs to know about cognitive development**
> - Teachers should be aware of Piaget's theory of development or his sequence of developmental stages in order to exercise appropriate professional scepticism towards pedagogic claims and approaches based upon them.
> - Accommodation as a theory of conceptual change appears to be falsified by the persistence of misconceptions – we may never really *change* our prior ideas. The strategy of introducing cognitive conflict, therefore, is unlikely to work for the reasons people think it does. Cognitive conflict might work because it stimulates intense thinking about a topic – though this is unlikely where students have low prior knowledge of the topic.
> - Don't expect to necessarily *change* students' prior conceptions. Therefore, don't rely on 'accommodation strategies' (e.g. discovery or practical-based methods) to successfully teach science conceptions.
> - New ideas should be represented in different ways in order to successfully link them with the prior knowledge students possess. Rather than focusing on misconceptions early on, when students have little prior knowledge to help them get to grips with the contradiction, it may be better to start with careful and explicit teaching of key scientific facts and concepts.
> - Rather than worry about the age or stage of a student, it may be better to think out their development in terms of prior knowledge. Where learning involves 'formal operations', we can use concrete analogies to help explain the abstract concepts.
> - Scaffolding helps makes students engage with challenging material but it must be removed to prevent them from becoming dependent on it.
> - Peer influences can have important effects on students' learning, but teachers exert huge influences on social norms. We should be mindful of the way we shape this and the culture of our classrooms.

---

*   We should point out that this is not a settled question and there is much disagreement between sociologists, economists and psychologists on the effects of peer culture on cognitive development.

References

Bjorklund, D. F. (2012) *Children's thinking: Cognitive development* and individual differences (5th ed.), Belmont, CA: Wadsworth.

Bruner, J. (1960) *The Process of Education*. Cambridge, MA: Harvard University Press.

Donaldson, M. (1978) *Children's minds*, New York, NY: Norton.

Harris, J. R. (1998) *The Nurture Assumption*, New York: Free Press.

Miller, P. H. (2011) *Theories of developmental psychology* (5th ed.), New York, NY: Worth.

Mayer, R. (2008) *Learning and instruction*, Upper Saddle River, NJ: Pearson.

Metz, K. (1985) 'The development of children's problem solving in a gears task: A problem space perspective', *Cognitive Science*, 9, 431-472.

Nuthall, G. (2007) *The Hidden Lives of Learners*, Wellington, NZ: NZCER Press.

Piaget, J. (1952) *The Child's Concept of Number*, New York: Norton.

Piaget, J. & Inhelder, N. (1956, 1997) *The Child's Conception of Space* (trans. Langdon, F. J. & Lunzer, J. L.), London: Routledge.

Rogoff, B. (2003) *The cultural nature of human development*, New York, NY: Oxford University Press.

Repacholi, B. M. & Gopnik, A. (1997) 'Early reasoning about desires: Evidence from 14- and 18-month-olds', *Developmental Psychology*, 33, 12-21.

Schauble, L. (1990) 'Belief revision in children: The role of prior knowledge and strategies for generating evidence', *Journal of Experimental Child Psychology*, 49, 31-57.

Shtulman, A. & Valcarcel, J. (2012) 'Scientific knowledge suppresses but does not supplant earlier intuitions', *Cognition*, 124(2), 209-215.

Siegler, R. S. (1994) 'Cognitive variability: A key to understanding cognitive development', *Current Directions in Cognitive Science*, 3(1), 1-5.

Siegler, R. S. (1995) 'How does change occur: A microgenetic study of number conservation', *Cognitive Psychology*, 28, 225-273.

Siegler, R. S., deLoache, J. S. & Eisenberg, N. (2003) *How Children Develop*, New York: Worth.

Siegler, R. S. & Jenkins, E. (1989) *How Children Discover New Strategies*. Hillsdale, NJ: Erlbaum.

Willingham, D. T. (2008) 'What is Developmentally Appropriate Practice?' *American Educator*, Summer 2008, pp. 34-39.

Wimmer, H. & Perner, J. (1983) 'Beliefs about beliefs: Representation and constraining function of wrong beliefs in young children's understanding of deception', *Cognition*, 13, 103-128.

Yvon, F., Chaiguerova, L. A. & Newnham, D. S. (2013) Vygotsky under debate: two points of view on school learning, *Psychology in Russia: State of the art*, 6(2).

Zahn-Waxler, C., Radke-Yarrow, M., Wagner, E. & Chapman, M. (1992) Development of concern for others, *Developmental Psychology*, 28, 126-136.

Chapter 22
Attachment

Attachment theory is included in this section on myths and misconceptions not because the theory itself or the psychiatric disorders associated with the theory are dubious, but because application of the theory within mainstream teaching is, potentially, misguided. There's certainly no harm in developing an understanding of this branch of developmental psychology, but teachers should be sceptical of advice suggesting they should change the way they teach or how they apply school behaviour management policy based on labels relating to attachment.

John Bowlby: Attachment theory

British psychologist John Bowlby's clinical work with 'juvenile delinquents' over the course of World War Two led to the formulation of his ideas about the role of early and prolonged separation from parents in the problems he identified in those children's social and emotional development. The core of his theory is that attachment is an evolutionary adaptation, characterised by a child seeking proximity to the caregiver when that child perceives a threat or suffers discomfort. Given the intense needs of human infants, it is perhaps unsurprising that the formation of a "deep and enduring emotional bond that connects one person to another across time and space"* evolved to improve the chances of an infant's survival.

---

*   Ainsworth, M. D. S. (1973) 'The development of infant-mother attachment', in Cardwell, B. & Ricciuti, H. (eds.) *Review of child development research* (Vol. 3), Chicago: University of Chicago Press, pp. 1-94.

Over the first year of life, an infant begins to develop attachments with parents or carers. As these attachments form we tend to see characteristic behaviour in infant interactions with their attachment figure:

- **Stranger anxiety** – the infant responds with fear or distress to the arrival of a stranger.
- **Separation anxiety** – when separated from parent or carer the infant shows distress and upon that attachment figure's return a degree of proximity seeking for comfort.
- **Social referencing** – the infant looks at the parent or carer to see how they respond to something novel in the environment. The infant looks at the facial expressions of the parent or carer (e.g. smiling or fearful) which influences how they behave in an uncertain situation.

Attachment figures aren't simply individuals who spend a lot of time with the infant, or the ones who feed them, but typically the individuals who respond the most sensitively, for example often playing and communicating with the infant. For many infants the principal attachment figure is their mother, but fathers, grandparents or siblings may also fulfil this role. By about 18 months, most infants enjoy multiple attachments though these may be hierarchical with a primary attachment figure of particular importance. The behaviour relating to attachment develops over early childhood, for example babies tend to cry because of fear or pain, whereas by about two years old they may cry to beckon their caregiver (and cry louder or shout if that doesn't work!).

Bowlby believed these early experiences of attachment formed an 'internal working model' which the child used to form relationships with secondary attachment figures, later friendships with peers, and eventually romantic and parenting relationships in adult life.

Mary Ainsworth: Types of attachment

There are individual differences in the behaviour related to attachment. Famous observation studies by Mary Ainsworth (who worked with Bowlby during the 1950s) identified that in normal children there were a range of attachment types:

- **Secure attachment:** The majority of infants, across different cultures, tend to have an attachment style typified by strong stranger and separation anxiety along with enthusiastic proximity seeking with the parent upon reunion.
- **Insecure-avoidant:** Slightly more common in western cultures, an insecure-avoidant attachment tends to be characterised by avoiding or ignoring the caregiver and showing little emotion (whilst experiencing

inward anxiety) when the caregiver leaves the room, and displaying little enthusiasm when the caregiver returns.
- **Insecure-resistant:** Perhaps more common in 'collectivist cultures', an insecure-resistant (sometimes also called insecure-ambivalent) attachment tends to be characterised as showing intense distress during separation, and being difficult to comfort when the caregiver returns. Infants with this attachment type may also show some rejection or resentment towards the caregiver after a separation.
- **Disorganised attachment:** Added in the 1990s, infants with a disorganised attachment tend to show no consistent pattern in behaviour towards their caregiver. For example, they may show intense proximity-seeking behaviour one moment, then avoid or ignore the caregiver the next.

Many children who have an 'insecure' attachment type may find it harder to form peer friendships, and this possibly underlies an association between insecure and disorganised attachment and higher levels of behaviour problems in school. However, it's not certain that differences in attachment are specifically the cause of behaviour problems. For example, a meta-analysis by Fearnon et al (2010) found that socio-economic status accounted for a considerable portion of the variance in behaviour problems in childhood.

So, whilst there's reasonable evidence to suggest that these individual differences in attachment correlate to differences in behaviour within school, it is very important to note that the presence of behaviour problems doesn't necessarily indicate whether a student has a secure or insecure attachment with their parent.

Reactive Attachment Disorder (RAD)

A popular misconception about attachment is a conflation between the types of attachment that make up the range of normal attachments children possess, and an 'attachment disorder'. For example, the British Association for Adoption and Fostering, a leading adoption and fostering charity, argues that the lack of clarity about the use of attachment concepts in describing children's relationship difficulties can create confusion and advises extreme caution. Even when used by those trained to do so, attachment classifications cannot be equated with a clinical diagnosis of disorder. While insecure patterns may indicate a risk factor in a child's development, they do not by themselves identify disorders. A diagnosis of an attachment disorder can only be undertaken by a psychiatrist.

Reactive Attachment Disorder is a psychiatric condition and often accompanied by other psychiatric disorders. It refers to a highly atypical set of behaviours indicative of children who experience extreme difficulty in forming close attachments. The prevalence of attachment disorders in the general population is not well established, but is likely to be low. However there are substantially higher rates among young children raised in institutional care or who have been exposed to abuse or neglect. The Office for National Statistics report for the Department of Health in 2002 estimated that somewhere between 2.5% to 20% of looked after children had an attachment disorder (depending on how broad a definition was used).

There is a broad distinction between two classifications of RAD:

- **Inhibited attachment disorders:** Characterised by significant difficulties with social interactions such as extremely detached or withdrawn – usually attributed to early and severe abuse from 'attachment figures' such as parents.
- **Disinhibited attachment disorders:** Characterised by diffuse attachments, as shown by indiscriminate familiarity and affection without the usual selectivity in choice of attachment figures – often attributed to frequent changes of caregiver in the early years.

Unfortunately, there is no widely applicable, evidence-based set of therapies for RAD and there has been concern expressed about some forms of therapy. One example is 'holding therapy' involving holding a child in a position which prevents escape whilst engaging in an intense physical and emotional confrontation. There is nothing in attachment theory to suggest that holding therapy is either justifiable or effective for the treatment of attachment disorders. Furthermore, a report for the APSAC (American Professional Society on the Abuse of Children) Task Force advised that any techniques involving physical coercion should not be used because of risk of harm and absence of proven benefit. Less controversial therapies involve counselling to address the issues that are affecting the carer's relationship with the child and teaching parenting skills to help develop attachment.

Into the classroom

Infants tend to develop attachment relationships with their early childhood teachers, so relationship quality is likely to be a central feature of early childhood programmes. However, certainly by the time students reach secondary school, they are unlikely to form attachments to their teachers (in the technical sense). Therefore, whilst some background in attachment theory is probably useful for early years (EY) teachers, its applications are extremely limited for teachers of older students. However, even in early years there is an argument that too much enthusiasm for attachment theory isn't necessarily helpful.

For example, Degotardi and Pearson argue that the role of an early childhood teacher shouldn't overly focus on the security-focused features of attachment relationships. By emphasising the formation of a strong 'parental' bond, attachment theory advances the image of the EY teacher as a 'mother-substitute'. While this notion may encourage early years teachers to respond sensitively to children's physical and emotional needs, there's a danger this may blur the distinct roles of parents and early childhood practitioners. Essentially, a teacher shouldn't be expected to feel, react, and behave as parents do – as their roles are very different. Instead, they suggest, early years teachers need to adopt a wider approach to relationships that includes, but extends beyond, attachment theory. There are many important goals beyond the focus on emotional security which early years teachers shouldn't neglect: including the facilitation of thinking and communication, socialisation and modelling, scaffolding and mediating, etc.

So whilst attachment theory is much more relevant to early years teachers (compared to secondary school for example) – there's an argument for teachers (of all stages) not to get too eager about applying attachment theory in the classroom. Occasionally, materials relating to how (secondary) teachers should modify their approach with students depending on that student's attachment type are circulated through INSET and CPD sessions, and this seems problematic for a number of reasons.

Firstly, identifying attachment type from patterns of behaviour in the classroom isn't something teachers are qualified to do. Developmental psychologists classically used careful, structured observation methods to study interactions between an infant and parent in order to identify attachment behaviours. More recently, clinical interviews and self-report questionnaires have become more common methods of assessment, but these should be administered and interpreted by a psychologist rather than a teacher. Quite simply, making judgements about the quality of attachment a student has with their parent isn't something teachers should be doing. Therefore, it's hard to see how a teacher's 'diagnosis' of a student's attachment type could be remotely valid or applicable. Whether or not you might think a child has an insecure attachment really isn't a teacher's professional call.

Secondly, individual differences in attachment are not 'pathological'. For example, given that about 30-35% of representative populations have an insecure attachment, it is unhelpful to view insecure attachment as an 'attachment problem'. Labelling a student as having an 'insecure attachment' (even assuming that label has been applied with some validity) doesn't really explain anything about their behaviour (as not all insecurely attached children misbehave – there's merely a correlation) or provide reliable insight into what behaviour management strategies a teacher should use to help the student improve their behaviour in the classroom. In the worst case, the use of attachment labels simply pathologises perfectly normal student (mis)behaviour.

Lastly, there appears to be no robust evidence to support the idea that a teacher differentiating for a student's attachment type actually helps that student in any way. Teachers should be highly sceptical of advice suggesting they should change the way they teach or how they apply school behaviour management policy based on labels relating to attachment.

Teachers may have a student in their class who has a reactive attachment disorder. It's a relatively uncommon psychiatric disorder to find in mainstream schools, and therefore SEND coordinators would likely brief teachers about a specific student coming into the school with the disorder. Some teachers might argue that a deeper knowledge of attachment theory is needed to work with students with attachment disorder for a couple of reasons.

Firstly, given the relationship between attachment disorders and abusive or neglectful relationships, perhaps some teachers are worried that they need to know about attachment disorder in order to fulfil their statutory safeguarding responsibilities. However, it's important to note that whilst some children with RAD have suffered abuse or neglect, that doesn't mean that problematic behaviour is evidence of such. The teacher isn't in a position to make either the clinical judgement or investigate the cause of problematic behaviour they suspect may relate to a safeguarding concern. Therefore, sensible advice would be that if a student is behaving in a way which concerns you, then report that concern to your designated member of SLT (as you would *any* safeguarding concern).

Secondly, it may be that some teachers feel they need to know more about attachment in order to support students with behaviour problems in school. However, teachers should not confuse their role with that of the primary caregiver for a child. For example, the Center for Family Development is an attachment centre based in New York specialising in the treatment of adopted and foster families with trauma and attachment disorder. In their 'Overview of Reactive Attachment Disorder for Teachers' they point out that, as a teacher, you are not the primary caregiver for a child you teach. Teachers are not parents or therapists, and that the relatively transient relationships that students form with different teachers from year to year is something entirely normal that a student with RAD needs to learn.

A common recommendation approaching behaviour management of children with RAD is the explicit teaching of consequences: helping the student by explicitly linking cause and effect – showing that there's a consequence associated with good behaviour and there's a consequence for poor behaviour.

Other suggestions include:

- Creating a structured environment with extremely consistent rules.
- Being consistent and specific when giving praise or confronting poor behaviour.
- Providing the child with choices, but choices provided by you, the teacher.
- Maintaining your professional boundaries (avoid attempting to create 'friendship' or 'intimacy' with the child).
- Keep your calm and avoid losing your temper; communicate directly, positively, and firmly.
- Implementing consequences in an unemotional way and adopting a 'business-like' tone that indicates that any sanction or reward is 'nothing personal'.

In short, a lot of the advice relating to working with students with RAD is pretty good advice for working with *any* student who has challenging behaviour. Beyond generic advice, however, it is likely that an educational psychologist or child psychiatrist working with the student may recommend specific strategies that might help an individual student with RAD achieve some stability and success in school. As with any student with SEND, teachers would be well advised to consider such guidance in detail and (ideally) have some time to work with the SEND coordinator in effectively implementing such strategies.

What every teacher needs to know about attachment

- Whilst there's a relationship between insecure and disordered attachment and behaviour problems in the classroom, teachers are not qualified to 'diagnose' a student's attachment type nor engage in any kind of 'therapy' with that student. We'd recommend that teachers should be highly sceptical of any encouragement to relate student behaviour back to the quality of attachment with the parent. Teachers running training or teacher development materials might do well to remember that 'attachment' is a technical psychological term and that in many cases you might be better off swapping it for a more general term like 'relationship'.

- There is a condition called Reactive Attachment Disorder which has a higher incidence within 'looked after' students. Again, teachers are not qualified to make this psychiatric diagnosis.

- There is an important difference between the professional role of a teacher and the role of a primary caregiver, and even in early years practice, where infants tend to form attachments with their teachers, it's vital that recent interest in attachment theory within the profession doesn't blur that line.

- Where teachers are concerned that behaviour presented in the classroom might indicate abuse or neglect, then they are already obliged by law to report these concerns (but not investigate them or try to involve themselves in resolving them).

- In terms of managing the behaviour of students with attachment problems, so that they can overcome the difficulties of their family background and experience success within school, the guidance suggests things like a structured environment, consistent rules, professional distance and focusing feedback on behaviour not the child – advice that forms the basis of good behaviour management regardless of the cause of problematic behaviour.

- It may be the case that specific children with RAD will have individual strategies beyond basic behaviour management which will help them achieve in school. However, that's also the case for any student with special educational needs and disabilities. Rather than generic training on attachment theory, perhaps what is more important is an opportunity to take the time to read, implement and work with specialist coordinators to ensure any specific strategies suggested by an educational psychologist or child psychiatrist are employed effectively.

References

Brandon U Teacher Tools. 'Reactive Attachment Disorder.' Retrieved on 11 March 2016 from http://www.brandonuteachertools.net/reactive-attachment-disorder.html

Bretherton, I. (1992) 'The origins of attachment theory: John Bowlby and Mary Ainsworth', *Developmental psychology*, 28(5), 759.

British Association for Adoption and Fostering (2006) *Attachment Disorders, their Assessment and Intervention/Treatment BAAF Position Statement 4.*

Center for Family Development (2015) *An Overview of Reactive Attachment Disorder for Teachers.* Retrieved on 11 March 2016 from http://www.center4familydevelop.com/helpteachrad.htm

Chaffin, M., Hanson, R., Saunders, B. E., Nichols, T., Barnett, D., Zeanah, C., Berliner, L., Egeland, B., Newman, E., Lyon, T. & LeTourneau, E. (2006) 'Report of the APSAC task force on attachment therapy, reactive attachment disorder, and attachment problems', *Child maltreatment*, 11(1), 76-89.

Degotardi, S. & Pearson, E. (2009) 'Relationship theory in the nursery: Attachment and beyond', *Contemporary Issues in Early Childhood*, 10(2), 144-155.

Fearon, R. P., Bakermans-Kranenburg, M. J., Van IJzendoorn, M. H., Lapsley, A. M. & Roisman, G. I. (2010) 'The significance of insecure attachment and disorganization in the development of children's externalizing behavior: a meta-analytic study', *Child development*, 81(2), 435-456.

Gatward, R., Corbin, T., Goodman, R. & Ford, T. (2003) *The mental health of young people looked after by local authorities in England,* HM Stationery Office.

Moullin, S., Waldfogel, J. & Washbrook, E. (2014) *Baby Bonds: Parenting, attachment and a secure base for children,* Sutton Trust.

National Collaborating Centre for Mental Health (UK) (2015) *Children's Attachment: Attachment in Children and Young People Who Are Adopted from Care, in Care or at High Risk of Going into Care.*

Van Ijzendoorn, M. H. & Kroonenberg, P. M. (1988) 'Cross-cultural patterns of attachment: A meta-analysis of the strange situation', *Child Development*, 147-156.

Verschueren, K. & Koomen, H. M. (2012) 'Teacher–child relationships from an attachment perspective', *Attachment & human development*, 14(3), 205-211.

Chapter 23
Stress and resilience

Fear, like pain, is a feature of the human condition generally considered to be a 'bad thing'. That said, it's almost certain that you are alive today, reading this book, because fear has saved your life at some stage. Whether it was spotting the speeding car just as you were about to step into the road, or causing you to cross the road when a group of rowdy drunks, spoiling for a fight, spilled out into the street, fear tells us we are in danger and prompts us to act (most of the time) in a way which reduces the possibility of injury and gets the body ready to run away or defend ourselves should the need arise. Stress and fear are inescapable and essential parts of life, and experiencing and overcoming them are an important part of our learning and development.

Although our stress response has evolved to deal well with threats humans faced over the course of evolutionary history, it can sometimes be a maladaptive, unhelpful response in many everyday contexts. It's highly unlikely that you'll have to stay alert for a wild animal stalking you on your way home this evening; it's much more likely you'll encounter those stresses typical of modern life (e.g. traffic jams, late trains, pestering emails etc.) which are especially tough during periods of significant life-changing events (e.g. getting married or divorced, losing a loved one, or starting a new job). Whilst the body gearing up to run or fight is useful in the context of surviving predation, it can be downright unhelpful today.

The stress response

The autonomic nervous system – which regulates our internal organs outside of our conscious control and (usually) awareness – is broadly divided into two branches: the sympathetic nervous system (SNS) which prepares the body to deal with threats (often referred to as 'fight or flight') and the opposing parasympathetic nervous system (PNS) which winds the body down again ('rest and digest'). On perceiving a threat in the environment, our bodies trigger a sequence of physiological changes which prepare us to respond to danger. The SNS stimulates the heart to beat faster, our breathing to become faster and deeper, and glucose to be released into the bloodstream, so that muscles have the energy they need for intense work. Other responses occur too, for example our muscles will tense up (which is why we might feel aches and pains), our capillaries near the surface of the skin contract (which is why we may appear pale), we start to sweat, our pupils dilate and the activity of the PNS is inhibited (including digestion, which is why our mouths go dry and we might feel butterflies in the stomach). It also makes us more alert and vigilant and, in some contexts, more likely to behave aggressively.

Of course, even after an immediate emergency has been dealt with there may still be a need to stay ready for action – having escaped from the sabre-toothed tiger, it may still be in the area looking for a meal. When we perceive an ongoing threat, the body maintains a state of readiness through the release of corticosteroids (e.g. cortisol). This ongoing response to stress has positive and negative effects; the short-term survival advantages come with some longer-term costs. For example, we become less sensitive to pain, but our blood sugar and pressure will remain high – which over the long term may increase the chance of cardiovascular problems. Long term, it may also suppress the response of the immune system a degree, potentially increasing the chances of catching colds or slowing recovery from an injury or illness.

Stress is neither good nor bad. We need some stress in order to perform well, but too much or too little impairs our performance. The relationship between stress and performance follows the Yerkes-Dodson Law, an inverted 'U' shaped curve (see Figure 1).

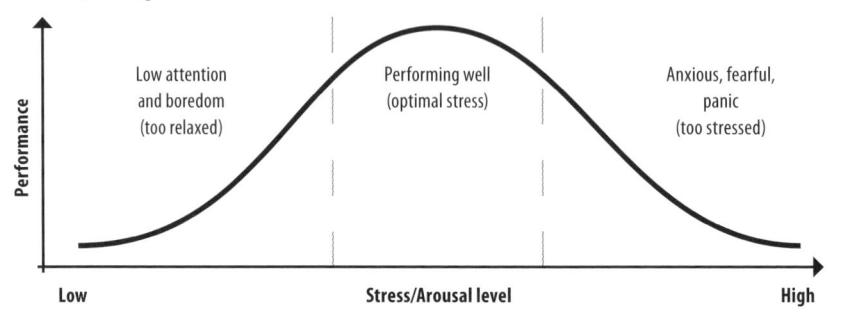

Figure 1: Yerkes-Dodson Law – the relationship between arousal and performance.

Too little arousal and we become inattentive and bored. We may start to react to irrelevant stimuli in the environment and tend to feel sleepy and indolent. Too much arousal is also unhelpful, impairing the performance of memory and the ability to perform complex reasoning. Both states are pretty unpleasant, though in education we tend to overlook the fact that 'underload' can be a problem and perhaps get fixated with the effects of very high stress. It's easy to understand why; if you've ever had a panic attack, it can feel like you're dying! Although we actively seek and enjoy stress – perhaps going on rollercoasters or bungee jumping, or turning the lights off to enjoy a good horror movie – where individuals suffer frequent panics, obsessions and overwhelming phobias, stress can be debilitating and benefits from clinical intervention*.

Perception and response to stress

There's almost certainly a genetic component to how our bodies react to stress; it's possible that some people inherit an oversensitive fear response. For most people, however, whether we perceive stress to be 'good' or 'bad' depends upon a number of factors.

Self-efficacy: A term created by the psychologist Albert Bandura, self-efficacy represents a person's belief in their ability to succeed in specific situations or in accomplishing a particular task. If we feel that a situation or a task is within our capabilities, then we tend not to become overly stressed by it. Our self-efficacy is likely to be improved if we have prior experience of success and feel that we have a good degree of control regarding the outcome. When faced with similar situations or tasks in future, we won't feel overly stressed by them. On the other hand, repeated experience of failure or the belief that there's nothing within our control that will influence the outcome will undermine that sense of self-efficacy and make the situation or task feel more stressful.

Social support: The presence and support of friends and family provides a stable, socially rewarding context which appears to help us deal with stressful situations. Part of this is likely the simple effect of having a sense of predictability and stability. However, there's also some evidence that social support can act a bit like a buffer to stress. Having friends and family around may reassure us that a situation is less threatening than we may have at first perceived: for example, that our perception of the importance of a task is exaggerated. Alternatively, they may reassure us that the possible harm the threat represents is less than we thought, for example by guiding us through a reassuring 'what's the worst that can happen'-type conversation.

---

*   As with any other aspect of health, anyone who has a concern about mental health should seek the advice of a GP, not a teacher.

Accumulation and amplification: Our perception of stress is likely cumulative – we can brush off a single, quite stressful event – but when stress events combine, we may find ourselves overwhelmed. A combination of significant or traumatic life events and everyday strains make a maladaptive response to a stress much more likely. This is exacerbated by the resources we have available – there are higher rates of distress and psychiatric disorders among social groups with fewer assets, including young adults, members of ethnic minority groups, women and members of lower socio-economic groups generally.

The way we react when under stress is complex. There are many individual and situational factors which can influence the way someone responds and whether that response is appropriate. A traditional idea within psychology is the 'approach–avoidance' continuum. In general, the source of stress might be approached or confronted in some way, perhaps through adopting a problem-solving approach, or taking control of the situation. Alternatively, the source of stress might be avoided or ignored in some way, perhaps by distracting ourselves, procrastinating or avoiding exposure to the person or situation we perceive as stressful.

These approaches have strengths and limitations depending on the situation and resources available. For example, with exam stress, clearly avoiding revision, or skipping school is not a helpful way of tackling the situation. Avoiding a situation which triggers anxiety may temporarily reduce that anxiety, which is likely to negatively reinforce unhelpful behaviour (see Chapter 14). On the other hand, when there is genuinely nothing you can do about a situation, ruminating on worries likely won't help and finding constructive ways to distract yourself from worry, or coming to terms with things and emotionally accepting the situation, is probably more helpful.

Into the classroom

Resilience and well-being

There's a fairly widespread, popular view that mental disorders like anxiety amongst young people have been increasing over the course of the 21st century. Certainly some studies have shown that the reported incidences of psychological disorders have been increasing, but it is difficult to know for sure whether this is an actual increase within the population or reflects changes in recognition and diagnosis of such disorders. A review of recently conducted longitudinal psychiatric studies by Bor et al (2014) found little evidence that the mental health of young people was deteriorating over recent years. They did find evidence of an increase in internalising disorders amongst adolescent girls (which includes anxiety), though the source of this increase was unclear.

Although it could be that a combination of worries about things like success in school and social expectations about weight and appearance underlie this reported increase, changing attitudes, media attention and increased awareness of problems like eating disorders may have had a role in girls' willingness to talk about such issues, possibly leading to greater likelihood of reporting.

However, the study found no increase in internalising disorders amongst adolescent boys; no increase in externalising disorders (such as attention deficit hyperactivity disorder, oppositional defiance disorder or conduct disorder) for either boys or girls; and for both children and toddlers, no evidence of a worsening of mental health symptoms (most studies reporting an improvement or no change in recent years).

The focus upon well-being in schools may not be an entirely positive or beneficial movement in social policy. There are concerns that the ordinary feelings, common when growing up, are being unnecessarily pathologised. Kathryn Ecclestone, a professor of education at the University of Sheffield, has long been a critic of the way ideas from psychotherapy have inveigled their way into schools. Emotional literacy, well-being and self-esteem are slippery, often contradictory concepts, she argues, which may inadvertently exacerbate feelings of emotional vulnerability and lead to a 'diminished self'. The sociologist Frank Furendi is also a fierce critic of the emerging preoccupation with emotional well-being within schools and wider culture. He points out that there's something of an 'emotionally correct hierarchy' of virtuous behaviours which often castigates boys for their emotional illiteracy and a refusal to accept emotional vulnerability as a fundamental flaw of the male psyche.

Although well intentioned, this kind of a approach risks making it seem a normal view that we are all in some way unstable, vulnerable and emotionally damaged. If we want children to be resilient – i.e. adapt and cope appropriately to stressful situations and adversity – then the pseudotherapeutic language of well-being may not be the best way of doing this. It's possible that we may end up unintentionally persuading children that they are emotionally defenceless and mentally fragile. Are we also in danger of turning normal expressions of human emotion like bereavement or shyness, or normal childhood behaviours like being noisy or disruptive in a classroom, into a swathe of quasi-medical problems? In our quest to develop resilience we might paradoxically be exacerbating children's perceptions of adversity and risk.

It's interesting to relate this to some of the evidence that suggests that, over time, young people have become more external in their locus of control. Locus of control (LoC) refers to the extent to which a person believes they can control events affecting them. For example, when exam time looms, a student with a high *internal* LoC might feel that their performance in the tests will be determined primarily by their adequate revision and good preparation. A student with high *external* LoC might feel that their chances in the exam are determined by the quality of their teacher, or simply good luck (e.g. the right questions coming up). Our LoC almost certainly varies in different contexts (depending in part on our self-efficacy), but a meta-analysis by Twenge et al (2004) which reviewed studies of LoC between 1960 to 2002 found evidence to suggest that, on average, the LoC of young people in the US had been steadily becoming more external. The report found evidence that the same was true for quite young children: "Children, even those as young as age 9, increasingly feel that their lives are controlled by outside forces rather than their own efforts" (p. 315).

Attempts to improve the resilience of pupils through soft-psychotherapeutic interventions have not, thus far, proved successful. For example, a report in 2011 for the Department for Education evaluated the UK Resilience Programme. The programme, based on the Penn Resiliency Program (a curriculum developed by a team of psychologists at the University of Pennsylvania) attempted to improve children's psychological well-being through resilience and the promotion of realistic thinking and coping skills. Cognitive behavioural therapy (see Chapter 18 for a brief outline of what CBT involves) was an explicit part of the training. Unfortunately, the studies met with limited success: the one-year follow-up found a small average impact on pupils' depression scores, school attendance, and English and maths grades; however even this modest effect had disappeared at the two-year follow-up, suggesting that, on average, pupils who had participated in resilience workshops were doing no better on these outcomes than pupils who had not.

One of the significant ethical problems with importing psychotherapeutic interventions into schools is the relative lack of research into the adverse effects and contraindications of therapy. It's widely held that any adverse effects of CBT-based therapies are far less severe and common than for pharmacotherapy (aka drugs). However, it seems fair to say that the tracking and monitoring of adverse reactions to psychotherapy hasn't been consistent (e.g. Linden, 2013; Fricchione 2013). That said, estimates suggest that on average, approximately 10 per cent of clients actually get worse after starting therapy[*], with perhaps 1 in 20 saying that they had experienced 'lasting bad effects' from therapy[†]. To what extent are schools implementing proper screening and monitoring for these therapeutic approaches improving resilience?

---

[*] Jarrett, C. (2008)
[†] Crawford, M., Thana, L., Farquharson, L., Palmer, L., Hancock, E., Bassett, P., Clarke, J. & Parry, G. (2016)

Is there a better way to help students cope and adapt to stressful situations and the current and future adversity they will face in life? Kathryn Ecclestone suggests we'd be better off focusing on "a stimulating, enriched, challenging curriculum and extra-curricular activities"* to help students develop the character and resilience we'd like them to have. A recent article by Paul Tough, the author of *Helping Children Succeed,* seems to go along with this view. His research led him to question whether we should think of character qualities, like grit, curiosity, self-control, optimism, or conscientiousness as skills which can be taught. Instead, none of the educators he encountered who appeared to be highly successful at engendering these traits gave pep-talks or motivational speeches to students; indeed many made no mention of these 'skills' at all. What appeared to work was talking to the child and giving detailed feedback about the mistakes they had made and what they could have done differently.

We enjoy rollercoasters and horror films because they give the thrill of adrenaline without the genuine presence of a threat, and perhaps this is a better guide for teachers wishing to develop student resilience than psychotherapy. That's not saying that a minority of children won't need more professional help, or a justification for underfunding Child and Adolescent Mental Health Services (CAMHS). However, for the majority of children, a challenging curriculum and a rich diet of extra-curricular activities may help develop resilience by providing an environment of 'safe adversity' for children to experience and develop a tolerance for stress. Regularly taking children out of their comfort zone, whether that's a challenging maths test, speaking in a debate or performing in a school play, gives them the experience of adversity in the safety of a low-stakes environment.

Encouraging students to take on stressful challenges as an opportunity to learn (about a subject or about themselves) rather than something to be scared of, may help them develop the self-efficacy they'll need in the face of the 'slings and arrows' that life will inevitably throw at them.

What every teacher needs to know about stress and resilience

- Stress is neither a good nor a bad thing – we need some to get out of bed in the morning – but too much is clearly unhelpful. We tend to experience high levels of stress when we perceive our resources or capability as insufficient for the challenge or threat we think we're

---

*   Jarrett, C. (2008)

facing. It's common in therapy to tackle this at the level of person perception – however, we can practically reduce stress by improving the resources available and capability of the individual so they can actually deal with the challenge they face
- Teachers are not psychotherapists or psychiatrists; if there's concern that a child has a genuine problem with anxiety they should be referred to a specialist.
- For most people, our sense of self-efficacy and our social support networks can help us deal with periods of adversity.
- Often taking a problem-solving approach to stress – breaking down a difficult situation and solving pieces of the problem one at a time – is a helpful approach.
- There's nothing pathological with being occasionally sad or anxious or lonely – it's all part of the human condition. When there genuinely is nothing that can be done, distracting yourself and expressing emotions can often help us deal with the situation.
- When it comes to exams – arguably the biggest source of stress we impose upon students – it's useful to watch for avoidance strategies, like skipping lessons or procrastination with revision.
- Remember that as teachers, we influence the context for students' experience of stress. If you are stressing about the exams, don't be surprised if your students pick up on that and start to worry overly.
- When it comes to building resilience – the ability to adapt and cope with stressful situations – therapeutic approaches have yet to demonstrate their effectiveness and may, in rare instances, do more harm than good.
- Self-efficacy – our belief that we can succeed at a challenging task – appears to influence our experience of stress. Building opportunities for students to experience success in the face of adversity, within the safe and caring environment of school, provides a fairly good bet for developing resilience.

References

Aldao, A., Nolen-Hoeksema, S. & Schweizer, S. (2010) 'Emotion-regulation strategies across psychopathology: A meta-analytic review', *Clinical psychology review*, 30(2), 217-237.

Bor, W., Dean, A. J., Najman, J. & Hayatbakhsh, R. (2014) 'Are child and adolescent mental health problems increasing in the 21st century? A systematic review', *Australian and New Zealand Journal of Psychiatry*, 48(7), 606-616, doi:0004867414533834.

Challen, A., Noden, P., West, A. & Machin, S. (2011) *UK resilience programme evaluation: Final report*, Department for Education.

Chrousos, G. P. (2009) 'Stress and disorders of the stress system', *Nature Reviews Endocrinology*, 5(7), 374-381.

Cohen, S. & Wills, T. A. (1985) 'Stress, social support, and the buffering hypothesis', *Psychological bulletin*, 98(2), 310.

Crawford, M., Thana, L., Farquharson, L., Palmer, L., Hancock, E., Bassett, P., Clarke, J. & Parry, G. (2016) 'Patient experience of negative effects of psychological treatment: results of a national survey', *The British Journal of Psychiatry*, 208(3), 260-265.

Ecclestone, K. (2007) 'Resisting images of the 'diminished self': the implications of emotional well-being and emotional engagement in education policy', *Journal of Education Policy*, 22(4), 455-470.

Ecclestone, K. (2012) 'From emotional and psychological well-being to character education: challenging policy discourses of behavioural science and 'vulnerability'', *Research Papers in Education*, 27(4), 463-480.

Ecclestone, K. (2015) 'Well-being programmes in schools might be doing children more harm than good'. Retrieved from https://theconversation.com/well-being-programmes-in-schools-might-be-doing-children-more-harm-than-good-36573 on 1 June 2016

Ellis, B. J., Jackson, J. J. & Boyce, W. T. (2006) 'The stress response systems: Universality and adaptive individual differences' *Developmental Review*, 26(2), 175-212.

Fricchione, V. P. (2013) 'The problem of side effects in psychotherapy: adverse treatment reactions or unwanted events', *European Psychiatry*, 28,(1).

Furedi, F. (2003) *Therapy culture: Cultivating vulnerability in an uncertain age*, London: Routledge.

Jarrett, C. (2008) 'When therapy causes harm', *Psychologist*, 21(1), 10-12.

Linden, M. (2013) 'How to define, find and classify side effects in psychotherapy: from unwanted events to adverse treatment reactions', *Clinical psychology & psychotherapy*, 20(4), 286-296.

Lupien, S. J., McEwen, B. S., Gunnar, M. R. & Heim, C. (2009) 'Effects of stress throughout the lifespan on the brain, behaviour and cognition' *Nature Reviews Neuroscience*, 10(6), 434-445.

Maciejewski, P. K., Prigerson, H. G. & Mazure, C. M. (2000) 'Self-efficacy as a mediator between stressful life events and depressive symptoms Differences based on history of prior depression', *The British Journal of Psychiatry*, 176(4), 373-378.

Mendl, M. (1999) 'Performing under pressure: stress and cognitive function', *Applied Animal Behaviour Science*, 65(3), 221-244.

Roth, S. & Cohen, L. J. (1986) 'Approach, avoidance, and coping with stress', *American psychologist*, 41(7), 813.

Skinner, E. A., Edge, K., Altman, J. & Sherwood, H. (2003) 'Searching for the structure of coping: a review and critique of category systems for classifying ways of coping, *Psychological bulletin*, 129(2), 216.

Thoits, P. A. (2010) 'Stress and health major findings and policy implications', *Journal of health and social behavior*, 51(1 suppl), S41-S53.

Tough, P. (2016) 'Why Character Can't Be Taught Like The Pythagorean Theorem'. Retrieved from: http://ww2.kqed.org/mindshift/2016/06/09/why-character-cant-be-taught-like-the-pythagorean-theorem/ on 9 June 2016

Twenge, J. M., Zhang, L. & Im, C. (2004) 'It's beyond my control: A cross-temporal meta-analysis of increasing externality in locus of control, 1960-2002', *Personality and Social Psychology Review*, 8(3), 308-319.

Chapter 24
Neuroscience

With the advent of increasingly inexpensive access to brain imaging technology, neuroscience has entered a fascinating period of rapid advancement. Although techniques like electroencephalography (EEG) were being used in the 1920s and magnetic resonance imaging (MRI) since the 1970s, the most recent advances have allowed scientists to analyse functional changes caused by neuronal activity[*] in the brain (fMRI). The ability to generate images of what's going on in our brains is hugely exciting, and the enthusiasm for trying to apply this science to education should come as no surprise.

However, neuroscience is probably the wrong level of description to provide meaningful insight into classroom practice: observing the actions of particular groups of neurons, or activity in various regions in the brain, is a long way from teaching a classroom full of children. Concepts like neuroplasticity, or findings about the role of dopamine in learning, provide little to no insight into how best to teach maths to 11-year-olds.

Instead, the hugely important way in which neuroscience can be useful to education is by helping scientists test cognitive theories and models relevant to how children learn. Daniel Willingham gives the example of dyslexia. For a long time, competing explanations for why some children struggle to learn to read were contended: some psychologists arguing it was a disorder of the visual perception system, others maintaining it was related to phonology (e.g. the conversion of written characters to their corresponding phonemes). Brain

---

[*] To be more precise, fMRI looks at how blood-oxygen levels (which correlate with neural activity) change over time.

imagining techniques have been able to shed significant light on which of these rival hypotheses provides the better explanation. A study finding reduced activation in the left temporoparietal cortex suggested that dyslexia was better explained by phonological rather than visual perception explanations.

Neuroscience provides a phenomenal way of testing cognitive theories about how children learn. However, well meaning but misguided attempted to apply neuroscience to teaching have led to a number of myths and misconceptions. Back in 2002, the OECD reported concerns that a number of misconceptions based on flawed interpretations of neuroscience were widespread within education. Sometimes these misconceptions are based upon 'hyped' versions or distortions of genuine findings, other times they appear entirely spurious, merely cloaking themselves in the language of neuroscience to give the ideas a veneer of plausibility.

It appears people are easily persuaded by ideas when presented alongside neurological jargon. Experiments by Deena Weisberg and colleagues at Yale give us an insight into how neuroscientific explanations exert a powerful influence on our beliefs. Participants were divided into four groups, each of which read brief explanations of psychological phenomena (none of which required a neuroscientific explanation); half the participants read good explanations, the other half bad explanations (i.e. they merely restated a description of the phenomenon). In addition, half the participants saw spurious neuroscientific justifications for the explanation specifying an area of activation in the brain (irrelevant to the explanation), whilst the other half did not. Participants then had to rate how satisfied they were with the explanations given for each phenomenon.

Participants could tell the difference between the good and bad explanations, but for novices and students taking a cognitive neuroscience course, the presence of the irrelevant neuroscientific information led them to judge the explanations, particularly the bad explanations, more favourably. On the other hand, the expert participants (who had completed advanced degrees in subjects like cognitive neuroscience or cognitive psychology) rated the good explanations a bit worse when accompanied by a spurious neuroscientific explanation (though this has yet to be replicated in other experiments).

Perhaps unsurprisingly, non-experts tend to be persuaded by explanations which use technical language and scientific terminology, perhaps because they sound more scientific, even where those terms are irrelevant to the explanation. This probably isn't limited to merely neuroscientific terms, but probably many other areas of psychology as well. How readily are we, as teachers, swayed by claims about child psychology or pedagogical techniques which appear to have the stamp of authority offered by scientific-sounding jargon?

There's even evidence that we may find scientific articles more credible when merely a picture of a brain scan is included (e.g. McCabe and Castel, 2008). It seems our enthusiasm for neuroscience and our bias towards finding 'brain-based' ideas more plausible (regardless of their scientific validity) means that neuro-myths can spread easily within education. Given these biases in our judgements, we should be particularly sceptical of any innovation in teaching which uses the prefix 'neuro-' or the word 'brain' in its title. This might perhaps explain why we were so completely taken in by Brain Gym.

Into the classroom

Development in early infancy

Some of these myths relate to early brain development in childhood. One of these is the idea that there is a sharply defined critical period of brain development within the first three years of a child's life, and that the changes which occur during this period determine later development and success in life. This belief was held by a third of UK teachers according to a study by Dekker et al (2012). A more common belief held by 95% of UK teachers was that the brains of pre-school children are improved or enhanced by environments rich in stimuli. You see evidence of this belief occasionally on social media, for example people sharing an apparent brain scan of a 'normal' child versus the much smaller brain of a child which has been deprived or neglected.

There's no doubt that some things are easier to learn in early childhood than later on in life. The degree of 'neuroplasticity' (the capacity of the brain to change and form new synaptic connections) varies by the stimulus involved. So, whilst there are sensitive periods for some stimuli, other types of stimuli may affect changes within the brain across our whole lives. For example, the ability to learn the sounds and the grammar of a language appears to be easiest to learn in the early to middle childhood years. Therefore, neuroscientists sometimes refer to 'sensitive' periods, ages during which development of such abilities appears to be optimal. However, many other aspects of cognition, not least the acquisition of semantic knowledge, continue to develop throughout life.

The second more common misconception appears related to the first. The idea that early childhood is a critical period for brain development encourages the idea that an 'enriched' environment during this time will enhance brain development. One source of these myths may come from experiments on animals involving severely impoverished environments. For example, a famous study by Blakemore and Cooper (1970) placed kittens in an environment where either they could only see horizontal or vertical lines. After five months, the kittens appeared to be blind to lines which were perpendicular to the orientation they had experienced. However, whilst these extreme studies appear to confirm that ordinary experience is necessary for normal neural development, it doesn't tell us that 'enriched' stimulation will lead to enhanced neural development. This kind of belief overlooks the fact that the brain shows plasticity throughout life, not just during early childhood.

However, it may be that the enduring popularity of this idea in teaching isn't explained by animal studies but is more likely an influence of prevalence of Piagetian theory in teacher training. As we saw in Chapter 21, Piaget claimed that cognitive development in the sensorimotor stage involved the infant engaging in intense experimentation with their environment, and it may be that educators have taken this to imply that a 'rich' environment will enhance that development. Perhaps as a consequence of this influential theory, there is a common belief – often revealing itself in discussions about play-based learning – that exposure to an 'enriched' environment in early childhood will lead to more cognitive development. Once again, this falls foul of the notion that there is a critical period for brain development in early infancy, and rarely tries to define what an 'enriched' or 'enhanced' environment might actually look like.

Another possible reason for the popularity of this myth in education is the Mozart effect: the idea that listening to Mozart can increase intelligence. Back in the 1990s studies reporting an increase in IQ scores, particularly for spatial reasoning abilities, became widely publicised and generated considerable excitement. Lynn Waterhouse (2006) reports that the Governor of Georgia requested over $100,000 to provide a tape of classical music for every newborn to 'help their brains develop faster'. It's not hard to see why such simple, effortless ways to apparently achieve education gains are so popular, but as usual the accumulating evidence didn't justify the hype. Certainly listening to music may increase emotional arousal, but the balance of evidence doesn't support the notion that listening to Mozart increases children's intelligence.

Localisation of brain function

Another set of neuro-myths involve the idea that different functions of human behaviour lie in localised areas of the brain and that education needs to accommodate individual differences in the extent to which these areas are active, or encourage some sort of integration between these areas.

For example, Dekker et al (2012) found that 91% of UK teachers believed that 'Differences in hemispheric dominance (left brain or right brain) can help to explain individual differences amongst learners', 88% believed 'Short bouts of coordination exercises can improve integration of left and right hemispheric brain function' and nearly half (48%) thought 'We mostly only use 10% of our brain'.

The last claim perhaps taps into the admirable belief of most educators that everyone has untapped potential, but the claim is "so wrong it is almost laughable" (Boyd, 2008). Whilst at any one time some parts of the brain will be highly active and other areas less active, over any 24-hour period most regions of the brain are continually active. In other words, we use almost every part of the brain and most regions of the brain are almost constantly active.

However, the idea that some parts of the brain remain 'untapped' perhaps explains the other two neuro-myths. The idea that some people are left-brained (e.g. logical, mathematical, scientific) and others are right-brained (e.g. artistic, poetic, creative) is equally laughable in our opinion, but it is not uncommon to find this claim being repeated on social media and in teacher professional development.

The origins of this myth likely have some foundation in the pioneering work in the 1960s of neuroscientists like Roger Sperry and Michael Gazzaniga. The idea that there are highly differentiated functions of the left and right hemisphere has its origin in a series of strange and fascinating experiments on 'split-brain' patients. As a desperate last resort to control epilepsy, patients had the complex nerve fibres which connect and coordinate processes between the two hemispheres of the brain (the *corpus callosum*) severed. This allowed researchers to run a sequence of experiments to see whether each hemisphere was able to act as an independent entity (was there one consciousness operating in the brain, or two?).

Of course, even if evidence to support exclusive lateralisation of functioning within one or other brain hemisphere was reliable, we couldn't generalise this finding to everyone else. However, over the years studies do appear to have found evidence that some cognitive functions appear to be associated with activity in particular regions of the brain. As it happens, this evidence doesn't support the simplistic idea of a 'creative' right brain and a 'logical' left. For example, language processing (presumably needed for poetry) appears to be localised in the left hemisphere, and attentional processes (presumably needed for logical and mathematical reasoning) appear to be localised in the right.

Furthermore, even if there were localised functions consistent with the 'left-brained, right-brained' idea, there would also be the question of whether activity in one or other hemisphere was 'dominant'. Again, it doesn't appear to be the case. Nielsen et al (2013) found evidence that there appear to be some lateralisation of networks in the left and right hemispheres, but that there was no evidence of one hemisphere having more global dominance over the other. In short, there's no evidence that people are left-brained or right-brained.

It's hard to believe any of our readers won't be aware of Brain Gym or Ben Goldacre's systematic demolition of its major claims in *Bad Science* nearly a decade ago. What appears to have surprised many commentators is the persistence of teachers advocating the techniques in the absence of good evidence for their effectiveness. However, given that many people appear to believe that there are valuable abilities related to one or other hemisphere of the brain – and believe that we tend to use one hemisphere less than the other – it's perhaps unsurprising that the idea that special exercises can be used to 'join up' or 'improve coordination' between the hemispheres of the brain has continued to find enthusiastic proponents within the teaching profession.

What every teacher needs to know about neuroscience

- As professionals, we should be ready to challenge neuro-myths in the staff room as much as we would tackle misconceptions in our classrooms.
- Perhaps the first step is simply to be aware of common misconceptions related to how children learn, so that we can challenge bogus ideas about teaching.
- Given the limitations of directly applying neuroscientific evidence to classroom settings, as a rule of thumb we should probably exercise professional scepticism when anyone claims that a method of teaching is 'brain-based' or supported by neuroscience. There's a chance that such terminology is being included to persuade us rather than genuinely justify the approach to teaching.

References

Blakemore, C. & Cooper, G. F. (1970) 'Development of the brain depends on the visual environment', *Nature*, 228, 477-478.

Bruer, J. T. (1999) 'Neural connections: Some you use, some you lose', *The Phi Delta Kappan*, 81(4), 264-277.

Dekker, S., Lee, N., Howard-Jones, P. & Jolles, J. (2012) 'Neuromyths in education: Prevalence and predictors of misconceptions among teachers', *Frontiers in psychology*, 3, 429.

Gazzaniga, M. (1998) 'The Split Brain Revisited', *Scientific American* 279 (1), 35-39.

Geake, J. (2008) 'Neuromythologies in education', *Educational Research*, 50(2), 123-133.

Goldacre, B. (2008) *Bad Science*, London, Fourth Estate.

Goldacre, B. (2006) 'Brain Gym exercises do pupils no favours', *The Guardian*. Accessed from: http://www.theguardian.com/commentisfree/2006/mar/18/comment.badscience on 20th May 2016

Howard-Jones, P. A. (2014) 'Neuroscience and education: myths and messages', *Nature Reviews Neuroscience*, 15(12), 817-824.

Howard-Jones, P. A., Franey, L., Mashmoushi, R. & Liao, Y. C. (2009) 'The neuroscience literacy of trainee teachers', *in British Educational Research Association Annual Conference* (pp. 1-39). University of Manchester.

McCabe, D. P. & Castel, A. D. (2008) 'Seeing is believing: The effect of brain images on judgments of scientific reasoning', *Cognition*, 107(1), 343-352.

Nielsen, J., Zielinski, B., Ferguson, M., Lainhart, J. & Anderson, J. (2013) 'An evaluation of the left-brain vs. right-brain hypothesis with resting state functional connectivity magnetic resonance imaging', *PLoS ONE* 8(8): e71275. doi:10.1371/ journal.pone.0071275

Organisation for Economic Co-operation, and Development (2002) *Understanding the Brain: Towards a New Learning Science*, Paris: OECD.

Pasquinelli, E. (2012) 'Neuromyths: why do they exist and persist?' *Mind, Brain, and Education*, 6(2), 89-96.

Waterhouse, L. (2006) 'Multiple intelligences, the Mozart effect, and emotional intelligence: A critical review', *Educational Psychologist*, 41(4), 207-225.

Weisberg, D., Keil, F., Goodstein, J., Rawson, E. & Gray, J. (2008) 'The Seductive Allure of Neuroscience Explanations', *Journal of cognitive neuroscience*, 20 (3), 470-477.

Willingham, D. T. (2009) 'Three problems in the marriage of neuroscience and education', *Cortex*, 45(4), 544-545.

Wilson, R. (2012) 'The emperor's new clothes: Learning styles and multiple Intelligences', *Colleagues*, 8(2), 7.

Chapter 25
Individual differences

The study of individual differences, whether in terms of personality or character traits, is an area of psychology frequently applied to education. However, is this really a helpful approach to developing classroom practice? At best, teachers learning about or trying to measure differences in students' personality or character wastes time and resources which could be better spent within schools. At worst, it applies inaccurate and unhelpful labels to children, which may have unintended and sometimes negative consequences.

Although it's true that all snowflakes are unique, this tells us nothing about how to build a snowman or design a better snowplough. For all their individuality, useful applications depend upon the underlying physical and chemical similarities of snowflakes. The same applies to teaching children. Of course children are all unique; genetically, developmentally, cognitively and socially, no two children are exactly alike. However, for all their individuality, any application of psychology to teaching is typically best informed by understanding the underlying similarities in the way children learn and develop, rather than trying to apply ill-fitting labels to define their differences.

Whether individual differences are framed as variances in personality or character traits, to be useful to a teacher, these psychometric differences would need to establish two key things:

1. There would have to be a valid measure identifying differences between students (see Chapter 8).

2. There would have to be evidence that interventions in the classroom informed by these differences helped students learn.

Most attempts to define the differences between children fail the first of these tests. Even where they appear to meet robust tests of validity, the evidence of the latter test is usually absent or too weak to apply with any confidence.

What is personality?

In psychological terms 'personality' is the characteristic patterns of thoughts and behaviours (including emotional responses) that are consistent within an individual across time and not dependent upon context. However, personality measures are little better than horoscopes in defining useful differences between individuals. In *The Cult of Personality*, Annie Murphy Paul investigated the industry surrounding personality testing and found flawed theories and invalid methods being used to create inaccurate descriptions of people who in reality are "complicated, contradictory, changeable across time and place". Businesses waste millions of dollars every year using personality measures which appear more focused on indulging our obsessive interest in our 'selves' than providing any predictive or useful knowledge about that 'self'.

Myers-Briggs Type Indicator

A classic example of a problematic personality measure would be the Myers-Briggs Type Indicator (MBTI) – the most frequently used test of personality used in businesses across the world. The MBTI is based on Carl Jung's theory of personality types. Through a sequence of 'yes' and 'no' forced choice questions, the inventory sorts individuals using four dimensions of personality so that a person is categorised into one of 16 types. The dimensions are 'extrovert' versus 'introvert' (how outgoing and sociable a person is compared to how reserved and how comfortable they are being alone); 'sensing' versus 'intuition' (whether a person prefers concrete and detailed information, or prefers to identify general patterns using insight rather than analysis); 'thinking' versus 'feeling' (valuing objective truth and deductive logic, or giving greater value to people's motives and emotions); 'judging' or 'perceiving' (whether a person prefers a structured and organised environment, or a more flexible one with minimal planning). All very intriguing, but does the test tell us anything valid about the person who takes it?

Probably not. It uses forced choice questions (e.g. *Do you prefer to arrange dates, parties, etc., well in advance – or – be free to do whatever looks like fun when the time comes?*) which means, for people in the middle of any dimension, relatively small differences in the way the questions are answered will push them into one category or another. This creates enormous problems with the test-retest reliability of the measure i.e. if you take the test again, do you come out as the same personality type – a big deal if you're claiming to be able to measure stable features of personality. The test-retest reliability of the MBTI appears to be very poor. If after a short time period of five weeks you retake the test, there's a 50% chance that you'd end up in a different personality category. If a measure is not reliable, it cannot be valid; so the poor reliability of the MBTI implies that it's not a valid measure of personality.

Despite these problems, the MBTI has been used to try to identify the learning styles, or learning preferences of students. But, if the measure isn't valid, any claim that adapting teaching to match these different personality types will advantage students must be treated with extreme scepticism. A review of many different learning styles by Frank Coffield and colleagues suggested that commercial forces have increasingly led the MBTI being used by institutions to assess student strengths and weaknesses, despite the fact that there is no clear evidence that types are stable over time or offer clear practical applications to teaching. The science writers Joseph Stromberg and Estelle Caswell argue that the MBTI has as "about as much scientific validity as your astrological sign". It appears to be a test designed to make people feel "happy after taking it" rather than providing valid predictive insight into an individual's behaviour, performance or preferences.

The 'Big Five' personality traits

Another construct of personality is the 'Big Five' or OCEAN: openness (appreciation of art, emotion and unusual ideas versus a more pragmatic and perseverant stance), conscientiousness (being organised, dependable and self-disciplined versus flexible, spontaneous but a bit unreliable), extraversion (as described for the MBTI above), agreeableness (compassionate and cooperative versus hostile or suspicious) and neuroticism (the extent to which the person experiences unpleasant emotions like anxiety or depression versus having fairly stable mood states).

This construct receives more attention within psychology and is widely perceived to have greater validity (despite the fact that it more-or-less shares four dimensions with the MBTI, which lacks a measure of neuroticism) because it delivers more reliable ratings of personality. A reasonable question, given the interest in schools developing students' personality traits, is the extent to which a person's scores on measures of the 'Big Five' correlate with job performance. We might expect each of the traits to influence job performance to an extent, but perhaps conscientiousness would seem the most valuable (and perhaps most strongly related to character traits like grit and resilience). Indeed, it's hard to think of a job where the traits associated with conscientiousness might not be desirable!

Surprisingly though, the relationship between personality and job performance seems pretty weak. A meta-analysis by Barrick and Mount (1991) found that the OCEAN characteristics only correlated modestly with job performance. They relate findings that suggest that conscientiousness and cognitive ability are only weakly linked – presumably the basis for claims that personality characteristics may be more important than academic ability to potential employers.

In schools, it seems reasonable to propose that students will be more or less conscientious in their studies depending upon their relationship with a particular subject rather than a generic conscientiousness trait. A student might be very dependable in one context (e.g. turning up for training for every school football match) but highly unreliable in another (e.g. 'forgetting' their science homework). Does a personality questionnaire measuring the conscientiousness of that student really tell us anything useful?

Even if we accepted that conscientiousness predicted job performance, there would still be a question of whether interventions intended to develop that trait would successfully improve student performance in school or at work (it would be fair to say psychologists have typically been more interested in measuring differences rather than changing them). Lots of things correlate (see Part 3: Professional scepticism). We should ask whether this modest correlation hides the genuine cause behind the association of conscientiousness and job performance. Perhaps it is not a 'conscientiousness trait' that causes people to be more committed and responsible at work but rather job satisfaction which drives the individual to work more conscientiously. It seems plausible that people with high job satisfaction are less anxious, more outgoing and harder working than those who find their jobs unfulfilling, unrewarding or unbearably stressful. There have certainly been plenty of studies which have looked at the relationship between job satisfaction and job performance. A review of these studies (Judge et al, 2001) found an average correlation of 0.3 – a similarly weak relationship to that of a conscientious trait.

The fact that other studies don't find a relationship between conscientiousness and career success also casts doubt upon the idea that a trait is driving successful performance at work. The Sutton Trust recently published 'A Winning Personality', which detailed some analysis of a very large BBC survey in which respondents took a personality test (measuring the OCEAN traits) and provided some demographic information. They found that respondents who claimed to have a high income (more than £40,000 per year) were also more likely to rate themselves as extroverts. High earners were also more likely to claim that their parents had professional jobs (suggesting more advantaged backgrounds) and express higher economic aspirations (implying they were generally keen to earn more money).

Most of the papers reported these findings as evidence supporting some sort of 'character education' intervention. The *TES* headline read 'Extrovert personality traits could boost poor pupils' career prospects'. *Schools Week* went with the even bolder claim 'Schools must teach 'extrovert' traits – or social mobility will suffer'. However, the report itself makes clear that there is no way of telling what the causal mechanism might be that link these factors. Whilst the study was reported as an influence of personality upon income, it seems equally plausible that achieving success and promotion in your work will make you more assertive and sociable.

Even if we accept that extraversion is a valid, measurable difference between students and that higher extraversion (rather than conscientiousness) would lead to more social mobility, there would still be a question of whether personality interventions for children from low-income backgrounds would have the intended consequences. What wasn't widely reported was the fact that high earners in the survey were also less likely to be 'agreeable'. High agreeableness is typified as kind, considerate or generous. Low agreeableness is said to reflect selfish, suspicious and uncooperative traits. High-earning women in the survey were also more likely to score low on 'openness'. People with high 'openness to experience' are typified as imaginative, curious and interested in art, whereas low 'openness' may regard art or science with suspicion and prefer familiarity over novelty. Would we want these to be traits children possess when they leave school? How would we know that interventions designed to boost 'extraversion' wouldn't inadvertently promote less desirable traits?

Another issue takes us right back to one of founding fathers of personality psychology, Gordon Allport. Allport thought that when it comes to character traits, context is more important than people. He argued that personality is a series of traits, human relationships, current context and motivation. As he said, "Types exist not in people or in nature, but rather in the eye of the observer." He saw any theory that regarded personality as stable, fixed or invariable as wrong. If this is the case, is it possible to meaningfully alter students' characters, or can we only change the contexts within which their character traits are apparent?

Character education

In 1899 William James, to many the grandfather of psychology, collected together a series of lectures he'd given to teachers over the years. There are many debates within education related in his work which resonate over a century later. Not least of these echoes, perhaps, is the parallel between James's belief in the importance of students developing virtuous habits and the current preoccupation with children's character:

> "So far as we are thus mere bundles of habit, we are stereotyped creatures, imitators and copiers of our past selves. And since this, under any circumstances, is what we always tend to become, it follows first of all that the teacher's prime concern should be to ingrain into the pupil that assortment of habits that shall be most useful to him throughout life. Education is for behavior, and habits are the stuff of which behavior consists."*

Schools have been working to instil such 'good habits' ever since. Every time a teacher gives a late detention or chases up an absence they are developing time-keeping. Is there a greater example of resilience than a child who suffers long-term illness, loses a parent or cares for a sibling yet continues their studies in school? Flexibility is exemplified in the secondary school timetable where a child may go from the very different demands required for PE, maths, art and English in a single day. Problem solving is one area where children in England appear to excel according to PISA and the development of communication skills is routinely developed within every subject curriculum.

However, to say that schools should focus on developing character education is best described as 'not even wrong'[†]. The concept lacks either a clear definition, or intended outcomes. Character education seems to encompass everything and exclude nothing.

For example, a recent 'Character Nation' report by Demos illustrates this problem. Their discussion of character education includes: perseverance, resilience and grit; confidence and optimism; motivation, drive and ambition; neighbourliness and community spirit; tolerance and respect; honesty, integrity and dignity; curiosity and focus; moral virtues such as courage, temperance, generosity, magnificence, pride, gentleness, friendliness, honesty, wit or charm; humility and modesty; empathy and compassion; a sense of fairness and gratitude; a

---

* James, W. (1899) 'Talks to teachers'. *Chapter 8, The Laws of Habit*. Retrieved from http://www.uky.edu/ eushe2/Pajares/tt8.html 29 June 2016

† The exact quote comes from Peierls' biography of the theoretical physicist, Wolfgang Pauli: "Quite recently, a friend showed him the paper of a young physicist which he suspected was not of great value but on which he wanted Pauli's views. Pauli remarked sadly, 'It is not even wrong.'" Peierls, R. E. (1960) *Wolfgang Ernst Pauli, 1900-1958. Biographical Memoirs of Fellows of the Royal Society*, 5, 174-192. p. 186

love or zest of learning; creativity; locus of control and self-efficacy; discipline and/or a sense of agency; critical thinking; application and self-regulation; civic virtues such as acts of service and volunteering; performance virtues such as social and emotional skills; emotional intelligence and skills for life and work; self-perceptions, self-awareness and self-control; the ability to bounce back and cope; OCEAN personality traits like 'openness', 'conscientiousness' and 'agreeableness'; the attitudes, dispositions and behaviour that are vital to education. This isn't even an exclusive list. It appears that anything beyond exam results could be included as an example of character education.

Demos argue that 'character' is the right term because although no one can define it, "everyone knows what it means". But do they? In this context it seems to mean 'everything except possibly exam grades'. This then means the priorities for schools should be good exam grades and ... everything else. This fundamental flaw is treated as a virtue, however. Demos suggest the loose definition is ideal as individual schools can develop an approach and language suitable to their school context. However, a term that means everything means nothing.

Amongst this bewildering array of traits and dispositions, perhaps one of the best defined concepts of character education has been the idea of 'grit'. Grit is defined as 'perseverance and passion for long-term goals' and research by Angela Duckworth has suggested it is a factor[*] underlying success for groups as disparate as Ivy league undergraduates, West Point military cadets, elite athletes and National Spelling Bee competitors. The proposal is an optimistic one; achievement of difficult goals in life depends not upon talent alone, but 'a sustained and focused application of talent over time'.

However, despite the enthusiasm for the idea amongst teachers, a recent meta-analysis[†] has suddenly cast doubts about whether the concept stands up to scrutiny. The research (in press at the time of writing) looked at results of studies from 88 different samples involving over 66,000 individuals. They appeared to find that grit was only modestly correlated (0.18) with performance and strongly correlated to the personality trait of conscientiousness. Given these problems, can teachers have any confidence that interventions or character education initiatives based on the idea of developing grit will have an effect on student outcomes? Certainly, there's no robust evidence to suggest so. Even Duckworth has admitted her findings of the independent impact of grit are what personality psychologists would place in the 'small-to-medium' range.

---

[*] A pretty small factor, for example 'grit' increased the probability of the West Point Cadets successfully completing their training from 97% to 99%.

[†] Crede, M., Tynan, M. & Harms, P. (in press)

One of the common issues is that evaluations of programmes designed to develop character are often intensely subjective. Many of the glowing, positive claims come from evaluations carried out by those who were implementing the initiative in the first place! We need to remove confirmation bias, expectancy effects and plain wishful thinking to provide anything genuinely helpful for our children. Where more robust evaluation has been conducted, interventions to develop character have not always demonstrated long-term positive outcomes for students.

For example, an evaluation of the UK Resilience Programme reported only modest and short-term gains for students (see Chapter 23 – Stress and resilience). However, for the majority of school-based character education interventions, we don't really know what the impact has been. It is possible that schools have wasted teaching time and added to teachers' workloads all to no positive effect. But this isn't the worst possible outcome. As noted earlier, professor of education Kathryn Ecclestone suggests that there may be a darker side to this well-intentioned focus on character. She warns that our attempts to develop resilience and emotional well-being may inadvertently have negative outcomes for students (see Chapter 23).

Into the classroom

People vary in innumerable ways, and so finding differences between groups of individuals (for example, students who achieve well at school compared to ones that don't) is easy. However, there are significant questions about the validity and reliability of many personality tests. Even where reasonably valid psychometric differences can be measured, there is the serious but typically unanswered question as to whether the differences apparently detected by these tests provide any pedagogical insight which might inform teaching.

Character education arguably suffers even more problems. Firstly, what constitutes 'character' is poorly defined and risks becoming so vague and all-encompassing that it's impossible to examine the concept in any meaningful or rigorous way. Secondly, even where a character trait *is* well defined and appears to have some relationship with student outcomes, it's not clear whether interventions designed to develop that trait provide any benefit to students. Attempts to evaluate character education programmes are often subjective and suffer from researcher bias. Consequently, teachers should be highly sceptical of apparent character education success stories. Finally, potential negative effects of such programmes are frequently ignored. Our first priority before implementing any kind of psychological intervention in a school should be ensuring that it will not harm our students.

The entire concept of personality and character may be misleading. Teachers would do better to focus on useful applications arising from what children have in common in terms of how they learn (see Chapter 10 – Effective instruction). It's important to consider that focusing on personality and character may be an example of what psychologists call the 'fundamental attribution error'.

A term first coined by Lee Ross in 1977, the fundamental attribution error describes our tendency emphasise personality or character traits when explaining the behaviour of a person rather than considering external factors related to the situation. When evaluating the behaviour of others we tend to naturally overemphasise the role of traits – if someone we don't know appears discourteous or brusque, we assume that person is ill-mannered – and underestimate the role of context and the influence of the situation – that the rudeness is not typical of that person, who was merely tired and stressed when we met them. Through implementing interventions to develop character traits, is the profession at risk of acting upon this bias? Are we, in essence, erroneously attributing aspects of student success to trait characteristics which may be better understood and improved by understanding the situational factors which cause students to behave in ways which encourage that success?

What every teacher needs to know about individual differences

- In some cases, the concept and measurement of 'personality' may be little better than astrology in providing useful information about individuals.
- The correlation between personality characteristics and outcome measures like job performance is rather more modest than some claims teachers might believe.
- Personality differences – even where they can be measured with some validity – may be a consequence rather than the cause of children achieving or underachieving in school.
- Character education risks being such an open-ended and vague concept that it will be impossible to rigorously evaluate whether interventions actually provide benefits for students.
- Even where well defined, interventions to develop positive character traits have often lacked proper evaluation, and even where robustly evaluated the effects sometimes appear disappointingly short-lived.

- Finally, the whole notion of personality and character traits may be predicated on a common bias in human thinking – falsely attributing success or failure to the characteristics of a student which may be better understood and improved by understanding the situational factors instead.

References

Allport, G. W. (1937) *Personality: A psychological interpretation*, New York: Holt.

Allport, G. W. (1955) *Becoming: Basic considerations for a psychology of personality*, New Haven, CT: Yale University Press.

Allport, G. W. (1966) 'Traits revisited', *American Psychologist*, 21, 1–10.

Barrick, M. R. & Mount, M. K. (1991) 'The big five personality dimensions and job performance: a meta-analysis', *Personnel psychology*, 44(1), 1-26.

Challen, A., Noden, P., West, A. & Machin, S. (2011) *UK resilience programme evaluation: Final report*. Research Report DFE-RR097. Department for Education.

Coffield, F., Moseley, D., Hall, E. & Ecclestone, K. (2004) *Learning styles and pedagogy in post 16 learning: a systematic and critical review*. The Learning and Skills Research Centre.

Credé, M., Tynan, M. C. & Harms, P. D. (in press) *Much Ado about Grit: A Meta-Analytic Synthesis of the Grit Literature*.

Demos (2015) *Character Nation*. Retrieved from http://www.demos.co.uk/project/character-nation-2/ on 31 May 2016

Duckworth, A. L., Peterson, C., Matthews, M. D. & Kelly, D. R. (2007) 'Grit: perseverance and passion for long-term goals', *Journal of personality and social psychology*, 92(6), 1087.

Ecclestone, K. (2015) 'Well-being programmes in schools might be doing children more harm than good'. Retrieved from https://theconversation.com/well-being-programmes-in-schools-might-be-doing-children-more-harm-than-good-36573 on 31 May 2016

Ecclestone, K. & Hayes, D. (2009) *The dangerous rise of therapeutic education*, UK and US: Routledge.

James, W. (1899) 'Talks to teachers', *Chapter 8, The Laws of Habit*. Retrieved from http://www.uky.edu/ eushe2/Pajares/tt8.html 29th June 2016.

Judge, T. A., Thoresen, C. J., Bono, J. E. & Patton, G. K. (2001) 'The job satisfaction–job performance relationship: A qualitative and quantitative review', *Psychological bulletin*, 127(3), 376.

Krznaric, R. (2013) 'Have we all been duped by the Myers-Briggs test?', *Fortune*, May 15.

Paul, A. M. (2004) *The cult of personality*, New York: Free Press.

Ross, L. (1977) 'The intuitive psychologist and his shortcomings: Distortions in the attribution process', *Advances in experimental social psychology,* 10, 173-220.

Schools Week (2016) 'Schools must teach 'extrovert' traits – or social mobility will suffer'. Retrieved from http://schoolsweek.co.uk/schools-must-teach-personality-traits-or-social-mobility-will-suffer/ on 31 May 2016.

Stromberg, J. & Caswell, E (2014) 'Why the Myers-Briggs test is totally meaningless'. Retrieved from http://www.vox.com/2014/7/15/5881947/myers-briggs-personality-test-meaningless on 31 May 2016.

TES (2016) 'Extrovert personality traits could boost poor pupils' career prospects'. Retrieved from https://www.tes.com/news/school-news/breaking-news/extrovert-personality-traits-could-boost-poor-pupils-career-prospects on 31 May 2016.

Vries, R. D. & Rentfrow, J. (2016) 'A winning personality: the effects of background on personality and earnings.' Retrieved from http://www.suttontrust.com/wp-content/uploads/2016/01/Winning-Personality-FINAL.pdf on 31 May 2016.

Chapter 26
Creativity

Creativity, psychologists assure us, can be fostered. That may be so, but there are a number of problems with such a proposition. Firstly, what exactly do we mean by creativity? The American Psychological Association define creativity as "the generation of ideas that are new and useful in a particular situation".[*]

Whatever our definition of creativity, how can we measure it? In the 1960s, J. P. Guilford came up with an interesting proxy for measuring creativity –'divergent thinking': the idea that there are multiple solutions to any problem. He devised a number of tests to quantify divergent thinking including the 1967 Alternative Uses Test which asked participants to suggest as many alternative uses as they are able for everyday objects including toothpicks, bricks and paper clips.

In 1968, George Land conducted a research study to test the creativity of 1,600 children ranging in ages from three-to-five years old. This was the same creativity test he devised for NASA to help select innovative engineers and scientists, sometimes referred to as 'the paper clip test' in which participants have to come up with as many different uses for a paper clip as they can think of. Most people are able to come up with 10 to 15 uses. People who are good at divergent thinking come up with around 200.

Unfortunately, at least according to some interpretations, our capacity for divergent thinking deteriorates with age. Land's longitudinal study found 98% of children at aged five were assessed as having genius levels of divergent thinking. Five years later, when they were aged eight to 10 years, those at genius

---

[*] Top 20 Principles From Psychology For Prek–12 Teaching And Learning. p. 14

level had dropped to 30%. By the time they were 15, the average score was just 12%. Adults taking the same test tend score around 2%. Creativity guru Ken Robinson argues that the main intervention these children have had is a conveyor belt education that tells them, "There's only one answer. It's at the back. And don't look. That's called cheating."

Despite the fact that a great many of the creative people who've ever lived – including Robinson – have been products of the school system, the real problem with Land's analysis is that simply giving us percentages tells us nothing about the quality of the answers the children provided. It is possible that adults think of fewer uses for a paper clip because they have the ability to filter out nonsense answers? Students naturally possess a relatively limited set of schemata, and thus their ability to be creative (to combine schemata from different domains to generate interesting variations) is also fairly limited. What probably impresses us as adults is the uninhibited way children make productions based on these limited schemata. Princesses are painted, doctors and nurses are role-played, cardboard robots are constructed without embarrassment, and these unselected productions are usually (and quite naturally) rewarded by praise and attention.

However, as we get older we begin to identify more with our peers and, even if our parents still encourage us, our creativity starts to undergo more internal selection before production. Over time we come to understand that the first thoughts that pop into our heads are rarely true expressions of genius, and the nature of our creativity starts to expand and change. As we learn more the schemata available to us expands, and we become more discerning about what represents quality.

John Baer argues that much of what is supposed about divergent thinking may be wrong. Divergent thinking, as with any other form of creativity, is not a stable trait that can be transferred between domains of knowledge. We are all capable of being creative in one area without being able to be creative in others, but the strategies a student might use to be creative on the sports field, or when writing an essay, will not necessarily make them creative in mathematics or science, and vice versa. Although it seems intuitive that linking of unusual uses for a paper clip must be similar to thinking of unusual recipes for soufflé, simply lumping things together and giving them the same name doesn't actually make them the same.

This was demonstrated by Ellis Paul Torrance, the leading developer of creativity tests. He created two different versions of a test to measure figural (thinking creatively with pictures) and verbal (thinking creativity with words) divergent thinking*, and gave the same tests to different groups of people. There was almost no correlation between scores on these two tests of divergent thinking, indicating that the two sets of divergent thinking skills were completely unrelated.

It seems that divergent thinking is many completely different sets of skills. Unfortunately, many school districts, and even some researchers who use Torrance's tests, frequently forget this and act as if these tests were measuring some readily transferable, domain-general skill. The result has been confusion about what creativity is and the likelihood that many research findings that should have been rejected have been accepted uncritically.

The problem is, although divergent thinking tests produce easily quantifiable data, what is that data actually telling us? How could teachers really know if students had become more creative as a result of their efforts? Attempts to measure creativity suffer from a lack of validity and reliability. Creativity covers many different forms and fields. A test which assesses a proxy like counting uses of a paper clip suffers from a lack of validity. How, say, might Mozart or Van Gogh have performed on this test? If they were unable to think of many uses would that make their music or art less creative? If creativity is not, as seems likely, a global trait, the tests will also suffer from poor reliability as it would be unlikely that people would get the same score in different situations.

One way around the problem would be to measure a more global trait, which is highly correlated with creativity. There's been much debate in the psychological literature about whether intelligence and creativity are part of the same process (the conjoint hypothesis) or represent distinct mental processes (the disjoint hypothesis). Some researchers believe that creativity is the outcome of the same cognitive processes as intelligence, and that it is only labelled when the outcome of a cognitive process happens to produce something novel. If this is the case, maybe we could measure students' creativity simply by giving them an IQ test?

Can we teach creativity?

There's also the issue of whether creativity can actually be taught. Of course it's desirable that students are able to identify problems, generate potential solutions, evaluate the effectiveness of those strategies, and then communicate with others about the value of the solutions, but how do we go about teaching them how to do these things?

Any discussion of creativity in the classroom needs to distinguish between

---

*   For an explanation of figural and verbal tests see http://www.ststesting.com/ngifted.html

student creativity and 'creative approaches' to teaching. One argument is that if teachers take a creative approach to teaching, students will become more creative. While it's probably true that creativity can be nurtured and that environmental factors will affect how creative students are, simply being exposed to a teacher striving to be creative is unlikely to make much of a difference. Encouraging divergent work is no guarantee of quality. We need to accept that experts learn differently to novices (see Chapter 7) and that certain kinds of creative approaches to teaching may backfire. If teachers design instruction to allow for students to find multiple ways of solving problems, this might lead to some being able to make interesting connections, but it's more likely to lead to cognitive overload (see Chapter 4). Teachers would be better advised to concentrate on the principles discussed in Chapter 10 – Effective instruction.

It may be that creativity is not always desirable. Kaufman and Beghetto (2013) argue that teachers need to encourage restraint in students and that often it is much more efficient to follow well-established processes rather than trying to think of new ways to solve old problems. Instead, they suggest it might be more productive to teach students when and in what contexts it is useful to be creative. Character traits associated with creativity are often those displayed by students considered disruptive or unruly. Kaufman and Beghetto argue that such students may benefit from being explicitly taught the value of conforming to pro-social norms (see Chapter 19) and self-control. There are certain brands of 'creativity' that are, perhaps, misplaced in the classroom. That's not to say enquiring minds should be crushed or that enthusiasm should be stemmed, but it does mean that the concept of self-regulation discussed in Chapter 17 should be given at the very least equal weight. Creativity without self-control is unlikely to result in anything useful.

Understanding creativity is hideously complex, and the appeal of grand, overarching, generic theories of creativity is that they tend to be simple and easy to understand. Their simplicity is also their weakness. While we can't pretend to know exactly what creativity is or how to instil it in students, we are certain that any attempt to reduce it to a set of easy-to-teach principles is undoubtedly wrong.

Into the classroom

It might be that it's helpful to teach students how to develop a broader understanding of creativity and recognise that creativity has costs as well as benefits. Alongside this we should probably help students recognise their creative strengths and limitations. Most usefully though, teachers should develop students' contextual knowledge about creative expression. This involves not only clarifying the constraints and expectations of particular tasks and activities, but also giving them a rationale for our expectations and constraints. For example: "The reason why I am asking you to follow this procedure, rather than come up with your own, is because we want to first understand how these procedures result in the chemical reaction we have been studying."

If Baer is correct in claiming that creativity is domain specific, students will best learn to be creative by developing their long-term memories within and between subject domains. Understanding the deeper similarities between two different domains allows us to creatively take an idea from one domain and apply it to another. It may also be worth specifically nurturing creativity separately within each discipline.

Creativity requires knowledge of form. This is as true of mathematics, art, music, science and engineering as it is of writing. As well as all the other knowledge needed to to write a sonnet, one also has to understand the rules of the sonnet form. In order to play with the form, to experiment with the rules and yes, to break them, you still need to know what those rules are. If you don't know how a sentence operates how can you truly be creative in the way you construct your sentences? Just having ideas and tossing them at the page simply isn't good enough. Providing a clear, comprehensible framework for how to structure these ideas will help pupils to have a greater ability to process their ideas into a form which has worth.

You can't make students be creative just by giving them 'creative' tasks. Asking students to use their imaginations without giving them a clear structure is an invitation to either daydream or imitate. You can't question a belief unless you know what that belief entails. You can't make unusual connections unless you know enough to connect seemingly unrelated ideas. However, once students have access to rich knowledge of at least two or more domains of knowledge they will be able to use what they know to question, make connections and explore alternatives.

Finally, we're encouraged to be creative role models. If, the reasoning goes, we show students how we use multiple strategies to solve problems across various aspects of our lives, they will be inspired to do the same. If only life were that simple. Teachers' power as role models comes from our ability to guide and shape peer culture; peers have more influence than anyone else. We should definitely value, encourage and seek out opportunities for showing how students can think creativity in our subjects, but we should be realistic about our ability to turn it on or off in students. Received wisdom often suggests that to make students creative we need first to make them happy and comfortable.

As we saw in Chapter 23, although there's a body of thinking which supposes stress and anxiety erode the creative faculties, actually moderate stress is likely to make students more creative.

To conclude, we *can* foster creativity but explicitly trying to promote creativity might actually stifle it. By teaching students the richness and range of the subjects on offer at school we will best set them up to be able to see links and connections, solve problems and think along the edges of what is known.

> **What every teacher needs to know about creativity**
>
> - Teachers should teach students that creativity is not always desirable. Sometimes it is better to follow tried and tested procedures.
> - Asking students to be creative without support is likely to lead to cognitive overload. Instead design well-structured tasks with clear constraints for them to overcome.
> - A creative approach to problem solving requires experience and expertise. Students need to be given an experience of success before being expected to approach tasks independently.
> - Teach students how to be creative within subject areas by modelling subject-specific processes and explaining how to apply what they have learned in similar contexts.
> - Once students have a firm grasp of the foundational knowledge in the subject areas they are studying, only then should we get them to question and critique what they have learned.

References

Baer, J. (2011) 'How Divergent Thinking Tests Mislead Us: Are the Torrance Tests Still Relevant in the 21st Century? The Division 10 Debate', *Psychology of Aesthetics, Creativity, and the Arts*, 5(4), 309–313.

Beghetto, R. A. (2013) *Killing ideas softly? The promise and perils of creativity in the classroom*, Charlotte, NC: Information Age Press.

Jauk, E. (2013) 'The relationship between intelligence and creativity: New support for the threshold hypothesis by means of empirical breakpoint detection', *Intelligence*, 41(4): 212–221.

Kaufman, J. C. & Beghetto, R. A. (2013) 'In praise of Clark Kent: Creative metacognition and the importance of teaching kids when (not) to be creative', *Roeper Review: A Journal on Gifted Education*, 35, 155–165. doi:10.1080/02783193.2013.799413

Land, G. & Jarman, B. (1993) *Breaking Point and Beyond*, San Francisco: Harper Business.

Nusbaum, E.C. & Silvia, P.J. (2011) 'Are intelligence and creativity really so different? Fluid intelligence, executive processes and strategy use in divergent thinking', *PLoS ONE*, 9.

Plucker, J., Beghetto, R. A. & Dow, G. (2004) 'Why isn't creativity more important to educational psychologists? Potentials, pitfalls, and future directions in creativity research', *Educational Psychologist*, 39, 83-96. doi.10.1207/s15326985ep3902_1

Robinson, K. (2010) *The Element: How Finding Your Passion Changes Everything*, London: Penguin.

Runco, M. A. & Pritzker, S. R. (eds.) (2011) *Encyclopedia of creativity* (2nd ed.). Boston, MA: Academic Press.

Sawyer, R. K. (2012) *Explaining Creativity: The Science Of Human Innovation*, 2nd edition, Oxford: Oxford University Press.

Scott, G., Leritz L. E. & Mumford, M. D. (2004) 'The Effectiveness of Creativity Training', *Creativity Research Journal*, 16(4), 361-388.

Silvia, P. J., Winterstein, B. P., Willse, J. T., Barona, C. M., Cram, J. T., Hess, K. I., Martinez, J. L. & Richard, C. A. (2008) 'Assessing creativity with divergent thinking tasks: Exploring the reliability and validity of new subjective scoring methods', *Psychology of Aesthetics, Creativity, and the Arts*, 2, 68-85.

Sternberg, R. J., Grigorenko, E. L. & Singer, J. L. (eds.) (2004) *Creativity: From potential to realization*, Washington, DC: American Psychological Association.

Torrance, E. P. & Presbury, J. (1984) 'The criteria of success used in 242 recent experimental studies of creativity', *Creative Child & Adult Quarterly*, 9, 238-243.

Conclusions and Further reading

So, there you have it: our admittedly biased view of what we think every teacher ought to know about psychology. As we've already said, there's plenty more you might like to know about and probably lots you should know about, but this is what we think is most important.

Part 1 on learning and thinking is, we believe, the most uncontentious section of the book. All of the available research seems to confirm what we've written about, although we've tried to ensure that where there is legitimate disagreement we've signposted it. Part 2 is more contested. The psychology of motivation is dauntingly complex and we've only really scratched the surface here. What we've chosen to include is, we hope, useful in the classroom and some of what we chose not to include we felt would have offered conflicting, possibly unhelpful advice at odds with some of the findings from cognitive science discussed in Part 1. The final part is an attempt to set the record straight on some of the least helpful areas of psychology that have permeated into schools. In most cases, it's not that the science is bad – although sometimes that is a problem – it's more that research, which might be useful in other areas, has been adopted uncritically into schools.

We hope readers recognise that we're not claiming to be right about everything we've written, but we're right to the best of our understanding and knowledge. We're sure that in the coming years some, if not all, of what we've written about will be contested and cast into doubt. Psychology is a young science and that is as it should be. We learn from testing assumption, finding mistakes and making new and better theories.

Conclusions and Further reading

Although, of course, we hope you enjoyed reading the book, beyond that we hope it proves useful as an ongoing source of reference and professional development, as well as a springboard for further investigation. Our ultimate motivation is to stimulate informed discussion about how students learn and how we can help them learn (regrettably, in our experience as teachers, meetings too often revolved around admin rather than the genuinely interesting and most important aspects of our jobs!). We've tried to make each chapter 'stand alone' so that a busy teacher or group of teachers can read through a chapter at a time rather than tackle the whole book in one go – in the hope that this facilitates its use within school professional development as well as for your personal interest and enjoyment.

If nothing else, we hope to have inoculated you against some of the worst excesses of psychology and introduced you to some of the more promising. We hope that this will be the start rather than the end of a journey and, as such, we want to take the opportunity to recommend a reading list (see overleaf) that will take you deeper into the sometimes murky, but always fascinating realm of psychology as it applies to education.

Thanks for reading and keep on thinking.

Further reading

Some of our favourite books

Shaun Allison and Andy Tharby, *Making Every Lesson Count*.

Tom Bennett, *Teacher Proof*.

Peter C. Brown, Henry L. Roediger & Mark McDaniel, *Make It Stick: The Science of Successful Learning*.

Pedro De Bruyckere, Paul A. Kirschner and Casper Hulshof, *Urban Myths about Learning and Education*.

Benedict Carey, *How We Learn*.

Daisy Christodoulou, *Seven Myths About Education*.

Ruth Colvin Clark, *Evidence-Based Training Methods* (2nd edition).

David Didau, *What if everything you knew about education was wrong?*

Kathryn Ecclestone and Dennis Hayes, *The Dangerous Rise of Therapeutic Education*.

Daniel Kahneman, Thinking, Fast and Slow.

Dean Koretz, *Measuring Up*.

Carl Sagan, *The Demon-Haunted World: Science as a Candle in the Dark*.

Dylan Wiliam, *Leadership for Teacher Learning: Creating a Culture Where All Teachers Improve So That All Students Succeed*.

Daniel Willingham, *Why Don't Students Like School?*

Richard Wiseman, *59 Seconds: Think a little, change a lot*.

Blogs

Nick's blog: evidenceintopractice.wordpress.com

David's blog: www.learningspy.co.uk

The Learning Scientists: www.learningscientists.org/blog

Greg Ashman's blog: gregashman.wordpress.com

Daisy Christodoulou's blog: thewingtoheaven.wordpress.com

Pedro De Bruyckere's blog: theeconomyofmeaning.com

Cristina Milos's blog: momentssnippetsspirals.wordpress.com

Andrew Old's blog: teachingbattleground.wordpress.com

James Theobald's blog: othmarstrombone.wordpress.com

Dan Willingham's blog: www.danielwillingham.com/daniel-willingham-science-and-education-blog

You Are Not So Smart: youarenotsosmart.com

Alex Quigley's blog: www.theconfidentteacher.com

Publications

Deans for Impact: The Science of Learning http://www.deansforimpact.org/pdfs/The_Science_of_Learning.pdf

Top 20 Principles From Psychology for PreK–12 Teaching and Learning: http://www.apa.org/ed/schools/cpse/top-twenty-principles.pdf

The Sutton Trust: What Makes great Teaching? http://www.suttontrust.com/wp-content/uploads/2014/10/What-Makes-Great-Teaching-REPORT.pdf

Index

A

Abrams, Dominic 201
Accomodation 95, 220, 226
ADHD 38, 172, 174, 178-179
Age Related Expectations 224
Ainsworth, Mary 228-229, 236
Allport, Gordon 258, 263
Alternative Uses Test 265
American Professional Society on the Abuse of Children 231
American Psychological Association 107, 144, 157, 161, 167, 265, 271
Aronson, Elliot 132, 137-138, 150, 202, 206
Asch, Solomon 191, 198
Assessment 12, 89-108, 116, 138, 149, 223, 232
        for learning, 100-103
        formative, 100-103
        summative, 100-107
Attachment theory 231-236
Attribution theory 83-84

B

Baddeley, Alan 35, 37, 41, 53, 61
Baer, John 266, 269
Bandura, Albert 173, 179, 194, 198, 239
Barnett, Susan 63-64, 66, 68, 179, 236
Bartlett, Frederic 19, 54, 60

Baumeister, Roy 169, 173-174, 179
behaviour 5-12, 17, 21, 44, 52, 54, 71, 83, 120-121, 126, 130, 134, 141, 143,-144, 151-162, 165, 171, 173, 176, 181-184, 186-188, 190, 192-198, 201, 207, 228-230, 232-235, 240, 245, 250, 256, 260, 262
behaviourism 151
Biederman, Joseph 172, 179
Big five – see OCEAN 263
Bjork, Robert 9, 15-16, 49, 56-57, 60, 65-69, 84-88, 101, 108
Blackmore, Susan 18, 24
Bloom's taxonomy 114
Bowlby, John 228-229, 236
Brain Gym 249, 252-253
Brain Training 38, 175
Bruner, Jerome 224, 227
Butler, Andrew 69, 87
Butler, Ruth 167, 170

C

Carey, Benedict 65, 69, 198
Ceci, Stephen 63-64, 66, 68
Center for Family Development 233, 236
character education 175, 182, 245, 258-262
Chi, Michelene 32, 73, 80
Child and Adolescent Mental Health Services 243
chunking 37, 43, 109
Cialdini, Robert 192, 198

Index

Clark, Ruth 112
Coe, Robert 5, 7, 9, 24, 121-123
Coffield, Frank 256, 263
cognitive behavioural therapy 181, 184, 188
cognitive conflict 29-31, 59, 219, 220, 226
cognitive dissonance 192
Cognitive Load Theory 43-44, 46-47, 49, 50
Cohen, Geoffrey 22-24, 133, 203, 207, 245-246
comparative judgement (CJ) 104-106, 191
conceptual competition 27
conceptual conflict 29

D

Deci, Edward 150, 161, 166, 170
Demos 259-260, 263
Dennett, Daniel 17, 21, 24
desirable difficulties 9, 15, 47, 66
discrimination 138, 199, 201, 205
divergent thinking 265-267, 271
Dolan, Paul 166, 170
Dual Coding Theory 38
Duckworth, Angela 260, 263
Dweck, Carol 124-128, 132-133, 161

E

Ebbinghaus, Hermann 52, 55, 58, 61
Ecclestone, Katherine 241, 243, 245, 261, 263
Education Endowment Foundation 128, 132
EEF Toolkit 214
effort 19-21, 23, 46, 47-49, 52, 58, 72, 75, 84, 86, 95, 106, 112, 114, 116-117, 122, 124-131, 136, 143, 146-149, 156, 158, 160, 165, 167-169, 176, 183, 202, 205, 209, 215
Electroencephalography 247
Ericsson, K. Anders 42, 71, 80, 87
evolution 17-19, 21, 23-24, 42, 212
expectations 57, 60, 77-78, 86, 98, 121-122, 129, 134-139, 144, 148-149, 156, 158, 160, 165, 173, 176, 185, 190, 197-198, 215, 220, 223, 224, 241, 269
experts 8, 41, 63, 67-68, 71-75, 80, 104, 209, 216-217, 223, 225, 248
explicit instruction 49, 66, 113, 116, 117, 118
extinction 154
extraversion 256-258

F

False Consensus effect 213
false negatives 210
false positives 210
feedback 15, 71-72, 82-88, 106, 116, 126, 129, 138, 148-149, 156, 165, 168-170, 173, 220, 235, 243
    reducing feedback 15, 84-85
Fitts, Paul 71
forgetting 5, 14-16, 47, 49, 51-60, 66, 110, 122, 257
Franklin effect 192
Fundamental Attribution Error 83, 262
Furendi, Frank 241

G

Gazzaniga, Michael 251, 253
Geary, David 18, 19, 20, 23, 24, 28, 32, 45, 49, 61, 218, 223
goals 33, 48, 72, 84, 124-125, 132, 133, 140-147, 150, 164-177, 183, 187, 201, 205-206, 232, 260, 263
Goldacre, Ben 218, 252, 253
grit 147, 243, 257, 259, 260, 263
group dynamics 199, 203, 206
groups 73, 94, 106, 120, 122, 136-137, 148, 155, 175, 190-191, 195, 199-206, 215, 225, 240, 247-248, 260, 261, 267
    in-groups 204-206
    out-groups 205-206
Guilford, J. P. 33, 265

H

Haidle, Miriam 17, 24
halo effect 105, 136-137, 139
Hattie, John 82-83, 87, 145
Hawthorne effect 134
Haydn, Terry 151, 162
Heider, Fritz 83
Hitch, Graham 35, 41
Hyperthymesia 34

I

introversion 255

J

Jacob, Robin 175, 179
James, William 258
Jensen, Frances 162
Jung, Carl 255
Jussim & Harber 135, 139, 206

K

Kahneman, Daniel 19-20, 25, 104, 137, 139, 141, 145, 153, 163, 274
King & Burton 140, 141, 144
Klapp, Alli 167, 170
knowledge
    folk knowledge, 18-20, 23, 28
    primary knowledge, 19, 45, 75, 110
    subject knowledge 73

L

Laming, Donald 103, 108
Land, George 265
Landsberger, Henry 134
learned helplessness 125, 132
Lemov, Doug 195-196, 198
Lepper, Mark 155, 162, 170
locus of control (LoC) 241, 246, 260
Loftus, Elizabeth 54, 61

M

Magnetic Resonance Imaging (MRI) 247, 253
Marshmallow Test 172, 174, 179
Maslow, Abraham 183
mastery 71-72, 146-150, 165-168
Mastery Motivation 146, 150
Mayer, Richard 33, 69, 111-112, 119, 227
McGrath, Helen 183, 189
Meltzoff, Andrew 22, 25
memory
    central executive, 36
    declarative 51-54
    episodic buffer 36-37
    executive functioning, 36, 171-178
    long-term memory, 15, 19, 27, 34, 36, 40-41, 43-48, 51-60, 70, 74-75, 79, 100-101, 109-110, 114-118, 220
    Multi-Store Model 35
    non-declarative 51-52
    phonological loop 36-37, 39, 111
    semantic 52-54, 57-58
    short-term memory 37, 41, 60
Messick, Samuel 97, 108
metacognition 76-77, 80, 115, 176-178, 225, 270
method of the loci 58
Meyer, George 33
Meyer and Land 29
Miller, George 37, 42, 69, 189, 227
mindfulness 182
mindset
    fixed 124, 126-128, 131
    growth 38, 124, 126-128, 131-132, 195, 203, 205
Mischel, Walter 172, 179
misconceptions 5, 19, 23, 26-28, 30-33, 44, 54, 59, 60, 70, 101, 105, 110-111, 114, 117, 218, 220, 226, 228, 248, 252
mnemonics 38, 39, 40, 77, 115
motivation 6, 12, 18, 21, 41, 55, 70, 72, 76-77, 95, 120-122, 128, 132-133, 139-140, 143-144, 146, 150, 155-156, 159,-161, 164-170, 178, 180, 192, 206, 258-259, 272-273
    extrinsic 122, 144, 164-169
    intrinsic 144, 146, 164-169
Mozart effect 250, 253
multiple choice questions 103
Muraven, Mark 169, 174, 179
Myers-Briggs Type Indicator 255

N

neuroscience 6, 51, 61, 132, 218, 245,-249, 252-253
Noble, Toni 183, 189
no excuses 158
novices 41, 48, 63, 67-68, 72-75, 80, 177, 224, 248, 268
Nuthall, Graham 26-27, 33, 66, 69, 102, 108, 121, 123, 164, 170, 225, 227

O

OCEAN 256-257, 260
OECD 248, 253
orientation 146-149, 250

P

Palmer, John 54, 61, 242, 245
Paluck, Elizabeth 195, 198
Parkinson, Julia 175, 179
Pauli, Wolfgang 259
Pavlov, Ivan 52, 151
pedagogical content knowledge 27
Penn Resiliency Program 242
performance 4, 15-16, 30, 53, 63, 70,-72, 74, 77, 80, 82, 84-89, 92-94, 96, 98-104, 106-107, 116, 124, 126-127, 130-133, 135, 136, 138, 141-144, 147-149, 165, 167-168, 170, 173, 177, 203-204, 206, 210, 212, 238-239, 242, 256, 257, 260, 262, 263
PERMA 183
personality 83, 132-133, 139, 144, 162, 169, 170, 178-179, 196, 246, 254- 264
Piaget, Jean 8-9, 19, 25, 172, 219, 220-223, 226-227, 250
Pink, Daniel 163-164, 165, 170
placebo effect 134
Polanyi, Michael 104, 108
Popper, Karl 213
Positive Educational Practices 183
positive psychology 150, 181-184, 187-189
Posner 29, 33, 71, 81, 179
practice 5-17, 26, 30, 33, 47-49, 57-60, 64, 66, 69- 72, 74, 75- 81, 83, 85, 87, 90, 93-94, 96-97, 101, 107-108, 111, 114-115, 117-118, 122, 124-125, 139, 143, 162, 165, 170, 177, 179-187, 210, 212-213, 215, 227, 235, 247, 254
        deliberate 71, 79, 80, 87
        purposeful 71-72
praise 1, 85, 129, 133, 148, 156, 157, 160, 161, 163, 234, 266, 270
Proust, Marcel 65
psychometrics 89
publication bias 186
punishment 151-153, 159, 161, 183
Pygmalion effect 135

R

randomised controlled trials (RCT) 9, 214
REDI programme 175
regression to the mean 94, 215
reliability 89-90, 108, 150
restorative justice 181, 185, 187, 189
restorative practices 122, 183, 187, 188
rewards 6, 122, 151, 153-156, 159-161, 164-166
Rich Harris, Judith 225
Robber's Cave 199, 200-201
Robinson, Sir Ken 7, 17, 132, 266, 271
Rogers, Carl 183
Rosenthal and Jacobson 135, 139
Ross, Lee 262
Ryan, Richard 150, 161, 166, 170

S

Sagan, Carl 208, 215-216, 218, 274
sanctions 6, 122, 151, 153, 157, 159-160, 166, 185-186, 197
Sapir-Whorf Hypothesis 16
satiation 154
scaffolding 59, 76-77, 130, 144, 148- 149, 177, 224-226, 232
schemas 23, 26, 28, 44-45, 48, 54, 56, 59-60, 73-74, 109, 114, 117, 219, 220, 221, 225
Schultz, P. W. 193, 198
self-concept 192
Self Determination Theory 166
self-regulation 122, 171-180, 260, 268
Sherif, Muzafer 199, 200, 201, 204, 206
short-term 15, 30, 37, 38, 41, 60, 68, 78, 101, 134, 147, 149, 159, 160, 164, 166, 174, 238, 261
Siegler, Robert 27, 33, 223, 227
Skinner, B. F. 58, 61, 151-154, 159, 162, 246
Skinner box 152, 153
Smith and Guthrie 62
social norms 83, 121, 122, 152, 153, 159, 160, 176, 190-198, 201, 226, 268
spacing effect 66
Sperry, Roger 251
Staw, Barry 136, 139
stereotypes 19, 139, 157, 203, 220

stereotype threat 132, 203, 204, 205, 206
Sutton Trust 257, 275
Sweller, John 43-44, 49-50, 73, 80, 81, 117-119

T

Tajfel, Henri 200, 207
testing effect 47,-49, 69, 76, 102, 114-116
Tetlock, Philip 165, 170
Theory of Mind (ToM) 21
Thorndike, Edward 62, 69, 136, 139, 151
threshold concepts 29
Timperley, Helen 82-83, 87
Torrance, Ellis Paul 266-267, 270-271
Tough, Paul 243, 246
transfer
    far 63-64
    near 64
Tversky, Amos 141, 145, 153, 163, 212, 218

U

UK Resilience Programme 242

V

validity 89-100, 102- 103, 107, 108, 121, 150, 215, 232, 249, 255, 256, 261, 262, 267, 271, 282
Vigen, Tyler 213, 218
Visuo-spatial sketchpad 37, 39, 110-111
Vygotsky, Lev 8-9, 16, 221, 227

W

Walton, Gregory 133, 203, 207
Wason selection task 45
Waterhouse, Lynn 250, 253
Watson, John 151
Weiman, Carl 11, 13
Weisberg, Denna 248, 253
Wiliam, Dylan 1, 7, 11, 13, 84, 88, 89, 92, 102, 107-108, 148, 150, 152, 274
Willingham, Daniel 20, 24-25, 27, 33, 40, 42, 53, 60-61, 67, 69, 72-74, 80-81, 118-119, 160, 163, 170, 218, 227, 247, 253, 274-275
Wooldridge, Cindy 7, 64, 69
worked examples 48, 75, 78-79, 114, 116-118
Working Memory Model (WMM) 174

Y

Yerkes-Dodson Law 238
Young, Cliff 142

Z

zero-tolerance 157-158, 182, 187
Zone of Proximal Development 8, 223